LETTERS TO YOUNG CHURCHES

Religious Books in the Fontana Series

SEX, LOVE AND MARRIAGE	Roland H. Bainton
THE PLAIN MAN'S BOOK OF PRAYERS	William Barclay
THE MAN NEXT TO ME	Anthony Barker
THE FAITH OF THE CHURCH	Karl Barth
JESUS AND THE WORLD	Rudolf Bultmann
CHRISTIANITY AND HISTORY	Herbert Butterfield
THE TARTAN PIMPERNEL	Donald Caskie
SCIENCE AND CHRISTIAN BELIEF	C. A. Coulson
THE MEANING OF PAUL FOR TODAY	C. H. Dodd
THE AUTHORITY OF THE BIBLE	C. H. Dodd
NAUGHT FOR YOUR COMFORT	Trevor Huddleston
THE PERENNIAL PHILOSOPHY	Aldous Huxley
EDIFYING DISCOURSES	Søren Kierkegaard
DYING WE LIVE	Trs. Reinhard C. Kuhn
SACRED WRITINGS	Günter Lanczkowski
REFLECTIONS ON THE PSALMS	C. S. Lewis
THE FOUR LOVES	C. S. Lewis
THE PLAIN MAN LOOKS AT THE BIBLE	William Neil
THE MEANING OF PROTESTANTISM	James Nichols
THE GOSPELS IN MODERN ENGLISH	J. B. Phillips
THE BOOK OF REVELATION	J. B. Phillips
THE PLAIN MAN LOOKS AT HIMSELF	William Purcell
THE RESURRECTION OF CHRIST	A. M. Ramsey
THE CHRISTIAN EXPERIENCE OF THE HOLY SPIRIT	H. Wheeler Robinson
ON THE EDGE OF THE PRIMEVAL FOREST	Albert Schweitzer
MORE FROM THE PRIMEVAL FOREST	Albert Schweitzer
DOES GOD EXIST?	A. E. Taylor
WAITING ON GOD	Simone Weil
CHRISTIAN DOCTRINE	J. S. Whale
THE SCROLLS FROM THE DEAD SEA	Edmund Wilson
PRAYER	Olive Wyon

Letters to
Young Churches

A translation of the
New Testament Epistles

J. B. PHILLIPS

With an introduction by C. S. Lewis

COLLINS

fontana books

First published *1947*
First Edition in Fontana Books *1955*
Second Impression in Fontana Books *1956*
Third Impression in Fontana Books January, *1957*
Fourth Impression in Fontana Books October, *1957*
Fifth Impression in Fontana Books February, *1958*
Sixth Impression in Fontana Books October, *1958*
Second Edition (revised) in Fontana Books *1960*
Eighth Impression in Fontana Books March, *1963*

PRINTED IN GREAT BRITAIN
COLLINS CLEAR-TYPE PRESS: LONDON AND GLASGOW

CONTENTS

Introduction	*page* 7
Translator's Preface	13
The Letter to the Christians at Rome	19
The First Letter to the Christians at Corinth	58
The Second Letter to the Christians at Corinth	92
The Letter to the Christians in Galatia	114
The Letter to the Christians at Ephesus	126
The Letter to the Christians at Philippi	138
The Letter to the Christians at Colossae	146
The First Letter to the Christians in Thessalonica	154
The Second Letter to the Christians in Thessalonica	161
The First Letter to Timothy	165
The Second Letter to Timothy	174
The Letter to Titus	181
The Letter to Philemon	185
The Letter to Jewish Christians	187
The Letter of James	214
The First Letter of Peter	224
The Second Letter of Peter	233
The First Letter of John	239
The Second Letter of John	248
The Third Letter of John	250
The Letter of Jude	251

INTRODUCTION

By C. S. Lewis

It is possible that the reader who opens this volume on the counter of a bookshop may ask himself why we need a new translation of any part of the Bible, and, if of any, why of the Epistles. "Do we not already possess," it may be said, "in the Authorised Version the most beautiful rendering which any language can boast?" Some people whom I have met go even further and feel that a modern translation is not only unnecessary but even offensive. They cannot bear to see the time-honoured words altered; it seems to them irreverent.

There are several answers to such people. In the first place the kind of objection which they feel to a new translation is very like the objection which was once felt to any English translation at all. Dozens of sincerely pious people in the sixteenth century shuddered at the idea of turning the time-honoured Latin of the Vulgate into our common and (as they thought) "barbarous" English. A sacred truth seemed to them to have lost its sanctity when it was stripped of the poly-syllabic Latin, long heard at Mass and at Hours, and put into "language such as men do use"—language steeped in all the commonplace associations of the nursery, the inn, the stable, and the street. The answer then was the same as the answer now. The only kind of sanctity which scripture can lose (or, at least, New Testament scripture) by being modernised is an accidental kind which it never had for its writers or its earliest readers. The New Testament in the original Greek is not a work of literary art: it is not written in a solemn, eccles-iastical language, it is written in the sort of Greek which was spoken over the Eastern Mediterranean after Greek had become an international language and therefore lost its real beauty and subtlety. In it we see Greek used by people who have no real feeling for Greek words because Greek words are not the words they spoke when they were children. It is a sort of " basic " Greek ; a language without roots in the soil, a utilitarian, commercial and administrative language. Does this shock us ? It ought not to, except as the Incarnation itself ought to shock us. The same divine humility which decreed that God should become a baby at a peasant-woman's breast, and later an arrested field-preacher in the hands of the Roman police, decreed also that He should be preached in a vulgar, prosaic and unliterary language. If you can stomach the one, you can stomach the other. The Incarnation is in that sense an irreverent doctrine : Christianity, in that sense, an incurably irreverent religion. When we expect that it should have come before the World in all the beauty that we now feel in the Authorised Version we are as wide of the mark as the Jews were in expecting that the Messiah would come as a great earthly King. The real sanctity, the real beauty and sublimity of the New Testament (as of Christ's life) are of a different sort : miles deeper or *further in*.

In the second place, the Authorised Version has ceased to be a good (that is, a clear) translation. It is no longer modern English : the meanings of words have changed. The same antique glamour which has made it (in the superficial sense) so " beautiful," so " sacred," so " comforting," and so " inspiring," has also made it in many places unintelligible. Thus where St. Paul says " I know nothing against myself," it translates "I know nothing by myself." That was a good translation (though even then rather old-fashioned) in the sixteenth century : to the modern reader it means either nothing, or something quite different from what St. Paul said. The truth is that if we are to have translation at all we must have periodical re-translation. There is no such thing as translating a book into another language once and for all, for a language is a changing thing. If your son is to have clothes it is no good buying him a suit once and for all : he will grow out of it and have to be re-clothed.

And finally, though it may seem a sour paradox—we must

sometimes get away from the Authorised Version, if for no other reason, simply *because* it is so beautiful and so solemn. Beauty exalts, but beauty also lulls. Early associations endear but they also confuse. Through that beautiful solemnity the transporting or horrifying realities of which the Book tells may come to us blunted and disarmed and we may only sigh with tranquil veneration when we ought to be burning with shame or struck dumb with terror or carried out of ourselves by ravishing hopes and adorations. Does the word " scourged " really come home to us like " flogged " ? Does " mocked him " sting like " jeered at him "?

We ought therefore to welcome all new translations (when they are made by sound scholars) and most certainly those who are approaching the Bible for the first time will be wise not to begin with the Authorised Version—except perhaps for the historical books of the Old Testament where its archaisms suit the saga-like material well enough. Among modern translations those of Dr. Moffat and of Monsignor Knox seem to me particularly good. The present volume concentrates on the epistles and furnishes more help to the beginner : its scope is different. The preliminary abstracts to each letter will be found especially useful, and the reader who has not read the letters before might do well to begin by reading and reflecting on these abstracts at some length before he attempts to tackle the text. It would have saved me a great deal of labour if this book had come into my hands when I first seriously began to try to discover what Christianity was.

For a man who wants to make that discovery must face the epistles. And whether we like it or not, most of them are by St. Paul. He is the Christian author whom no one can by-pass.

A most astonishing misconception has long dominated the modern mind on the subject of St. Paul. It is to this effect : that Jesus preached a kindly and simple religion (found in the Gospels) and that St. Paul afterwards corrupted it into a cruel and complicated religion (found in the epistles). This is really quite untenable. All the most terrifying texts came from the mouth of our Lord : all the texts on which we can base such warrant as we have for hoping that all men will be saved come from St. Paul. If it could be proved that St. Paul altered the teaching of his Master in any way, he altered it in exactly the opposite way to that which is popularly supposed. But there is no real evidence for a pre-Pauline doctrine different from St. Paul's. The epistles are, for the most part, the earliest Christian documents we possess. The Gospels come later. They are not " the gospel," the statement of the Christian belief. They are written for those who had already been converted, who had already accepted " the gospel." They leave out many of the " complications " (that is, the theology) because they are intended for readers who have already been instructed in it. In that sense the epistles are more primitive and more central than the Gospels—though not, of course, than the great events which the Gospels recount. God's act (the Incarnation, the Crucifixion, and the Resurrection) comes first : the earliest theological analysis of it comes in the epistles : then, when the generation who had known the Lord was dying out, the Gospels were composed to provide for believers a record of the great Act and of some of the Lord's sayings. The ordinary popular conception has put everything upside down. Nor is the cause far to seek. In the earlier history of every rebellion there is a stage at which you do not yet attack the King in person. You say, " The King is all right. It is his Ministers who are wrong. They misrepresent him and corrupt all his plans—which, I'm sure, are good plans if only the Ministers would let them take effect." And the first victory consists in beheading a few Ministers : only at a later stage do you go on and behead the King himself. In the same way, the nineteenth-century attack on St. Paul was really only a stage in the revolt against Christ. Men were not ready in large numbers to attack Christ himself. They made the normal first move—that of attacking one of His principal ministers. Everything they disliked in Christianity was therefore attributed to St. Paul. It was unfortunate that their case could not impress anyone who had really read the Gospels and the Epistles with attention : but apparently few people had, and so the first victory was won

St. Paul was impeached and banished and the world went on to the next step—the attack on the King Himself. But to those who wish to know what St. Paul and his fellow-teachers really said the present volume will give very great help.

C. S. LEWIS

TRANSLATOR'S PREFACE

THIS VERSION of the New Testament Epistles is an attempt to translate these Letters into the English of to-day, with the following conditions borne constantly in mind:

1. As far as possible the language used must be such as is commonly spoken, written and understood at the present time.
2. When necessary the translator should feel free to expand or explain, while preserving the original meaning as nearly as can be ascertained.
3. The Letters should read like letters, not theological treatises. Where the Greek is informal and colloquial, the English should be the same.
4. The translation (or in some cases, the paraphrase) should "flow" and be easy to read. Artificial "verses" are to be discarded, though cross-headings can be introduced to divide the letters into what seems to be their natural sections.
5. Though every care must be taken to make the version accurate, the projected value of this version should lie in its "easy-to-read" quality. For close meticulous study, existing modern versions should be consulted.

Although it can hardly be claimed that this exacting ideal has been realised, it is hoped that in the following pages there will at any rate be times when the reader will completely forget that the words are a translation and will feel their sense as if they were "written for to-day." The Letters of the New Testament have been chosen for this attempt because many people, who are moderately familiar with the straightforward narrative of the four gospels, have not even a nodding acquaintance with the "epistles," and probably regard them as obscure and "difficult."

THE MESSAGE OF THE LETTERS

It is surely a remarkable accident, if it is not the Providence of God, that these human, un-selfconscious letters of the very early days of Christianity should have been preserved. What is even more remarkable is their astonishing relevance to-day. It seems that the men who wrote these letters concentrated upon the essential spiritual core of human life. They provide that spiritual vitamin, without which human life is at best sickly, and at worst dead. While scarcely touching on any "modern problem" they yet manage to give pointers of principle which show the way, and the spirit, in which the problems of even a highly complex age such as ours may be tackled successfully.

The present translator who has closely studied these letters for several years is struck by two things. First, their surprising vitality. Without holding fundamentalist views on "inspiration," he is continually struck by the living quality of the material on which he is working. Some will, no doubt, consider it merely superstitious reverence for "Holy Writ," yet again and again the writer felt rather like an electrician re-wiring an ancient house without being able to "turn the mains off." He feels that this fact is worth recording. Secondly, he is struck by the extraordinary unanimity of the letters. The cynic may suggest that these men were all in a conspiracy together (though it is difficult to see what motive they could have for such a thing), yet the fact remains that in their different ways and from their different angles they are all talking about the same thing, and talking with such certainty as to bring a wondering envy into the modern heart. Perhaps this could be made clearer by taking four illustrations, common to them all, in which their attitude to life differs fundamentally from that of most people to-day.

1. They all had a tremendous sense of the overwhelming Moral Perfection of God. To-day, when to many people God is a vague benevolence with about as much moral authority as Father Christmas, this may strike a strange, and possibly

salutary, note. The terrific "fuss" made about sin and salvation, and the insistence on the only safe approach to God being through Christ, are both due to this acute sense of the peril of a sinful being coming within range, as it were, of the blazing light and purity of God. God, by His very Nature, must mean instant destruction to all evil, and whereas all religions attempt "bridgeheads" towards Him, it is only through Christ that a real and safe bridge has been built between man, who has morally failed, and God the incredibly active and powerful Source of all Life, Love, Goodness, Truth and Beauty. The only safe approach to, and the only means of living in spiritual union with, such a Power lies in Christ—God-become-Man. Without special privilege, power or defence, Christ defeated Evil and then, overcoming a revulsion that men can hardly begin to imagine, He deliberately allowed Himself as Representative Man to experience in Person the ultimate consequence of Evil. These early Christians can hardly find words to express their awed appreciation of the free, but costly, Bridge that was built for Man by this Act of God.

2. In view of the above convictions we can hardly be surprised to find in these writers a condemnation of "false teachers." This condemnation may strike us at first as odd and even un-Christian. We commonly suppose that all roads of the human spirit, however divergent, eventually lead home to the Celestial Benevolence. But if we were seriously to think that they do not, that false roads in fact diverge more and more until they finally lead right away from God, then we can at any rate sympathise with what may seem to us a narrow attitude. For example, an "unorthodox" view of Christ which really means that the "Bridge" is still unbuilt, was anathema to these men who were sure of the truth, and had in many cases known Christ personally. It is at least possible that our "tolerance" has its root in inner uncertainty or indifference.

3. To the writers of these letters this present life was only an incident. It was lived, with a due sense of responsibility, as a preface to sharing the timeless life of God Himself. To these

men this world was only a part, and because of the cumulative result of human sin a highly infected and infectious part, of God's vast created universe, seen and unseen. They trained themselves therefore, and attempted to train others, not to be " taken in " by this world, not to give their hearts to it, not to conform to its values, but to remember constantly that they were only temporary residents, and that their rights of citizenship were in the unseen world of Reality. To-day when all the emphasis is thrown upon making the most of this life, and even Christianity is only seriously considered in many quarters because of its social implications, this point of view is comparatively rarely held. Yet as we read what they have to say we may perhaps find ourselves saying a little wistfully, " perhaps these men were right."

4. The great difference between present-day Christianity and that of which we read in these letters is that to us it is primarily a performance, to them it was a real experience. We are apt to reduce the Christian religion to a code, or at best a rule of heart and life. To these men it is quite plainly the invasion of their lives by a new quality of life altogether. They do not hesitate to describe this as Christ " living in " them. Mere moral reformation will hardly explain the transformation and the exuberant vitality of these men's lives—even if we could prove a motive for such reformation, and certainly the world around offered little encouragement to the early Christian ! We are practically driven to accept their own explanation, which is that their little human lives, had through Christ, been linked up with the very Life of God.

There is one other point that should be made before the letters are read. Without going into wearisome historical details, we need to remember that these letters were written, and the lives they indicate were led, against a background of paganism. There were no churches, no Sundays, no books about the Faith. Slavery, sexual immorality, cruelty, callousness to human suffering, and a low standard of public opinion, were universal ; travelling and communications were chancy and perilous ; most people were illiterate. Many Christians to-day talk about the " difficulties of our times " as though we should have to wait for better ones before the Christian religion can take root. It is heartening to remember that this faith took root and flourished amazingly in conditions that would have killed anything less vital in a matter of weeks. These early Christians were on fire with the conviction that they had become, through Christ, literally sons of God ; they were pioneers of a new humanity, founders of a new Kingdom. They still speak to us across the centuries. Perhaps if we believed what they believed, we might achieve what they achieved.

Although in making this version I have worked from the Greek Text used in the 1881 Revision, I wish to express my gratitude, especially for any unconscious reminiscences, to the modern translators, and in particular to Dr. James Moffat.

My thanks are also due to Dr. C. S. Lewis for his initial encouragement, and to the Rev. C. C. Wolters and Dr. Thornton Weekley for helpful suggestions.

And I wish specially to thank Miss Joan Carter who has never quailed at the seemingly innumerable typings and retypings which a work of this sort demands.

J. B. PHILLIPS

LONDON, 1941-REDHILL, 1946.

PREFACE TO THE
TWENTY-FIRST EDITION
GEOFFREY BLES EDITIONS

FOR SEVERAL years I have wished to make a thorough revision of this my first piece of New Testament translation, but owing to parochial duties and the pressure of other work this has hitherto not been possible. In this edition, however, the book has been thoroughly revised and a number of minor corrections has been made. A few sentences, or parts of sentences, which were quite inadvertently omitted in the original work have now been restored to their proper place. I would like to thank the many correspondents from various parts of the world who have made comments and useful suggestions, and particularly those scholars with far more knowledge of N.T. Greek than I possess myself who have taken the trouble to help me in this revision.

It must be said again that a translator is not a commentator, and while he may be well aware of the different interpretations which may be put upon certain passages he must, if he is to produce a readable and coherent whole, make decisions which remain his sole responsibility.

J. B. Phillips

swanage, 1956.

THE LETTER
TO THE CHRISTIANS AT ROME

AUTHOR. *Paul, probably written from Corinth (Acts XX, 3).*

DATE. *About 57.*

DESTINATION. *The Christians at Rome. No one knows how the church at Rome was founded, though it is perfectly possible that some Romans present on the day of Pentecost in Jerusalem (Acts 11, 10) carried back with them the Christian faith. The Roman Catholic tradition that Peter founded the Church in Rome is without reliable evidence.*

Paul is evidently writing to both converted Jews and converted pagans, which is what one would expect to find in the metropolitan city of the Roman Empire.

THEME. *This letter, with the possible exception of the " Letter to Jewish Christians," is the only one that appears to be written deliberately as a religious treatise and not merely in the ordinary way of correspondence. It is possible that Paul, naturally impressed that he was writing to the heart of the Empire, would take extra pains to " polish " this exposition of the faith.*

The theme is almost entirely that of God's " salvation " and needs a little explanation to the modern mind.

To Paul, brought up under the rigid Jewish Law, God was pre-eminently the God of Righteousness, i.e. moral perfection. In these days when the majority of people assume God to be a vague easy-going Benevolence it is difficult to appreciate the force of Paul's problem, or the wonder of its solution.

If we are prepared to grant the absolute Moral Perfection of God, eternally aflame with positive Goodness, Truth and Beauty, we can perhaps understand that any form of sin or evil cannot approach God without instant dissolution. This is as inevitable as, for example, the destruction of certain germs by the light of the sun.

How then, asks Paul, can man who has failed and, moreover, sinned deliberately, ever approach God or hope to share in His timeless existence?

The Law offers the first method. If men will themselves fully obey the law of God they will be free from moral taint and able to approach God in safety. Unhappily, as Paul points out at some length, men have signally failed to keep either the Law revealed to the Jews or the universal moral law of human conscience. If they have broken all the laws or only a few they have all failed and are all guilty. They can, moreover, do nothing to remove their guilt. The Law which ought to be a finger-post to God becomes to them nothing but a warning-notice. This is the crux of Paul's problem.

The heart of the Gospel is that God Himself meets this frightful deadlock by a Personal visit to this world. God, as Jesus Christ, became Representative Man, and as such deliberately accepted the eventual consequence of evil, namely, suffering and death. Any man therefore who sincerely entrusts his life to Christ can now be accepted by God by virtue of God's personal Act of Atonement. Salvation, i.e. being safe from the horrible long-term consequences of sin and safe in the presence of God's utter holiness, now becomes a matter of " believing " and not " achieving."

The theme is worked out in this letter, with a parenthetical passage about God's Chosen People, the Jews, and is closely followed by advice as to the sort of life that the " justified " and " saved " man should now live.

The letter closes with personal news and greetings.

THIS letter comes to you from Paul, servant of Jesus Christ, called as a Messenger and appointed for the service of that Gospel of God which was long ago promised by the prophets in the Holy Scriptures.

The Gospel is centred in God's Son, a descendant of David by human genealogy and patently marked out as the Son of God by the power of that Spirit of holiness which raised Him to life again from the dead. He is our Lord, Jesus Christ, from Whom we received grace and our commission in His name to forward obedience to the Faith in all nations. And of this great number you at Rome are also called to belong to Him.

To you all then, loved of God and called to be Christ's men and women, grace and peace from God the Father and from our Lord Jesus Christ.

A personal message   1 : 8

I must begin by telling you how I thank God through Jesus Christ for you all, since the news of your faith has become known everywhere. Before God, Whom I serve with all my heart in the Gospel of His Son, I assure you that you are always in my prayers. I am constantly asking Him that He will somehow make it possible for me now, at long last, to come to Rome. I am longing to see you : I want to bring you some spiritual strength, and that will mean that I shall be strengthened by you, each of us helped by the other's faith.

Then I should like you to know, my brothers, that I have long intended to come to you (but something has always prevented me), for I should like to see some results among you, as I have among other Gentiles. I feel myself under a sort of universal obligation, I owe something to all men, from cultured Greek to ignorant savage. That is why I want, as far as my ability will carry me, to preach the Gospel to you who live in Rome as well. For I am not ashamed of the Gospel. I see it as the very power of God working for the salvation of everyone who believes it, both Jew and Greek. I see in it God's plan for imparting righteousness to men, a process begun and continued by their faith. For, as the Scripture says :

The righteous shall live by faith.

The righteousness of God and the sin of man   1 : 18

Now the holy anger of God is disclosed from Heaven against the godlessness and evil of those men who render Truth dumb and inoperative by their wickedness. It is not that they do not know the truth about God : indeed He has made it quite plain to them. For since the beginning of the world the invisible attributes of God, e.g. His eternal Power and Divinity, have been plainly discernible through things which He has made and which are commonly seen and known, thus leaving these men without a rag of excuse. They knew all the time that there is a God, yet they refused to acknowledge Him as such, or to thank Him for what He is or does. Thus they became fatuous in their argumentations, and plunged their silly minds still further into the dark. Behind a façade of " wisdom " they became just fools, fools who would exchange the glory of the Eternal God for an imitation image of a mortal man, or of creatures that run or fly or crawl. They gave up God : and therefore God gave them up—to be the playthings of their own foul desires in dishonouring their own bodies.

The fearful consequence of deliberate atheism   1 : 25

These men deliberately forfeited the Truth of God and accepted a Lie, paying homage and giving service to the creature instead of to the Creator, Who alone is worthy to be worshipped for ever and ever, Amen. God therefore handed them over to disgraceful passions. Their women exchanged the normal practices of sexual intercourse for something which is abnormal and unnatural. Similarly the men, turning from natural intercourse with women, were swept into lustful passions for one another. Men with men performed these shameful horrors, receiving, of course, in their own personalities the consequences of sexual perversity.

Moreover, since they considered themselves too high and mighty to acknowledge God, He allowed them to become the slaves of their degenerate minds, and to perform unmentionable deeds. They became filled with wickedness, rottenness, greed and malice ; their minds became steeped in envy, murder, quarrelsomeness, deceitfulness and spite. They became whisperers-behind-doors, stabbers-in-the-back, God-haters ; they overflowed with insolent pride and boastfulness, and their minds teemed with diabolical invention. They scoffed at duty to parents, they mocked at learning, recognised no obligations of honour, lost all natural affection, and had no use for mercy. More than this—being well aware of God's pronouncement that all who do these things deserve to die, they not only continued their own practices, but did not hesitate to give their thorough approval to others who did the same.

Yet we cannot judge them, for we
also are sinners : God is the only judge   II : I

Now if you feel inclined to set yourself up as a judge of those who sin, let me assure you, whoever you are, that you are in no position to do so. For at whatever point you condemn others you automatically condemn yourself, since you, the judge, commit the same sins. God's Judgment, we know, is utterly impartial in its action against such evil-doers. What makes you think that you, who so readily judge the sin of others, can consider yourself beyond the judgment of God ? Are you, perhaps, misinterpreting God's generosity and patient mercy towards you as weakness on His part ? Don't you realise that God's kindness is meant to lead you to repentance ? Or are you by your obstinate refusal to repent simply storing up for yourself an experience of the wrath of God in the Day when, in His holy anger against evil, He shows His Hand in righteous judgment ?

There is no doubt at all that He will " render to every man according to his works," and that means eternal life to those who, in patiently doing good, aim at the unseen (but real) glory and honour of the eternal world. It also means anger and wrath for those who rebel against God's plan of life, and refuse to obey His rules, and who, in so doing, make themselves the very servants of evil. Yes, it means bitter pain and a fearful undoing for every human soul which works on the side of evil, for Jew and Greek alike. But, let me repeat, there is glory and honour and peace for every worker on the side of good, whether Jew or Greek. For there is no preferential treatment with God.

God's judgment is absolutely just   II : I2
All who have sinned without knowledge of the Law will die without reference to the Law ; and all who have sinned know-

ing the Law shall be judged according to the Law. It is not familiarity with the Law that justifies a man in the sight of God, but obedience to it.

When the Gentiles, who have no knowledge of the Law, act in accordance with it by the light of nature, they show that they have a law in themselves, for they demonstrate the effect of a law operating in their own hearts. Their own consciences endorse the existence of such a law, for there is something which condemns or commends their actions.

We may be sure that all this will be taken into account in the Day of True Judgment, when God will judge men's secret lives by Jesus Christ, as my Gospel plainly states.

You Jews are privileged—
do you live up to your privileges?   II : 17

Now you, my reader, who bear the name of Jew, take your stand upon the Law, and are, so to speak, proud of your God. You know His Plan, and are able through your knowledge of the Law truly to appreciate moral values. You can, therefore confidently look upon yourself as a guide to those who do not know the way, and as a light to those who are groping in the dark. You can instruct those who have no spiritual wisdom : you can teach those who, spiritually speaking, are only just out of the cradle. You have a certain grasp of the basis of true knowledge. You have without doubt very great advantages. But, prepared as you are to instruct others, do you ever teach yourself anything ? You preach against stealing, for example, but are you sure of your own honesty ? You denounce the practice of adultery, but are you sure of your own purity ? You loathe idolatry, but *how honest are you towards the property of heathen temples ?* Everyone knows how proud you are of the Law, but that means a proportionate dishonour to God when men know that you break it ! Don't you know that the very Name of God is cursed among the Gentiles because of the behaviour of Jews ? There is, you know, a verse of Scripture to that effect.

Being a true " Jew " is an inward
not an outward matter   II : 25

That most intimate sign of belonging to God that we call
circumcision does indeed mean something if you keep the
Law. But if you flout the Law you are to all intents and
purposes uncircumcising yourself! Conversely, if an uncircumcised man keep the Law's commandments, does he not
thereby " circumcise " himself? Moreover, is it not plain to
you that those who are physically uncircumcised, and yet
keep the Law, are a continual judgment upon you who, for
all your circumcision and knowledge of the Law, break it?

I have come to the conclusion that a true Jew is not the
man who is merely a Jew outwardly, and real circumcision is
not just a matter of the body. The true Jew is one who belongs
to God in heart, a man whose circumcision is not just an outward physical affair but is a God-made sign upon the heart
and soul, and results in a life lived not for the approval of
man, but for the approval of God.

Jews are privileged, but even they have failed   III : 1

Is there any advantage then in being one of the Chosen
People? Does circumcision mean anything? Yes, of course,
a great deal in every way. You have only to think of one
thing to begin with—it was the Jews to whom God's messages
were entrusted. Some of them were undoubtedly faithless,
but what then? Can you imagine that their faithlessness
could disturb the faithfulness of God? Of course not! Let
us think of God as true if every living man be proved a liar.
Remember the Scripture?

That thou mightest be justified in thy words,
And mightest prevail when thou comest into judgment.

But if our wickedness advertises the Goodness of God, do
we feel that God is being unfair to punish us in return? (I'm
using a human tit-for-tat argument.) Not a bit of it! What
sort of a Person would God be then to judge the world? It is
like saying that if my lying throws into sharp relief the Truth

of God and, so to speak, enhances His reputation, then why should He repay me by judging me a sinner? Similarly, why not do evil that good may be, by contrast, all the more conspicuous and valuable? (As a matter of fact, I am reported as urging this very thing, by some slanderously and others quite seriously! But, of course, such an argument is quite properly condemned.)

Are we Jews then a march ahead of other men? By no means. For I have shown above that all men from Jews to Greeks are under the condemnation of sin. The Scriptures endorse this fact plainly enough.

> There is none righteous, no, not one.
> There is none that understandeth,
> There is none that seeketh after God;
> They have all turned aside, they are together become unprofitable;
> There is none that doeth good, no, not so much as one:
> Their throat is an open sepulchre;
> With their tongues they have used deceit;
> The poison of asps is under their lips:
> Whose mouth is full of cursing and bitterness:
> Their feet are swift to shed blood;
> Destruction and misery are in their ways:
> And the way of peace have they not known;
> There is no fear of God before their eyes.

We know what the message of the Law is, to those who live under it—that every excuse may die on the lips of him who makes it and no living man may think himself beyond the judgment of God. No man can justify himself before God by a perfect performance of the Law's demands—indeed it is the straight-edge of the Law that shows us how crooked we are.

God's new plan—righteousness by faith,
not through the Law III : 21

But now we are seeing the righteousness of God declared quite apart from the Law (though amply testified to by both Law and prophets)—it is a righteousness imparted to, and operating in, all who have faith in Jesus Christ. (For there is no distinction to be made anywhere : everyone has sinned, everyone is falling short of the beauty of God's plan.) Under this divine system a man who has faith is now freely acquitted in the eyes of God by His generous dealing in the Redemptive Act of Jesus Christ. God has appointed Him as the means of propitiation, a propitiation accomplished by the shedding of His blood, to be received and made effective in ourselves by faith. God has done this to demonstrate His Righteousness both by the wiping out of the sins of the past (the time when He withheld His Hand), and by showing in the present time that He is a just God and that He justifies every man who has faith in Jesus Christ.

Faith, not pride of achievement III : 27

What happens now to human pride of achievement ? There is no more room for it. Why, because failure to keep the Law has killed it ? Not at all, but because the whole matter is now on a different plane—believing instead of achieving. We see now that a man is justified before God by the fact of his faith in God's appointed Saviour and not by what he has managed to achieve under the Law.

And God is God of both Jews and Gentiles, let us be quite clear about that ! The same God is ready to justify the circumcised by faith and the uncircumcised by faith also.

Are we then undermining the Law by this insistence on faith ? Not a bit of it ! We put the Law in its proper place.

Let us go back and consider our father Abraham IV : 1

Now how does all this affect the position of our ancestor Abraham ? Well, if justification were by achievement he could quite fairly be proud of what he achieved—but not, I am sure, proud before God. For what does the Scripture say about him ?

> And Abraham believed God, and it was reckoned unto him for righteousness.

Now if a man *works* his wages are not counted as a gift but as a fair reward. But if a man, irrespective of his work, has faith in Him who justifies the sinful, then that man's *faith* is counted as righteousness, and that is the gift of God. This is the happy state of the man whom God accounts righteous, apart from his achievements, as David expresses it :

> Blessed are they whose iniquities are forgiven
> And whose sins are covered.
> Blessed is the man to whom the Lord will not reckon sin.

It is a matter of faith, *not circumcision*   IV : 9

Now the question, an important one, arises : is this happiness for the circumcised only, or for the uncircumcised as well ?

Note this carefully. We began by saying that Abraham's faith was counted unto him for righteousness. When this happened, was he a circumcised man ? He was not, he was still uncircumcised. It was *afterwards* that the sign of circumcision was given to him, as a seal upon that righteousness which God was accounting to him *as yet an uncircumcised man*! God's purpose here is twofold. First, that Abraham might be the spiritual father of all who since that time, despite their uncircumcision, show the faith that is counted as righteousness. Then, secondly, that he might be the circumcised father of all those who are not only circumcised, but are living by the same sort of faith which he himself had before he was circumcised.

The promise, from the beginning, was made to faith   IV : 13

The ancient promise made to Abraham and his descendants, that they should eventually possess the world, was given not because of any achievements made through obedience to the Law, but because of the righteousness which had its root in faith. For if, after all, they who pin their faith to keeping the Law were to inherit God's world, it would make nonsense of faith in God Himself, and destroy the whole point of the Promise.

For we have already noted that the Law can produce no promise, only the threat of wrath to come. And, indeed, if there were no Law the question of sin would not arise.

The whole thing, then, is a matter of faith on man's part and generosity on God's. He gives the security of His own promise to all men who can be called " children of Abraham," i.e. both those who have lived in faith by the Law, and those who have exhibited a faith like that of Abraham. To whichever group we belong, Abraham is in a real sense our father, as the Scripture says :

A father of many nations have I made thee.

This faith is valid because of the existence of God Himself, Who can make the dead live, and speak His Word to those who are yet unborn.

Abraham was a shining example of faith IV : 18

Abraham, when hope was dead within him, went on hoping in faith, believing that he would become " a father of many nations." He relied on the word of God which definitely referred to " thy seed." With undaunted faith he looked at the facts—his own impotence (he was practically a hundred years old at the time) and his wife Sarah's apparent barrenness. Yet he refused to allow any distrust of a definite pronouncement of God to make him waver. He drew strength from his faith, and, while giving the glory to God, remained absolutely convinced that God was able to implement His own promise. This was the " faith " which was counted unto him for righteousness.

Now this counting of faith for righteousness was not recorded simply for Abraham's credit, but as a divine principle which should apply to us as well. Faith is to be reckoned as righteousness to us also, who believe in Him Who raised from the dead our Lord Jesus Christ, Who was delivered to death for our sins and raised again to secure our justification.

Faith means the certainty of God's Love, now and hereafter

V : I

Since then it is by faith that we are justified, let us grasp the fact that we *have* peace with God through our Lord Jesus Christ. Through Him we have confidently entered into this new relationship of grace, and here we take our stand, in happy certainty of the glorious things He has for us in the future.

This doesn't mean, of course, that we have only a hope of future joys—we can be full of joy here and now even in our trials and troubles. Taken in the right spirit these very things will give us patient endurance ; this in turn will develop a mature character, and a character of this sort produces a steady hope, a hope that will never disappoint us. Already we have some experience of the love of God flooding through our hearts by the Holy Spirit given to us. And we can see that it was while we were powerless to help ourselves that Christ died for sinful men. In human experience it is a rare thing for one man to give his life for another, even if the latter be a good man, though there have been a few who have had the courage to do it. Yet the proof of God's amazing love is this : that it was *while we were sinners* that Christ died for us. Moreover if He did that for us while we were sinners, now that we are men justified by the shedding of His blood, what reason have we to fear the wrath of God ? If, while we were His enemies, Christ reconciled us to God by *dying for us*, surely now that we are reconciled we may be perfectly certain of our salvation through His *living in us*. Nor, I am sure, is this a matter of bare salvation—we may hold our heads high in the light of God's love because of the reconciliation which Christ has made.

*A brief résumé—the consequence of
sin and the gift of God*   V : 12

This, then, is what has happened. Sin made its entry into the world through one man, and through sin, death. The entail of sin and death passed on to the whole human race, and no one could break it for no one was himself free from sin.

Sin, you see, was in the world long before the Law, though I suppose, technically speaking, it was not " sin " where there was no law to define it. Nevertheless death, the complement of sin, held sway over mankind from Adam to Moses, even over those whose sin was quite unlike Adam's.

Adam, the first man, corresponds in some degree to the Man who was to come. But the gift of God through Christ is a very different matter from the " account rendered " through the sin of Adam. For while as a result of one man's sin death by natural consequence became the common lot of men, it was by the generosity of God, the free giving of the grace of the One Man Jesus Christ, that the love of God overflowed for the benefit of all men.

Nor is the effect of God's gift the same as the effect of that one man's sin. For in the one case one man's sin brought its inevitable judgment, and the result was condemnation. But, in the other, countless men's sins are met with the free gift of grace, and the result is justification before God.

For if one man's offence meant that men should be slaves to death all their lives, it is a far greater thing that through Another Man, Jesus Christ, men by their acceptance of His more than sufficient grace and righteousness, should live all their lives like kings !

We see, then, that as one act of sin exposed the whole race of men to God's judgment and condemnation, so one Act of Perfect Righteousness presents all men freely acquitted in the sight of God. One man's disobedience placed all men under the threat of condemnation, but One Man's obedience has the power to present all men righteous before God.

Grace is a bigger thing than the Law   V : 20

Now we find that the Law keeps slipping into the picture to point the vast extent of sin. Yet, though sin is shown to be wide and deep, thank God His grace is wider and deeper still ! The whole outlook changes—sin used to be the master of men and in the end handed them over to death : now grace is the ruling factor, with righteousness as its purpose and its end the bringing of men to the eternal life of God through Jesus Christ our Lord.

Righteousness by faith, in practice   VI : I

Now what is our response to be ? Shall we sin to our heart's content and see how far we can exploit the grace of God ? What a ghastly thought ! We, who have died to sin— how could we live in sin a moment longer ? Have you forgotten that all of us who were baptised into Jesus Christ were, by that very action, sharing in His death ? We were dead and buried with Him in baptism, so that just as He was raised from the dead by that splendid revelation of the Father's power so we too might rise to life on a new plane altogether. If we have, as it were, shared His death, let us rise and live our new lives with Him ! Let us never forget that our old selves died with Him on the Cross that the tyranny of sin over us might be broken—for a dead man can safely be said to be immune to the power of sin. And if we were dead men with Him we can believe that we shall also be men newly alive with Him. We can be sure that the risen Christ never dies again— death's power to touch Him is finished. He died, because of sin, once : He lives for God for ever. In the same way look upon yourselves as dead to the appeal and power of sin but alive and sensitive to the call of God through Jesus Christ our Lord.

Do not, then, allow sin to establish any power over your mortal bodies in making you give way to your lusts. Nor hand over your organs to be, as it were, weapons of evil for the Devil's purposes. But, like men rescued from certain death, put yourselves in God's hands as weapons of good for His own purposes. For sin is not meant to be your master—

you are no longer living under the Law, but under grace.

The new service completely ousts the old   VI : 15

Now, what shall we do? Shall we go on sinning because we have no Law to condemn us any more, but are living under grace? Never! Just think what it would mean. You *belong* to the power which you choose to obey, whether you choose sin, whose reward is death, or God, obedience to Whom means the reward of righteousness. Thank God that you, who were at one time the servants of sin, honestly responded to the impact of Christ's teaching when you came under its influence. Then, released from the service of sin, you entered the service of righteousness. (I use an everyday illustration because human nature grasps truth more readily that way.) In the past you voluntarily gave your bodies to the service of vice and wickedness—for the purpose of becoming wicked. So, now, give yourselves to the service of righteousness—for the purpose of becoming really good. For when you were employed by sin you owed no duty to righteousness. Yet what sort of a harvest did you reap from those things that to-day you blush to remember? In the long run those things mean one thing only—death.

But now that you are employed by God, you owe no duty to sin, and you reap the fruit of being made righteous, while at the end of the road there is Life for evermore.

Sin *pays* its servants: the wage is death. But God *gives* to those who serve him: His free gift is eternal life through Jesus Christ our Lord.

How to be free from the Law   VII : 1

You know very well, my brothers (for I am speaking to those well acquainted with the subject), that the Law can only exercise authority over a man so long as he is alive. A married woman, for example, is bound by law to her husband so long as he is alive. But if he dies, then his legal claim over her disappears. This means that, if she should give herself to another man while her husband is alive, she incurs the stigma

L.Y.   B of adultery. But if, after her husband's death, she does exactly the same thing, no one could call her an adulteress, for the legal hold over her has been dissolved by her husband's death.

There is, I think, a fair analogy here. The death of Christ on the Cross has made you " dead " to the claims of the Law, and you are free to give yourselves in marriage, so to speak, to Another, the One Who was raised from the dead, that you may be productive for God.

While we were " in the flesh " the Law stimulated our sinful passions and so worked in our nature that we became productive—for Death ! But now that we stand clear of the Law, the claims which existed are dissolved by our " death," and we are free to serve God not in the old obedience to the letter of the Law, but in a new way, in the spirit.

Sin and the Law   VII : 7

It now begins to look as if sin and the Law were very much the same thing—can this be a fact ? Of course it cannot. But it must in fairness be admitted that I should never have had sin brought home to me but for the Law. For example, I should never have felt guilty of the sin of coveting if I had not heard the Law saying " Thou shalt not covet." But the sin in me, finding in the commandment an opportunity to express itself, stimulated all my covetous desires. For sin, in the absence of the Law, has no chance to function technically as " sin." As long, then, as I was without the Law I was, spiritually speaking, alive. But when the commandment arrived, sin sprang to life and I " died." The commandment, which was meant to be a direction to life, I found was a sentence to death. The commandment gave sin an opportunity, and without my realising what was happening, it " killed " me.

The Law is itself good   VII : 12

It can scarcely be doubted that in reality the Law itself is holy, and the commandment is holy, fair and good. Can it be that something that is intrinsically good could mean death to me ? No, what happened was this. Sin, at the touch of the Law, was forced to expose itself as sin, and *that* meant death for me. The contact of the Law showed the sinful nature of sin.

But it cannot make men good   VII : 14

After all, the Law itself is really concerned with the spiritual—it is I who am carnal, and have sold my soul to sin. In practice, what happens ? My own behaviour baffles me. For I find myself not doing what I really want to do but doing what I really loathe. Yet surely if I do things that I really don't want to do it cannot be said that " I " am doing them at all—it must be sin that has made its home in my nature. (And indeed, I know from experience that the carnal side of my being can scarcely be called the home of good !) I often find that I have the will to do good, but not the power. That is, I don't accomplish the good I set out to do, and the evil I don't really want to do I find I am always doing. Yet if I do things that I don't really want to do then it is not, I repeat, " I " who do them, but the sin which has made its home within me. When I come up against the Law I want to do good, but in practice I do evil. My conscious mind whole-heartedly endorses the Law, yet I observe an entirely different principle at work in my nature. This is in continual conflict with my conscious attitude, and makes me an unwilling prisoner to the law of sin and death. In my mind I am God's willing servant, but in my own nature I am bound fast, as I say, to the law of sin and death. It is an agonising situation, and who on earth can set me free from the clutches of my own sinful nature ? I thank God there *is* a way out through Jesus Christ our Lord.

The way out—new life in Christ   VIII : 1

No condemnation now hangs over the head of those who are " in " Jesus Christ. For the new spiritual principle of life " in " Christ lifts me out of the old vicious circle of sin and death.

The Law never succeeded in producing righteousness—the

failure was always the weakness of human nature. But God has met this by sending His own Son Jesus Christ to live in that human nature which causes the trouble. And, *while Christ was actually taking upon Himself the sins of men, God condemned that sinful nature.* So that we are able to meet the Law's requirements, so long as we are living no longer by the dictates of our sinful nature, but in obedience to the promptings of the Spirit. The carnal attitude sees no farther than natural things. But the spiritual attitude reaches out after the things of the spirit. The former attitude means, bluntly, death : the latter means life and inward peace. And this is only to be expected, for the carnal attitude is inevitably opposed to the purpose of God, and neither can nor will follow His laws for living. Men who hold this attitude cannot possibly please God.

What the presence of Christ within means   VIII : 9

But you are not carnal but spiritual if the Spirit of God finds a home within you. You cannot, indeed, be a Christian at all unless you have something of His Spirit in you. Now if Christ does live within you His presence means that your sinful nature is dead, but your spirit becomes alive because of the righteousness He brings with Him. I said that our nature is " dead " in the presence of Christ, and so it is, because of its sin. Nevertheless once the Spirit of Him Who raised Jesus from the dead lives within you He will, by that same Spirit, bring to your whole being new strength and vitality.

So then, my brothers, you can see that we have no particular reason to feel grateful to our instinctive nature, or to live life on the level of the instincts. Indeed that way of living leads to certain spiritual death. But if on the other hand you cut the nerve of your instinctive actions by obeying the Spirit, you are on the way to real living.

Christ is within—
follow the lead of His Spirit   VIII : 14

All who follow the leading of God's spirit are God's own sons. Nor are you meant to relapse into the old slavish

attitude of fear—you have been adopted into the very family
circle of God and you can say with a full heart, " Father, my
Father." The Spirit Himself endorses our inward conviction
that we really are the children of God. Think what that
means. If we are His children we share His treasures, and all
that Christ claims as His will belong to all of us as well ! Yes,
if we share in His sufferings we shall certainly share in His
glory.

Present distress is temporary and negligible   VIII : 18

In my opinion whatever we may have to go through now
is less than nothing compared with the magnificent future
God has planned for us. The whole creation is on tiptoe to
see the wonderful sight of the sons of God coming into their
own. The world of creation cannot as yet see Reality, not
because it chooses to be blind, but because in God's purpose
it has been so limited—yet it has been given hope. And the
hope is that in the end the whole of created life will be
rescued from the tyranny of change and decay, and have its
share in that magnificent liberty which can only belong to the
children of God !

It is plain to anyone with eyes to see that at the present
time all created life groans in a sort of universal travail. And
it is plain, too, that we who have a foretaste of the Spirit are
in a state of painful tension, while we wait for that redemption
of our bodies which will mean that at last we have realised our
full sonship in Him. We were saved by this hope, but in our
moments of impatience let us remember that hope always
means waiting for something that we haven't yet got. But
if we hope for something we cannot see, then we must
settle down to wait for it in patience.

This is not mere theory—the Spirit
helps us to find it true   VIII : 26

The Spirit of God not only maintains this hope within us,
but helps us in our present limitations. For example, we do
not know how to pray worthily as sons of God, but His
Spirit within us is actually praying for us in those agonising

longings which never find words. And God Who knows the heart's secrets understands, of course, the Spirit's intention as He prays for those who love God.

Moreover we know that to those who love God, who are called according to His Plan, everything that happens fits into a pattern for good. God, in his foreknowledge, chose them to bear the family likeness of His Son, that He might be the eldest of a family of many brothers. He chose them long ago ; when the time came He called them, He made them righteous in His sight and then lifted them to the splendour of life as His own sons.

We hold, in Christ, an impregnable position   VIII : 31

In face of all this, what is there left to say ? If God is for who can be against us ? He that did not hesitate to spare His own Son but gave Him up for us all—can we not trust such a God to give us, with Him, everything else that we can need ?

Who dares accuse us now ? The Judge Himself has declared us free from sin. Who is in a position to condemn ? Only Christ, and Christ died for us, Christ rose for us, Christ reigns in power for us, Christ prays for us !

Can anything separate us from the love of Christ ? Can trouble, pain or persecution ? Can lack of clothes and food, danger to life and limb, the threat of force of arms ? Indeed some of us know the truth of that ancient text :

> For Thy sake we are killed all the day long ;
> We were accounted as sheep for the slaughter.

No, in all these things we win an overwhelming victory through Him Who has proved His love for us.

I have become absolutely convinced that neither Death nor Life, neither messenger of Heaven nor monarch of earth, neither what happens to-day nor what may happen to-morrow, neither a power from on high nor a power from below, nor anything else in God's whole world has any power to separate us from the love of God in Jesus Christ our Lord !

The fly in the ointment—the
infidelity of my own race   IX : I

Before Christ and my own conscience I assure you that I am speaking the plain truth when I say that there is something that makes me feel very depressed, like a pain that never leaves me. It is the condition of my brothers, and fellow-Israelites, and I have actually reached the pitch of wishing myself cut off from Christ if it meant that they could be won for God.

Just think what the Israelites have had given to them. The privilege of being adopted as sons of God, the experience of seeing something of the glory of God, the receiving of the Agreements made with God, the gift of the Law, true ways of worship, God's own promises—all these are theirs. The patriarchs are theirs, and so too, as far as human descent goes, is Christ Himself, Christ Who is God over all, blessed for ever.

God's purpose is not utterly
defeated by this infidelity   IX : 6

Now this does not mean that God's word to Israel has failed. For you cannot count all "Israelites" as the true Israel of God. Nor can all Abraham's descendants be considered truly children of Abraham. The promise was that "in Isaac shall thy children be called." That means that it is not the natural descendants who automatically inherit the promise, but, on the contrary, that the children of the promise (i.e. the sons of God) are to be considered truly Abraham's children. For it was a promise when God said: "About this time I will come and Sarah shall have a son." (Everybody, remember, thought it quite impossible for Sarah to have a child.) And then, again, a word of promise came to Rebecca, at the time when she was pregnant with two children by the one man, Isaac our forefather. It came before the children were born or had done anything good or bad, plainly showing that God's act of choice has nothing to do with achievements, good or bad, but is entirely a matter of His will. The promise was :

The elder shall serve the younger.

And we get a later endorsement of this Divine choice in the words :

> Jacob I loved, but Esau I hated.

We must not jump to conclusions about God   IX : 14

Now do we conclude that God is monstrously unfair ? Never ! God said long ago to Moses :

> I will have mercy on whom I have mercy, and I will have compassion on whom I have compassion.

It is obviously not a question of human will or human effort, but of Divine mercy. The Scripture says to Pharaoh :

> For this very purpose did I raise thee up, that I might show in thee my power, and that my name might be published abroad in all the earth.

It seems plain, then, that God chooses on whom He will have mercy, and whom He will harden in their sin.

Of course I can almost hear your retort : " If this is so and God's Will is irresistible, why does God blame men for what they do ? " But the question really is this : " Who are you, a man, to make any such reply to God ? " When a craftsman makes anything he doesn't expect it to turn round and say, " Why did you make me like this ? " The potter, for instance, is always assumed to have complete control over the clay, making with one part of the lump a lovely vase, and with another a pipe for sewage. Can we not assume that God has the same control over human clay ? May it not be that God, though He must sooner or later expose His wrath against sin and show His controlling Hand, has yet most patiently endured the presence in His world of things that cry out to be destroyed ? Can we not see, in this, His purpose in demonstrating the boundless resources of His glory upon those whom He considers fit to receive His mercy, and whom He long ago planned to raise to glorious life? And by these chosen people I mean you and me, whom He has called out from both Jews and Gentiles. He says in Hosea:

I will call that my people, which was not my people;
And her beloved, which was not beloved.
And it shall be, that in the place where it was said unto them,
    Ye are not my people,
There shall they be called sons of the living God.

And Isaiah, speaking about Israel, proclaims:

If the number of the children of Israel be as the sand of the
    sea, it is the remnant that shall be saved:
For the Lord will execute his word upon the earth, finishing
    it and cutting it short.

And previously, Isaiah said:
Except the Lord of Sabaoth had left us a seed,
We had become as Sodom, and had been made like unto
    Gomorrah.

At present the Gentiles have gone
further than the Jews   IX : 30

Now, how far have we got? That the Gentiles who never had the Law's standard of righteousness to guide them, have attained righteousness, righteousness-by-faith. But Israel, following the Law of righteousness, failed to reach the goal of righteousness. And why? Because their minds were fixed on what they achieved instead of on what they believed. They tripped over that very stone the Scripture mentions:

Behold, I lay in Zion a stone of stumbling and a rock of
    offence:
And he that believeth on Him shall not be put to shame.

How Israel has missed the way   X : 1

My brothers, from the bottom of my heart I long and pray to God that Israel may be saved! I know from experience what a passion for God they have, but alas, it is not a passion based on knowledge. They do not know God's righteousness, and all the time they are going about trying to prove their own righteousness they have the wrong attitude to receive His. For Christ means the end of the struggle for righteousness-by-the-Law for everyone who believes in Him.

Moses writes of righteousness-by-the-Law when he says that the man who perfectly obeys the Law shall find life in it—which is theoretically right but impossible in practice. But righteousness-by-faith says something like this :

"You need not say in your heart, 'Who could go up to Heaven to bring Christ down to us, or who could descend into the depths to bring Him up from the dead?' For the secret is very near you, in *your own heart*, in *your own mouth*!" It is the secret of faith, which is the burden of our preaching, and it says, in effect, "If you openly admit by *your own mouth* that Jesus Christ is the Lord, and if you believe in *your own heart* that God raised Him from the dead you will be saved." For it is believing *in the heart* that makes a man righteous before God, and it is stating his belief by *his own mouth* that confirms his salvation. And the Scripture says : "Whosoever believes in Him shall not be disappointed." And that "Whosoever" means anyone, without distinction between Jew or Greek. For all have the same Lord, Whose boundless resources are available to all who turn to Him in faith. For :

Whosoever shall call upon the Name of the Lord shall be saved.

Can we offer the excuse of ignorance
on Israel's behalf?   X : 14

Now how can they call on One in Whom they have never believed? How can they believe in One of Whom they have never heard? And how can they hear unless someone pro-

claims Him ? And who will go to tell them unless he is sent ?
As the Scripture puts it :

> How beautiful are the feet of them that bring glad tidings
> of good things !

Yet all who have heard have not responded to the Gospel
Isaiah asks, you remember,

> Lord, who hath believed our report ?

(Belief, you see, can only come from hearing the message, and
the message is the word of Christ.)

But when I ask myself : " Did they never hear ? " I have to
answer that they *have* heard, for

> Their sound went out into all the earth,
> And their words unto the ends of the world.

Then I say to myself : " Did Israel not know ? " And my
answer must be that they did. For Moses says :

> I will provoke you to jealousy with that which is no nation,
> With a nation void of understanding will I anger you.

And Isaiah, more daring still, puts these words into the mouth
of God :

> I was found of them that sought me not.
> I became manifest unto them that asked not of me.

And then, speaking of Israel :

> All the day long did I spread out my hands unto a dis-
> obedient and gainsaying people.

Israel's failure—yet remember
the faithful few   XI : 1

This leads naturally to the question, " Has God then totally repudiated His People ? " Certainly not ! I myself, for one, am an Israelite, a descendant of Abraham and of the tribe of Benjamin. It is unthinkable that God should have repudiated His own People, the People whose destiny He Himself appointed. Don't you remember what the Scripture says in the story of Elijah ? How he pleaded with God on Israel's behalf :

> Lord, they have killed Thy prophets
> They have digged down Thine altars :
> And I am left alone, and they seek my life.

And do you remember God's reply ?

> I have left for myself seven thousand men
> Who have not bowed the knee to Baal.

In just the same way, there is at the present time a minority, chosen by the grace of God. And if it is a matter of the grace of God, it cannot be a question of their actions especially deserving God's favour, for that would make grace meaningless.

What conclusion do we reach now ? That Israel did not, on the whole, obtain the object of his striving, but a chosen few " got there," while the remainder became more and more insensitive to the righteousness of God. This is borne out by the Scripture :

> God gave them a spirit of stupor,
> Eyes that they should not see,
> And ears that they should not hear,
> Unto this very day.

And David says of them :

Let their table be made a snare, and a trap,
And a stumbling-block, and a recompense unto them :
Let their eyes be darkened, that they may not see,
And bow thou down their back alway.

In the providence of God disaster has
been turned to good account   XI : 11

Now I ask myself, "Was this fall of theirs an utter
disaster ? " It was not ! For through their failure the benefit
of salvation has passed to the Gentiles, with the result that
Israel is made to see and feel what it has missed. And if its
failure has meant such a priceless benefit for the world at
large, think what tremendous advantages its fulfilling of
God's plan could mean !

Now a word to you who are Gentiles. I should like you to
know that I make as much as I can of my ministry as " God's
Messenger to the Gentiles " so as to make my kinsfolk jealous
and thus save some of them. For if their exclusion from the
pale of Salvation has meant the reconciliation of the rest of
mankind to God, what would their inclusion mean ? It
would be nothing less than life from the dead ! If the flour is
consecrated to God so is the whole loaf, and if the roots of a
tree are dedicated to God every branch will belong to Him
also.

A word of warning   XI : 17

But if some of the branches of the tree have been broken off,
while you, like shoots of wild-olive, have been grafted in, and
share like a natural branch the rich nourishment of the root,
don't let yourself feel superior to those former branches. (If
you feel inclined that way, remind yourself that you do not
support the root, the root supports you.) You may make the
natural retort, " But the branches were broken off to make
room for my grafting ! " It wasn't quite like that. They lost
their position because they failed to believe ; you only maintain yours because you do believe. The situation does not call
for conceit but for a certain wholesome fear. If God removed
the natural branches for a good reason, take care that you

don't give Him the same reason for removing you. You must try to appreciate both the kindness and the strict justice of God. Those who fell experienced His justice, while you are experiencing His kindness, and will continue to do so as long as you do not abuse that kindness. Otherwise you too will be cut off from the tree. And as for the fallen branches, unless they are obstinate in their unbelief, they will be grafted in again. Such a restoration is by no means beyond the power of God. And, in any case, if you who were, so to speak, cuttings from a wild-olive, were grafted in, is it not a far simpler matter for the natural branches to be grafted back into the parent stem ?

God still has a plan for Israel   XI : 25

Now I don't want you, my brothers, to start imagining things, and I must therefore share with you my knowledge of God's secret plan. It is this, that the partial insensibility which has come to Israel is only to last until the full number of the Gentiles has been called in. Once this has happened, all Israel will be saved, as the Scripture says :

> There shall come out of Zion the Deliverer ;
> He shall turn away ungodliness from Jacob :
> And this is my covenant unto them,
> When I shall take away their sins.

As far as the Gospel goes, they are at present God's enemies —which is to your advantage. But as far as God's purpose in choosing is concerned, they are still beloved for their fathers' sakes. For once they are made, God does not withdraw His gifts or His calling.

The whole scheme looks topsy-turvy,
until we see the amazing wisdom of God!   XI : 30

Just as in the past you were disobedient to God but have found that mercy which might have been theirs but for their disobedience, so they, who at the present moment are disobedient, will eventually share the mercy which has been extended to you. God has all men penned together in the prison of disobedience, that He may have mercy upon them all.

Frankly, I stand amazed at the unfathomable complexity of God's wisdom and God's knowledge. How could man ever understand His reasons for action, or explain His methods of working? For:

Who hath known the mind of the Lord?

Or who hath been His counsellor?

Or who hath first given to Him, and it shall be recompensed unto him again?

For of Him, and through Him, and unto Him, are all things.

To Him be the glory for ever, Amen.

We have seen God's mercy and wisdom :
how shall we respond? XII : I

With eyes wide open to the mercies of God, I beg you, my brothers, as an act of intelligent worship, to give Him your bodies, as a living sacrifice, consecrated to Him and acceptable by Him. Don't let the world around you squeeze you into its own mould, but let God remould your minds from within, so that you may prove in practice that the Plan of God for you is good, meets all His demands and moves towards the goal of true maturity.

As your spiritual teacher I give this piece of advice to each one of you. Don't cherish exaggerated ideas of yourself or your importance, but try to have a sane estimate of your capabilities by the light of the faith that God has given to you all. For just as you have many members in one physical body and those members differ in their functions, so we, though many in number, compose one Body in Christ and are all members of one another. Through the grace of God we have different gifts. If our gift is preaching, let us preach to the limit of our vision. If it is serving others let us concentrate on our service : if it is teaching let us give all we have to our teaching ; and if our gift be the stimulating of the faith of others let us set ourselves to it. Let the man who is called to give, give freely ; let the man who wields authority think of

his responsibility; and let the sick visitor do his job cheerfully.

Let us have real Christian behaviour   XII : 9

Let us have no imitation Christian love. Let us have a
genuine break with evil and a real devotion to good. Let us
have real warm affection for one another as between brothers,
and a willingness to let the other man have the credit. Let us
not allow slackness to spoil our work and let us keep the fires
of the spirit burning, as we do our work for God. Base your
happiness on your hope in Christ. When trials come endure
them patiently; steadfastly maintain the habit of prayer. Give
freely to fellow-Christians in want, never grudging a meal or
a bed to those who need them. And as for those who try to
make your life a misery, bless them. Don't curse, bless. Share
the happiness of those who are happy, and the sorrow of those
who are sad. Live in harmony with each other. Don't
become snobbish but take a real interest in ordinary people.
Don't become set in your own opinions. Don't pay back a
bad turn by a bad turn, to *anyone*. Don't say "it doesn't matter
what people think," but see that your public behaviour is
above criticism. As far as your responsibility goes, live at
peace with everyone. Never take vengeance into your own
hands, my dear friends: stand back and let God punish if
He will. For it is written:

Vengeance belongeth unto Me: I will recompense.

And these are God's words:

If thine enemy hunger, feed him;
If he thirst, give him to drink:
For in so doing thou shalt heap coals of fire upon his head.

Don't allow yourself to be overpowered with evil. Take the
offensive—overpower evil by good!

The Christian and the civil law

XIII : 1

Every Christian ought to obey the civil authorities, for all legitimate authority is derived from God's Authority, and the existing authority is appointed under God. To oppose authority then is to oppose God, and such opposition is bound to be punished.

The honest citizen has no need to fear the keepers of law and order, but the dishonest man will always be nervous of them. If you want to avoid this anxiety just lead a law-abiding life, and all that can come your way is a word of approval. The officer is God's servant for your protection. But if you are leading a wicked life you have reason to be alarmed. The " power of the law " which is vested in every legitimate officer, is no empty phrase. He is, in fact, Divinely appointed to inflict God's punishment upon evil-doers.

You should therefore, obey the authorities, not simply because it is the safest, but because it is the right thing to do. It is right, too, for you to pay taxes for the civil authorities are appointed by God for the good purposes of public order and well-being. Give everyone his legitimate due, whether it be rates, or taxes, or reverence, or respect!

To love others is the highest conduct

XIII : 8

Keep out of debt altogether, except that perpetual debt of love which we owe one another. The man who loves his neighbour has obeyed the whole Law in regard to his neighbour. For the commandments, " Thou shalt not commit adultery," " Thou shalt not kill," " Thou shalt not steal," " Thou shalt not covet " and all other commandments are summed up in this one saying : " Thou shalt love thy neighbour as thyself." Love hurts nobody : therefore love is the answer to the Law's commands.

Wake up and live !

XIII : 11

Why all this stress on behaviour ? Because, as I think you have realised, the present time is of the highest importance, it is time to wake up to reality. Every day brings God's salvation nearer.

BITHYNIA & PONTUS

CAPPADOCIA

Troas

ASIA

EPHESUS
A.D. 62
(To Timothy)
A.D. 66

GALATIA
A D 56 or 57

●Lystra

●Antioch

Hierapolis

Laodicea●

COLOSSAE
A.D. 62 (Philemon)

●Tarsus

Hetus

●Antioch

●Jerusalem

PI

S.J.D.

The night is nearly over, the Day has almost dawned. Let us therefore fling away the things that men do in the dark, let us arm ourselves for the fight of the Day! Let us live cleanly, as in the daylight, not in the " delights " of getting drunk or playing with sex, nor yet in quarrelling or jealousies. Let us be Christ's men from head to foot, and give no chance to the flesh to have its fling.

Don't criticise each other's convictions   XIV : 1

Welcome a man whose faith is weak, but not with the idea of arguing over his scruples. One man believes that he may eat anything, another man, without this strong conviction, is a vegetarian. The meat-eater should not despise the vegetarian, nor should the vegetarian condemn the meat-eater—they should reflect that God has accepted them both. After all, who are you to criticise the servant of somebody else, especially when that Somebody Else is God ? It is to his own Master that he gives, or fails to give, satisfactory service. And don't doubt that satisfaction, for God is well able to transform men into servants who are satisfactory.

People are different—make allowances   XIV : 5

Again, one man thinks some days of more importance than others. Another man considers them all alike. Let every one be definite in his own convictions. If a man specially observes one particular day, he does so " to God." The man who eats, eats " to God," for he thanks God for the food. The man who fasts also does it " to God," for he thanks God for the benefits of fasting. The truth is that we neither live nor die as self-contained units. At every turn life links us to God, and when we die we come face to face with Him. In life or death we are in the hands of God. Christ lived and died that He might be the Lord in both life and death.

Why, then, criticise your brother's actions, why try to make him look small ? We shall all be judged one day, not by each other's standards or even our own, but by the standard of Christ. It is written :

As I live, saith the Lord, to me every knee shall bow,
And every tongue shall confess to God.

It is to God alone that we have to answer for our actions.

This should be our attitude   XIV : 13
Let us therefore stop turning critical eyes on one another.
If we must be critical, let us be critical of our own conduct
and see that we do nothing to make a brother stumble or fall.

I am convinced, and I say this as in the presence of Christ
Himself, that nothing is intrinsically unholy. But none the
less it is unholy to the man who thinks it is. If your habit of
unrestricted diet seriously upsets your brother, you are no
longer living in love towards him. And surely you wouldn't
let food mean ruin to a man for whom Christ died. You
mustn't let something that is all right for you look like an evil
practice to somebody else. After all, the Kingdom of Heaven
is not a matter of whether you get what you like to eat and
drink, but of righteousness and peace and joy in the Holy
Spirit. If you put these things first in serving Christ you will
please God and are not likely to offend men. So let us concentrate on the things which make for harmony, and on the
growth of one another's character. Surely we shouldn't wish
to undo God's work for the sake of a plate of meat !

I freely admit that all food is, in itself, harmless, but it can
be harmful to the man who eats it with a guilty conscience.
We should be willing to be both vegetarians and teetotallers
if by doing otherwise we should impede a brother's progress
in the faith. Your personal convictions are a matter of faith
between yourself and God, and you are happy if you have no
qualms about what you allow yourself to eat. Yet if a man
eats meat with an uneasy conscience about it, you may be sure
he is wrong to do so. For his action does not spring from his
faith, and when we act apart from our faith we sin.

Christian behaviour to one another   XV : 1
We who have strong faith ought to shoulder the burden of
the doubts and qualms of others and not just to go our own

sweet way. Our actions should mean the good of others—
should help them to build up their characters. For even
Christ did not choose His own pleasure, but as it is written :

The reproaches of them that reproached thee fell upon me.

For all those words which were written long ago are meant
to teach us to-day ; that when we read in the Scriptures of the
endurance of men and of all the help that God gave them in
those days, we may be encouraged to go on hoping in our own
time. May the God Who inspires men to endure, and gives
them a Father's care, give you a mind united towards one
another because of your common loyalty to Jesus Christ. And
then, as one man, you will sing from the heart the praises of
God the Father of our Lord Jesus Christ. So open your
hearts to one another as Christ has opened His heart to you,
and God will be glorified.

A reminder—Christ the Universal Saviour   xv : 8
    Christ was made a servant of the Jews to prove God's
trustworthiness, since He personally implemented the
promises made long ago to the fathers, and also that the
Gentiles might bring glory to God for His mercy to them.
It is written :

Therefore will I give praise unto Thee among the Gentiles
And sing unto Thy Name.

And again :

Rejoice, ye Gentiles, with His People.

And yet again :

Praise the Lord all ye Gentiles ;
And let all the peoples praise Him.

And then Isaiah says :

There shall be the root of Jesse,
And He that ariseth to rule over the Gentiles:
On Him shall the Gentiles hope.

May the God of Hope fill *you* with joy and peace in your
faith, that by the power of the Holy Spirit, your whole life
and outlook may be radiant with hope.

What I have tried to do   XV : 14
For myself I feel certain that you, my brothers, have real
Christian character and experience, and that you are capable
of keeping each other on the right road. Nevertheless I have
written to you with a certain frankness, to refresh your minds
with truths that you already know, by virtue of my commission as Christ's Minister to the Gentiles in the service of
the Gospel. For my constant endeavour is to present the
Gentiles to God as an offering which He can accept, because
they are sanctified by the Holy Spirit. And I think I have
something to be proud of (through Christ, of course) in my
work for God. I am not competent to speak of the work
Christ has done through others, but I do know that through
me He has secured the obedience of Gentiles in word and
deed, working by sign and miracle and all the power of the
Spirit. I have fully preached the Gospel from Jerusalem and
the surrounding country as far as Illyricum. My constant
ambition has been to preach the Gospel where the name of
Christ was previously unknown, and to avoid as far as possible
building on another man's foundation, so that :

They shall see, to whom no tidings of Him came,
And they who have not heard shall understand.

My future plans   XV : 22
Perhaps this will explain why I have so frequently been
prevented from coming to see you. But now, since my work
in these places no longer needs my presence, and since for
many years I have had a great desire to see you, I hope to
visit you on my way to Spain. I hope also that you will speed

me on my journey, after I have had the satisfaction of seeing you all. At the moment my next call is to Jerusalem, to look after the welfare of the Christians there. The churches in Macedonia and Achaia, you see, have thought it a good thing to make a contribution towards the poor Christians in Jerusalem. They have thought it a good thing to make this gesture and yet, really, they received " a good thing " from them first ! For if the Gentiles have had a share in the Jews' spiritual " good things " it is only fair that they should look after the Jews as far as the good things of this world are concerned.

When I have completed this task, then, and turned their gesture into a good deed done, I shall come to you *en route* for Spain. I feel sure that in this long-looked-for visit I shall bring with me the full blessing of Christ's gospel.

Now, my brothers, I am going to ask you, for the sake of Christ Himself and for the love we bear each other in the Spirit, to stand behind me in earnest prayer to God on my behalf—that I may not fall into the hands of the unbelievers in Judaea, and that the Jerusalem Christians may receive the gift I am taking to them in the spirit in which it was made. Then I shall come to you, in the purpose of God, with a happy heart, and may even enjoy with you a little holiday.

The God of peace be with you all, Amen.

Personal greetings and messages   XVI : 1

I want this letter to introduce to you Phoebe, our sister, a deaconess of the Church at Cenchrea. Please give her a Christian welcome, and any assistance with her work that she may need. She has herself been of great assistance to many, not excluding myself.

Shake hands for me with Priscilla and Aquila. They have not only worked with me for Christ, but they have faced death for my sake. Not only I, but all the Gentile churches, owe them a great debt. Give my love to the little church that meets in their house.

Shake the hand of dear Epaenetus, Achaia's first man to be won for Christ, and of course greet Mary who has worked so hard for you. A handshake too for Andronicus and Junias my kinsmen and fellow-prisoners; they are outstanding men among the Messengers and were Christians before I was.

Another warm greeting for Amplias, dear Christian that he is, and also for Urbanus, who has worked with me, and dear old Stachys, too.

>More greetings from me, please, to:
>Apelles, the man who has proved his faith,
>The household of Aristobulus,
>Herodion, my kinsman,
>Narcissus's household, who are Christians.

Remember me to Tryphena and Tryphosa, who work so hard for the Lord, and to dear old Persis who has also done great work.

Shake the hand of Rufus for me—that splendid Christian, and greet his mother, who has been mother to me too. Greetings to Asyncritus, Phlegon, Hermes, Patrobas, Hermas and their Christian group: also to Philologus and Julia, Nereus and his sister, and Olympas and the Christians who are with them.

Give each other a hearty handshake all round for my sake. The greetings of all the churches I am in touch with come to you with this letter.

A final warning   XVI : 17

And now I implore you, my brothers, to keep a watchful eye on those who cause trouble and make difficulties among you, in plain opposition to the teaching you have been given and steer clear of them. Such men do not really serve our Lord Jesus Christ at all but are utterly self-centred. Yet with their plausible and attractive arguments they deceive those who are too simple-hearted to see through them.

Your loyalty to the principles of the Gospel is known everywhere, and that gives me great joy. I want to see you experts in good, and not even beginners in evil. It will not be long before the God of peace will crush Satan under your feet. May the grace of our Lord Jesus Christ be with you.

Timothy, who works with me, sends his greetings, and so

do Lucius and Jason and Sosipater my fellow-countrymen. (Paul has just told me that I, Tertius, who have been taking down this epistle from his dictation, may send you my Christian greetings too.) Gaius, my host (and the host as a matter of fact of the whole church here), sends you his greetings. Erastus, our Town Clerk, and Quartus, another Christian brother, send greetings too.

Now to Him Who is able to set you on your feet as His own sons—according to my Gospel, according to the preaching of Jesus Christ Himself, and in accordance with the disclosing of that secret purpose which, after long ages of silence, has now been made known (in full agreement with the writings of the prophets long ago), by the command of the Everlasting God to all the Gentiles, that they might turn to Him in the obedience of faith—to Him, I say, the only God Who is wise, be glory for ever through Jesus Christ !

PAUL

THE FIRST LETTER TO
THE CHRISTIANS AT CORINTH

AUTHOR. *Paul, writing from Ephesus, where he stayed for more than two years. He had evidently written at least one previous letter to the Church at Corinth.*

DATE. *About 56.*

DESTINATION. *The Christian church at Corinth, which was then the largest town in Greece. Acts XVIII gives some account of the beginnings of the Church there. It is worth remembering that Corinth was a most important seaport, a garrison town, and a strategic road-junction. It was the capital of the Roman province of Achaia. It would have been full of a cosmopolitan crowd, and even in those days was a byword for immorality, probably largely because of the highly organised worship of Venus (Aphrodite).*

THEME. *The beginning of the letter is an impassioned indictment of the "party-spirit," which can have no place in a church where all men belong to Christ. Paul then proceeds to deal sternly with a particularly revolting case of sexual immorality, which the Corinthian Christians appear to treat with complacency. The litigiousness of the Corinthian Church is next censured. Paul's somewhat ascetic views on marriage follow, and modern readers need to remind themselves of the incredible sexual promiscuity existing in Corinth, against which Paul is obviously violently reacting.*

Butcher's meat in a city like Corinth had often been exposed before heathen idols before being offered for sale. This meant a practical difficulty for Christians and Paul advises upon it.

He then lays down some rules about public worship, particularly on the reverent conduct of what we now call the Holy Communion.

The question of the diversity of the gifts of God's Spirit is dealt with patiently and logically, and then follows the famous passage about the highest gift of all—Christian love.

Then comes the almost equally famous passage on the "Resurrection of the body," by no means irrelevant to modern ears.

The matter of the Jerusalem Sick and Poor Fund, and some interesting personal messages, close the letter.

PAUL, commissioned as Messenger of Jesus Christ, and Sosthenes, a Christian brother, to the Church of God at Corinth—to those whom Christ has made holy, who are called to be God's men and women, to all true believers in Jesus Christ, their Lord and ours—grace and peace be to you from God the Father and the Lord, Jesus Christ!

I am thankful for your faith   I : 4

I am always thankful to God for what the gift of His grace in Jesus Christ has meant to you—how, as the Christian message has become established among you, He has enriched your whole lives, from the words on your lips to the understanding in your hearts. And you have been eager to receive His gifts during this time of waiting for His final appearance. He will keep you steadfast in the faith to the end, so that when His Day comes you need fear no condemnation. God is utterly dependable, and it is He Who has called you into fellowship with His Son Jesus Christ, our Lord.

But I am anxious over your "divisions"   1 : 10

Now I do beg you, my brothers, by all that Christ means to you, to speak with one voice, and not allow yourselves to be split up into parties. All together you should be achieving a unity in thought and judgment. For I know, from what some of Chloe's people have told me, that you are each making different claims—"I am one of Paul's men," says one; "I am one of Apollos'" says another; or "I am one of Cephas'," ; while someone else says, "I owe my faith to Christ alone."

Do consider how serious these divisions are!   1 : 13

What *are* you saying? Is there more than one Christ? Was it Paul who died on the Cross for you? Were you baptised in the name of Paul? It makes me thankful that I didn't actually baptise any of you (except Crispus and Gaius), or perhaps someone would be saying I did it in my own name. (Oh, yes, I did baptise Stephanas' family, but I can't remember anyone else.) For Christ did not send me to see how many I could baptise, but to proclaim the Gospel. And I have not done this by the persuasiveness of clever words, for I have no desire to rob the Cross of its power. The preaching of the Cross is, I know, nonsense to those who are involved in this dying world, but to us who are being saved from that death it is nothing less than the power of God.

The Cross shows that God's wisdom is not
man's wisdom by any means   1 : 19

It is written :

> I will destroy the wisdom of the wise,
> And the prudence of the prudent will I reject.

For consider, what have the philosopher, the writer and the critic of this world to show for all their wisdom ? Has not God made the wisdom of this world look foolish ? For it was after the world in its wisdom had failed to know God, that He in His Wisdom chose to save all who would believe by the "simple-mindedness" of the Gospel message. For the Jews ask for miraculous proofs and the Greeks an intellectual panacea, but all we preach is Christ crucified—a stumbling-block to the Jews and sheer nonsense to the Gentiles, but for those who are called, whether Jews or Greeks, Christ the power of God and the wisdom of God. And this is really only natural, for God's "foolishness" is wiser than men, and His "weakness" is stronger than men.

Nor are God's values the same as man's   1 : 26

For look at your own calling as Christians, my brothers. You don't see among you many of the wise (according to this world's judgment) nor many of the ruling class, nor many from the noblest families. But God has chosen what the world calls foolish to shame the wise ; He has chosen what the world calls weak to shame the strong. He has chosen things of little strength and small repute, yes and even things which have no real existence to explode the pretensions of the things that are—that no man may boast in the presence of God. Yet from this same God you have received your standing in Jesus Christ, and He has become for us the true Wisdom, a matter, in practice, of being made righteous and holy, in fact, of being redeemed. And this makes us see the truth of the Scripture :

He that glorieth, let him glory in the Lord.

I came to you in God's strength not my own   II : 1

In the same way, my brothers, when I came to proclaim to you God's secret purpose, I did not come equipped with any brilliance of speech or intellect. You may as well know now that it was my secret determination to concentrate entirely on Jesus Christ Himself and the fact of His death upon the Cross.

As a matter of fact, in myself I was feeling far from strong ; I was nervous and rather shaky. What I said and preached had none of the attractiveness of the clever mind, but it was a demonstration of the power of the Spirit of God ! Plainly God's purpose was that your faith should rest not upon man's cleverness but upon the power of God.

*There is, of course, a real wisdom, which
God allows us to share with Him*   II : 6

We do, of course, speak " wisdom " among those who are spiritually mature, but it is not what is called wisdom by this world, nor by the powers-that-be, who soon will be only the powers that have been. The wisdom we speak of is that mysterious secret wisdom of God which He planned before the Creation for our glory to-day. None of the powers of this world have known this wisdom—if they had they would never have crucified the Lord of glory ! But, as it is written :

Things which eye saw not, and ear heard not,
And which entered not into the heart of man,
Whatsoever things God prepared for them that love him.

But God has, through the Spirit, let us share His Secret. For nothing is hidden from the Spirit, not even the deep wisdom of God. For who could really understand a man's inmost thoughts except the spirit of the man himself ? How much less could anyone understand the thoughts of God except the very Spirit of God ? And the marvellous thing is this, that we now receive not the spirit of the world but the Spirit of God Himself, so that we can actually understand something of God's generosity towards us.

*This wisdom is only understood
by the spiritual*   II : 13

It is these things that we talk about, not using the expressions of the human intellect but those which the Holy Spirit teaches us, explaining spiritual things to those who are spiritual.

But the unspiritual man simply cannot accept the matters which the Spirit deals with—they just don't make sense to him, for, after all, you must be spiritual to see spiritual things. The spiritual man, on the other hand, has an insight into the meaning of everything, though his insight may baffle the man of the world. This is because the former is sharing in God's wisdom, and

> Who hath known the mind of the Lord,
> That he should instruct Him?

Incredible as it may sound, we who are spiritual have the very thoughts of Christ!

But I cannot yet call you spiritual III : I

I, my brothers, was unable to talk to you as spiritual men: I had to talk to you as unspiritual, as yet babies in the Christian life. And my practice has been to feed you, as it were, with " milk " and not with " meat." You were unable to digest " meat " in those days, and I don't believe you can do it now. For you are still unspiritual; all the time that there is jealousy and squabbling among you you show that you are—you are living just like men of the world. While one of you says, " I am one of Paul's converts " and another says, " I am one of Apollos'," are you not plainly unspiritual?

After all, who is Paul? Who is Apollos? No more than servants through whom you came to believe as the Lord gave each man his opportunity. I may have done the planting and Apollos the watering, but it was God Who made the seed grow! The planter and the waterer are nothing compared with Him Who gives life to the seed. Planter and waterer are alike insignificant, though each shall be rewarded according to his particular work.

We work on God's foundation III : 9

In this work, we work with God, and that means that you are a field under God's cultivation, or, if you like, a house being built to His Plan. I, like an architect who knows his

job, by the grace God has given me, lay the foundation;
someone else builds upon it. I only say this, let the builder be
careful how he builds! The Foundation is laid already, and
no one can lay another, for it is Jesus Christ Himself. But any
man who builds on the Foundation using as his material gold,
silver, precious stones, wood, hay or stubble, must know that
each man's work will one day be shown for what it is. The
Day will show it plainly enough, for the Day will arise in a
blaze of fire, and that fire will prove the nature of each man's
work. If the work that a man has built upon the Foundation
will stand this test, he will be rewarded. But if a man's work
be destroyed under the test, he loses it all. He personally will
be safe, though rather like a man rescued from a fire.

Make no mistake : you are God's Holy Building   III : 16
➤ Don't you realise that you yourselves are the temple of God,
and that God's Spirit lives in you ? God will destroy anyone
who defiles His temple, for His temple is holy—*and that is
exactly what you are* ! ➤

Let no one be under any illusion over this. If any man
among you thinks himself one of the world's clever ones, let
him discard his cleverness that he may learn to be truly wise.
For this world's cleverness is stupidity to God. It is written :

He that taketh the wise in their craftiness.

And again :

The Lord knoweth the reasonings of the wise, that they are
vain.

So let no one boast of men. Everything belongs to you!
Paul, Apollos or Cephas ; the world, life, death, the present
or the future, everything is yours ! For you belong to Christ,
and Christ belongs to God !

Trust us, but make no hasty judgments   IV : I

You should look upon us as ministers of Christ, as trustees of the secrets of God. And it is a prime requisite in a trustee that he should prove worthy of his trust. But, as a matter of fact, it matters very little to me what you, or any man, thinks of me—I don't even value my opinion of myself. For I might be quite ignorant of any fault in myself—but that doesn't justify me before God. My only true Judge is God Himself.

The moral of this is that we should make no hasty or premature judgments. When the Lord comes He will bring into the light of day all that at present is hidden in darkness, and He will expose the secret motives of men's hearts. Then shall God Himself give each man his share of praise.

Having your favourite teacher is
not only silly but wrong   IV : 6

I have used myself and Apollos above as an illustration, so that you might learn from what I have said about us not to assess man above his value in God's sight, and may thus avoid the friction that comes from exalting one teacher against another. For who makes you different from somebody else, and what have you got that was not given to you? And if anything has been given to you, why boast of it as if it were something you had achieved yourself?

Think sometimes of what your
happiness has cost us !   IV : 8

Oh, I know you are rich and flourishing! You've been living like kings, haven't you, while we've been away? I would to God you were really kings in God's sight so that we might reign with you !

I sometimes think that God means us, the Messengers, to appear last in the procession of mankind, like the men who are to die in the arena. For indeed we are made a public spectacle before the angels of Heaven and the eyes of men. We are looked upon as fools, for Christ's sake, but you are wise in the Christian faith. We are considered weak, but

you have become strong : you have found honour, we little
but contempt. Up to this very hour we are hungry and thirsty,
ill-clad, knocked about and practically homeless. We still
have to work for our living by manual labour. Men curse us,
but we return a blessing : they make our lives miserable but
we take it patiently. They ruin our reputations but we go on
trying to win them for God. We are the world's rubbish, the
scum of the earth, yes, up to this very day.

A personal plea　　　　　　　　　　　　　　　　　　IV : 14

I don't write these things merely to make you feel un-
comfortable but that you may realise facts, as my dear
children. After all, you may have ten thousand teachers in the
Christian faith, but you cannot have many fathers ! For in
Jesus Christ I am your spiritual father through the Gospel ;
that is why I implore you to follow the footsteps of me your
father. I have sent Timothy to you to help you in this. For
he himself is my much-loved and faithful son in the Lord, and
he will remind you of those ways of living in Christ which I
teach in every church to which I go.

Please God it will not be long before I come to you in
person. Then I shall be able to see what power, apart from
their words, these pretentious ones among you really possess.
For the Kingdom of God is not a matter of a spate of words
but of the power of Christian living.

Now it's up to you to choose ! Shall I come to you ready to
chastise you, or in love and gentleness ?

A horrible sin and a stern remedy　　　　　　　　　　V : 1

It is actually reported that there is sexual immorality among
you, and immorality of a kind that even pagans condemn—a
man has apparently taken his father's wife ! Are you still
proud of your Church ? Shouldn't you be overwhelmed with
sorrow and shame ? The man who has done such a thing
should certainly be expelled from your fellowship !

I know I am not with you physically but I am with you in
spirit, and I assure you as solemnly as if I were actually present
before your assembly that I have already pronounced judg-

ment in the Name of the Lord Jesus on the man who has done this thing, and I do this with full Divine authority. My judgment is this : that the man should be left to the mercy of Satan so that while his body will experience the destructive powers of sin his spirit may yet be saved in the Day of the Lord Jesus.

Your pride in your Church is lamentably out of place. Don't you know how a little yeast can permeate the whole lump ? Clear out every bit of the old yeast that you may be new unleavened bread ! We Christians have had a Passover Lamb sacrificed for us—none other than Christ Himself ! So let us " keep the feast " with no trace of the yeast of the old life, nor the yeast of vice and wickedness, but with the unleavened bread of unadulterated truth !

In my previous letter I said, " Don't mix with the immoral." I didn't mean, of course, that you were to have no contact at all with the immoral of this world, or with any cheats or thieves or idolaters—for that would mean going out of the world altogether ! But in this letter I tell you not to associate with any professing Christian who is known to be an impure man or a swindler, an idolater, a man with a foul tongue, a drunkard or a thief. My instruction is : " Don't even eat with such a man." Those outside the Church it is not my business to judge. But surely it is your business to judge those who are inside the Church—God alone can judge those who are outside. It is your plain duty to expel from your Church this wicked man !

Don't go to law in pagan courts VI : 1

When any of you has a grievance against another, aren't you ashamed to bring the matter to be settled before a pagan court instead of before the Church ? Don't you know that Christians will one day judge the world ? And if you are to judge the world do you consider yourselves incapable of settling such infinitely smaller matters ? Don't you also know that we shall judge the very angels themselves—how much more then matters of this world only ! In any case, if you find you have to judge matters of this world, why choose as judges those who count for nothing in the Church? I say this deliberately to rouse your sense of shame. Are you really unable to find among your number one man with enough sense to decide a dispute between one and another of you, or must one brother resort to the law against another and that before those who have no faith in Christ! It is surely obvious that something must be seriously wrong in your Church for you to be having lawsuits at all. Why not *let* yourself be wronged or cheated? For when you go to law against your brother you yourself do him wrong, for you cheat him of Christian love and forgiveness.

Have you forgotten that the Kingdom of God will never belong to the wicked? Don't be under any illusion—neither the impure, the idolater or the adulterer; neither the effeminate, the pervert or the thief; neither the swindler, the drunkard, the foul-mouthed or the rapacious shall have any share in the Kingdom of God. *And such men, remember, were some of you!* But you have cleansed yourselves from all that, you have been made whole in spirit, you have been justified before God in the Name of the Lord Jesus and in His very Spirit.

Christian liberty does not mean
moral licence   VI : 12

As a Christian I *may* do anything, but that does not mean that everything is good for me to do. I may do everything, but I must not be the slave of anything. Food was meant for the stomach and the stomach for food; but God has no permanent purpose for either. But you cannot say that our physical body was made for sexual promiscuity; it was made for God, and God is the Answer to our deepest longings. The God Who raised the Lord from the dead will also raise us mortal men by His power. Have you realised the almost incredible fact that your bodies are integral parts of Christ Himself? Am I then to take parts of Christ and join them to a prostitute? Never! Don't you realise that when a man joins himself to a prostitute he makes with her a physical unity? For, God says, " the two shall be one flesh." On the other hand the man who joins himself to God is one with Him in spirit.

Avoid sexual looseness like the plague! Every other sin that a man commits is done outside his own body, but this is an offence against his own body. Have you forgotten that your body is the temple of the Holy Spirit, Who lives in you, and that you are not the owner of your own body? You have been bought, and at what a price! Therefore bring glory to God both in your body and your spirit, for they both belong to Him.

The question of marriage in present circumstances

VII : 1

Now let me deal with the questions raised in your letter.

It is a good principle for a man to have no physical contact with women. Nevertheless, because casual liaisons are so prevalent, let every man have his own wife and every woman her own husband. The husband should give his wife what is due to her as his wife, and the wife should be as fair to her husband. The wife has no longer full rights over her own person, but shares them with her husband. In the same way the husband shares his personal rights with his wife. Do not cheat each other of normal sexual intercourse, unless of course you both decide to abstain temporarily to make special opportunity for fasting and prayer. But afterwards you should resume relations as before, or you will expose yourselves to the obvious temptation of the Devil.

I give the advice above more as a concession than as a command. I wish that all men were like myself, but I realise that everyone has his own particular gift from God, some one thing and some another. Yet to those who are unmarried or widowed I say definitely that it is a good thing to remain unattached, as I am. But if they find they have not the gift of self-control in such matters, by all means let them get married. I think it is far better for them to be married than to be tortured by unsatisfied desire.

To those who are already married my command, or rather, the Lord's command, is that the wife should not leave her husband. But if she is separated from him she should either remain unattached or else be reconciled to her husband. A husband is not, in similar circumstances, to divorce his wife.

*Advice over marriage between
Christian and pagan*
VII : 12

To other people my advice (though this is not a Divine command) is this. For a brother who has a non-Christian wife who is willing to live with him he should not divorce her. A wife in a similar position should not divorce her husband. For the unbelieving husband is, in a sense, consecrated by being joined to the person of his wife; the unbelieving wife is similarly "consecrated" by the Christian brother she has married. If this were not so then your children would bear the stains of paganism, whereas they are actually consecrated to God.

But if the unbelieving partner decides to separate, then let there be a separation. The Christian partner need not consider himself bound in such cases. Yet God has called us to live in peace, and after all how can you, who are a wife, know whether you will be able to save your husband or not? And the same applies to you who are a husband.

I merely add to the above that each man should live his life with the gifts that God has given him and in the condition in which God has called him. This is the rule I lay down in all the churches.

For example, if a man was circumcised when God called him he should not attempt to remove the signs of his circumcision. If on the other hand he was uncircumcised he should not become circumcised. Being circumcised or not being circumcised, what do they matter? The great thing is to obey the orders of Almighty God. Everyone should stick to the calling in which he heard the call of God. Were you a slave when you heard the call? Don't let that worry you, though if you find the opportunity to become free you had better take it. But a slave who is called to life in Christ is set free in the eyes of God. And a man who was free when God called him becomes a slave—to Christ Himself! You have been redeemed, at tremendous cost; don't therefore sell yourselves as slaves to men! My brothers, let every one of us continue to live his life with God in the state in which he was when he was called.

In present circumstances it is really
better not to marry

VII : 25

Now as far as young unmarried women are concerned, I must confess that I have no direct commands from the Lord. Nevertheless, I give you my considered opinion as of one who is, I think, to be trusted after all his experience of God's mercy.

My opinion is this, that amid all the difficulties of the present time you would do best to remain just as you are. Are you married? Well, don't try to be separated. Are you unattached? Then don't try to get married. But if you, a man, should marry, don't think that you have done anything sinful. And the same applies to a young woman. Yet I do believe that those who take this step are bound to find the married state an extra burden in these critical days, and I should like you to be as unencumbered as possible. All our futures are so foreshortened, indeed, that those who have wives should live, so to speak, as though they had none! There is no time to indulge in sorrow, no time for enjoying our joys; those who buy have no time to enjoy their possessions, and indeed their every contact with the world must be as light as possible, for the present Scheme of Things is rapidly passing away. That is why I should like you to be as free from worldly entanglements as possible. The unmarried man is free to concern himself with the Lord's affairs, and how he may please Him. But the married man is sure to be concerned with matters of this world, that he may please his wife. You find the same difference in the case of the unmarried and the married woman. The unmarried concerns herself with the Lord's affairs, and her aim in life is to make herself holy, in body and in spirit. But the married woman must concern herself with the things of this world, and her aim will be to please her husband.

I tell you these things to help you; I am not putting difficulties in your path but setting before you an ideal, so that your service of God may be as far as possible free from worldly distractions.

But marriage is not wrong

VII : 36

But if any man feels he is not behaving honourably towards the woman he loves, especially as she is beginning to lose her first youth and the emotional strain is considerable, let him do what his heart tells him to do—let them be married, there is no sin in that. Yet for the man of steadfast purpose who is able to bear the strain and has his own desires well under control, if he decides not to marry the young woman, he too will be doing the right thing. Both of them are right, one in marrying and the other in refraining from marriage, but the latter has chosen the better of two right courses.

A woman is bound to her husband while he is alive, but if he dies she is free to marry whom she likes—but let her be guided by the Lord. In my opinion she would be happier to remain as she is, unmarried. And I think I am here expressing not only my opinion, but the will of the Spirit as well.

A practical problem : shall we be guided by superior knowledge or love ?

VIII : I

Now to deal with the matter of meat which has been sacrificed to idols. It is easy to think that we " know " over problems like this, but we should remember that while knowledge may make a man look big, it is only love that can make him grow to his full stature. For whatever a man may know, he still has a lot to learn, but if he loves God, he is opening his whole life to the Spirit of God.

In this matter, then, of eating meat which has been offered to idols, knowledge tells us that no idol has any real existence, and that there is no God but One. For though there are so-called gods both in heaven and earth, gods and lords galore in fact, to us there is only One God, the Father, from Whom everything comes, and for Whom we live. And there is one Lord, Jesus Christ, by Whom everything exists, and by Whom we ourselves are alive. But this knowledge of ours is not shared by all men. For some, who until now have been used to idols, eat the meat as meat really sacrificed to a god, and their delicate conscience is thereby injured. Now our acceptance by God is not a matter of meat. If we eat it, that does not make us better men, nor are we the worse if we do not eat it. You must be careful that your freedom to eat meat does not in any way hinder anyone whose faith is not as robust as yours. For suppose you with your knowledge of God should be observed eating meat in an idol's temple, are you not encouraging the man with a delicate conscience to do the same? Surely you would not want your superior knowledge to bring spiritual disaster to a weaker brother for whom Christ died? And when you sin like this and damage the weak conscience of your brethren you really sin against Christ. This makes me determined that, if there is any possibility of meat injuring my brother, I will have none of it as long as I live, for fear I might do him harm.

A word of personal defence to my critics   IX : 1

Is there any doubt that I am a genuine Messenger, any doubt that I am a free man? Have I not seen Jesus our Lord with my own eyes? Are not you yourselves samples of my work for the Lord? Even if other people should refuse to recognise my Divine commission, yet to you at any rate I shall always be a true Messenger, for you are a living proof of God's call to me. This is my real ground of defence to those who cross-examine me.

Aren't we allowed to eat and drink? May we not travel with a Christian sister like the other Messengers, like other Christian brothers, and like Cephas, whom some of you hold in such admiration? Are Barnabas and I the only ones not allowed to leave their ordinary work to give time to the ministry?

Even a preacher of the Gospel has some rights!   IX : 7

Just think for a moment. Does any soldier ever go to war at his own expense? Does any man plant a vineyard and have no share in its fruits? Does the shepherd who tends the flock never taste the milk? This is, I know, an argument from everyday life, but it is a principle endorsed by the Law. For is it not written in the Law of Moses :

Thou shalt not muzzle the ox when he treadeth out the corn ?

Now does this imply merely God's care for oxen, or does it include His care for us too ? Surely we are included ! You might even say that the words were written for us. For both the ploughman as he ploughs, and the thresher as he threshes should have some hope of an ultimate share in the harvest. If we have sown for you seed of spiritual things need you be greatly perturbed because we reap some of your material things ? And if there are others with the right to have these things from you, have not we an even greater right ? Yet we have never exercised this right and have put up with all sorts of things, so that we might not hinder the spread of the Gospel.

I am entitled to a reward, yet
I have not taken it   IX : 13

Are you ignorant of the fact that those who minister sacred things take part of the sacred food of the Temple for their own use, and those who attend the altar have their share of what is placed on the altar ? On the same principle the Lord has ordered that those who proclaim the Gospel should receive their livelihood from those who accept the Gospel.

But I have never used any of these privileges, nor am I writing now to suggest that I should be given them. Indeed I would rather die than have anyone make this boast of mine an empty one !

My reward is to make the Gospel
free to all men   IX : 16

For I take no special pride in the fact that I preach the Gospel. I feel compelled to do so ; I should be utterly miserable if I failed to preach it. If I do this work because I choose to do so then I am entitled to a reward. But if it is no choice of mine, but a sacred responsibility put upon me, what can I expect in the way of reward? This, that when I preach the Gospel, I can make it absolutely free of charge, and need not claim what is my rightful due as a preacher. For though I am no man's slave, yet I have made myself everyone's slave, that I might win more men to Christ. To the Jews I was a Jew that I might win the Jews. To those who were under the Law I put myself in the position of being under the Law (although in fact I stand free of it), that I might win those who are under the Law. To the weak I became a weak man, that I might win the weak. I have, in short, been all things to all sorts of men that by every possible means I might win some to God. I do all this for the sake of the Gospel; I want to play my part in it properly.

To preach the Gospel faithfully
is my set purpose

IX : 24

Do you remember how, on a racing-track, every competitor runs, but only one wins the prize? Well, you ought to run with your minds fixed on winning the prize! Every competitor in athletic events goes into serious training. Athletes will take tremendous pains—for a fading crown of leaves. But our contest is for an eternal crown that will never fade.

I run the race then with determination. I am no shadow-boxer, I really fight! I am my body's sternest master, for fear that when I have preached to others I should myself be disqualified.

Spiritual experience does not
guarantee infallibility

X : I

For I should like to remind you, my brothers, that our ancestors all had the experience of being guided by the cloud in the desert and of crossing the sea dry-shod. They were all, so to speak, "baptised" into Moses by these experiences. They all shared the same spiritual food and drank the same spiritual drink (for they drank from the Spiritual Rock which followed them, and that Rock was Christ). Yet in spite of all these wonderful experiences many of them failed to please God, and left their bones in the desert. Now in these events our ancestors stand as examples to us, warning us not to crave after evil things as they did. Nor are you to worship false gods as they did. The Scripture says—

The people sat down to eat and drink, and rose up to play.

Neither should we give way to sexual immorality as did some of them, for we read that twenty-three thousand fell in a single day ! Nor should we dare to exploit the goodness of God as some of them did, and fell victims to poisonous snakes. Nor yet must you curse the lot that God has appointed to you as they did, and met their end at the hand of the Angel of Death.

Now these things which happened to our ancestors are illustrations of the way in which God works, and they were written down to be a warning to us who are the heirs of the ages which have gone before us.

So let the man who feels sure of his standing to-day be careful that he does not fall to-morrow.

God still governs human experience   X : 13

No temptation has come your way that is too hard for flesh and blood to bear. But God can be trusted not to allow you to suffer any temptation beyond your powers of endurance. He will see to it that every temptation has a way out, so that it will never be impossible for you to bear it.

We have great spiritual privileges :
let us live up to them   X : 14

The lesson we must learn, my brothers, is at all costs to avoid worshipping a false God. I am speaking to you as intelligent men : think over what I am saying.

The Cup of blessing which we bless, is it not a very sharing in the Blood of Christ ? When we break the Bread do we not actually share in the Body of Christ ? The very fact that we all share one Bread makes us all one Body. Look at the Jews of our own day. Isn't there a fellowship between all those who eat the altar sacrifices?

Now am I implying that a false god really exists, or that sacrifices made to any god have some value? Not at all! I say emphatically that Gentile sacrifices are made to evil spiritual powers and not to God at all. I don't want you to have any fellowship with such powers. You cannot drink both the Cup of the Lord and the cup of devils. You cannot be a guest at the Lord's Table and at the table of devils. Are we trying to arouse the wrath of God? Have we forgotten how completely we are in His hands?

The Christian's guiding principle
is love not knowledge
X : 23

As I have said before, the Christian position is this: I may do anything, but everything is not useful. Yes, I may do anything, but everything is not constructive. Let no man, then, set his own advantage as his objective, but rather the good of his neighbour.

You should eat whatever is sold in the meat-market without asking any of the questions of an over-scrupulous conscience. The whole earth and all that is in it belongs to the Lord.

If a pagan asks you to dinner and you want to go, feel free to eat whatever is set before you, without asking any questions through conscientious scruples. But if your host should say straight out, "This meat has been offered to an idol," then don't eat it, for his sake—I mean for the sake of conscience, not yours, but his.

Now why should my freedom to eat be at the mercy of someone else's conscience? Or why should any evil be said of me when I have eaten meat with thankfulness, and have thanked God for it? Because, whatever you do, eating or drinking or anything else, everything should be done to bring glory to God.

Do nothing that might make men stumble, whether they are Jews or Greeks or members of the Church of God. I myself try to adapt myself to all men without considering my own advantage but *their* advantage, that if possible they may be saved.

Copy me, my brothers, as I copy Christ Himself.

The reasons that lie behind some
of the traditions　　　　　　　　　　　　　　　　XI : 2

I must give you credit for remembering what I taught you and adhering to the traditions I passed on to you. But I want you to know that Christ is the Head of every individual man, just as a man is the "head" of the woman and God is the Head of Christ. Thus it follows that if a man prays or preaches with his head covered, he is, symbolically, dishonouring Him Who is his real Head. But in the case of a woman, if she prays or preaches with her head uncovered it is just as much a disgrace as if she had had it closely shaved. For if a woman does not cover her head she might just as well have her hair cropped. And if to be cropped or closely shaven is a sign of disgrace to women (as it is with many peoples), then that is all the more reason for her to cover her head. A man ought not to cover his head, for he represents the very Person and Glory of God, while the woman reflects the person and glory of the man. For man does not exist because woman exists, but vice versa. Man was not created originally for the sake of woman, but woman was created for the sake of man. For this reason a woman ought to bear on her head an outward sign of man's authority for all the angels to see.

Of course, in the sight of God neither "man" nor "woman" has any separate existence. For if woman was made originally for man, no man is now born except by a woman, and both man and woman, like everything else, owe their existence to God. But use your own judgment, do you think it right and proper for a woman to pray to God bareheaded? Isn't there a natural principle here, that makes us feel that long hair is disgraceful to a man, but of glorious beauty to a woman? We feel this because the long hair is the cover provided by nature for the woman's head. But if anyone wants to be argumentative about it, I can only say that we and the Churches of God generally hold this ruling on the matter.

I must mention serious faults in your Church   XI : 17

But in giving you the following rules, I cannot commend your conduct, for it seems that your church meetings do you more harm than good! For first, when you meet for worship I hear that you split up into small groups, and I think there must be truth in what I hear. For there must be cliques among you or your favourite leaders would not be so conspicuous. It follows, then, that when you are assembled in one place you do not eat the *Lord's* Supper. For everyone tries to grab his food before anyone else, with the result that one goes hungry and another has too much to drink! Haven't you houses of your own to have your meals in, or are you making a convenience of the Church of God and causing acute embarrassment to those who have no other home?

Am I to commend this sort of conduct? Most certainly not!

To partake of the Lord's Supper is a
supremely serious matter   XI : 23

The teaching I gave you was given me personally by God Himself, and it was this: the Lord Jesus, in the same night in which He was betrayed, took bread, and when He had given thanks He broke it and said, "Take, eat, this is My Body which is being broken for you. Do this in remembrance of Me." Similarly, when supper was ended, He took the cup saying, "This cup is the New Agreement in My Blood: do this, whenever you drink it, in remembrance of Me."

This can only mean that whenever you eat this bread or drink of this cup, you are proclaiming that the Lord has died for you, and you will do that until He comes again. So that, whoever eats the bread or drinks the wine without due thought is making himself like one of those who allowed the Lord to be put to death without discerning Who He was.

No, a man should thoroughly examine himself, and only then should he eat the bread or drink of the cup. He that eats and drinks carelessly is eating and drinking a judgment on himself, for he is blind to the presence of the Lord's Body.

Careless Communion means spiritual
weakness : let us take due care   XI : 30

It is this careless participation which is the reason for the many feeble and sickly Christians in your Church, and the explanation of the fact that many of you are spiritually asleep.

If we were closely to examine ourselves beforehand, we should avoid the judgment of God. But when God does judge us, He disciplines us as His own sons, that we may not be involved in the general condemnation of the world.

Now, my brothers, when you come together to eat this bread, wait your proper turn. If a man is really hungry let him satisfy his appetite at home. Don't let your communions be God's judgment upon you !

The other matters I will settle in person, when I come.

The Holy Spirit inspires men's faith
and imparts spiritual gifts   XII : 1

Now I want to give you some further information in some spiritual matters. You have not forgotten that you were Gentiles, following dumb idols just as you had been taught. Now I want you to understand, as Christians, that no one speaking by the Spirit of God could call Jesus accursed, and no one could say that He is the Lord, except by the Holy Spirit.

Men have different gifts, but it is the same Spirit Who gives them. There are different ways of serving God, but it is the same Lord Who is served. God works through different men in different ways, but it is the same God Who achieves His purposes through them all. Each man is given his gift by the Spirit that he may make the most of it.

One man's gift by the Spirit is to speak with wisdom, another's to speak with knowledge. The same Spirit gives to another man faith, to another the ability to heal, to another the power to do great deeds. The same Spirit gives to another man the gift of preaching the word of God, to another the ability to discriminate in spiritual matters, to another speech in different tongues and to yet another the power to interpret the tongues. Behind all these gifts is the operation of the same Spirit, Who distributes to each individual man, as He wills.

*The human body is an example of
an organic unity*

XII : 12

As the human body, which has many parts, is a unity, and those parts, despite their multiplicity, comprise together one single body, so it is with the Body of Christ. For we were all baptised by the Spirit into one Body, whether we were Jews, Gentiles, slaves or free men, and we have all had experience of the same Spirit.

Now the body is not one member but many. If the foot should say, " because I am not a hand I don't belong to the body," does that alter the fact that the foot *is* a part of the body ? Or if the ear should say, " Because I am not an eye I don't belong to the body," does that mean that the ear really is no part of the body ? After all, if the body were all one Eye, for example, where would be the sense of hearing ? Or if it were all one Ear, where would be the sense of Smell ? But God has arranged all the parts in the one body, according to His design. So that the eye cannot say to the hand, " I don't need you ! " nor, again, can the head say to the feet, " I don't need you ! " On the contrary, those parts of the body which have no obvious function are the more essential to health ; and to those parts of the body which seem to us to be less deserving of notice we have to allow the highest honour of function. The parts which do not look beautiful have a deeper beauty in the work they do, while the parts which look beautiful may not be at all essential to life ! But God has harmonised the whole body by giving importance of function to the parts which lack apparent importance, that the body should work together as a whole with all the members in sympathetic relationship with one another. So it happens that if one member suffers all the other members suffer with it, and if one member is honoured all the members share a common joy.

Now you are together the Body of Christ, and individually you are members of Him. And in His Church God has appointed first some to be His Messengers, secondly some to be preachers of the word, thirdly teachers. After them He has appointed workers of spiritual power, men with the gift of healing, helpers, organisers and those with the gift of speaking in " tongues."

As we look at the Body of Christ do we find all are His Messengers, all are preachers, or all teachers ? Do we find all wielders of spiritual power, all able to heal, all able to speak with tongues, or all able to interpret the tongues ? No, we find God's distribution of gifts is on the same principles of harmony that He has shown in the human body.

You should set your hearts on the highest spiritual gifts, but I will show you what is the highest way of all.

Christian love—the highest and best gift   XIII : 1

If I speak with the eloquence of men and of angels, but have no love, I become no more than blaring brass or crashing cymbal. If I have the gift of foretelling the future and hold in my mind not only all human knowledge but the very secrets of God, and if I also have that absolute faith which can move mountains, but have no love, I amount to nothing at all. If I dispose of all that I possess, yes, even if I give my own body to be burned, but have no love, I achieve precisely nothing.

This love of which I speak is slow to lose patience—it looks for a way of being constructive. It is not possessive : it is neither anxious to impress nor does it cherish inflated ideas of its own importance.

Love has good manners and does not pursue selfish advantage. It is not touchy. It does not compile statistics of evil or gloat over the wickedness of other people. On the contrary, it is glad with all good men when Truth prevails.

Love knows no limit to its endurance, no end to its trust, no fading of its hope : it can outlast anything. It is, in fact, the one thing that still stands when all else has fallen.

All gifts except love will be
superseded one day   XIII : 9

For if there are prophecies they will be fulfilled and done with, if there are "tongues" the need for them will disappear, if there is knowledge it will be swallowed up in truth. For our knowledge is always incomplete and our prophecy is always incomplete, and when the Complete comes that is the end of the Incomplete.

When I was a little child I talked and felt and thought like a little child. Now that I am a man my childish speech and feeling and thought have no further significance for me.

At present all we see is the baffling reflection of reality ; we are like men looking at a landscape in a small mirror. The time will come when we shall see reality whole and face to face ! At present all I know is a little fraction of the truth, but the time will come when I shall know it as fully as God now knows me !

In this life we have three great lasting qualities—faith, hope and love. But the greatest of them is love.

"Tongues" are not the greatest gift   XIV : 1

Follow, then, the way of love, while you set your heart on the gifts of the Spirit. The highest gift you can wish for is to be able to speak the messages of God. The man who speaks in a "tongue" addresses not men (for no one understands a word he says) but God : and only in his spirit is he speaking spiritual secrets. But he who preaches the word of God is using his speech for the building up of the faith of one man, the encouragement of another or the consolation of another. The speaker in a "tongue" builds up his own soul, but the preacher builds up the Church of God.

I should indeed like you all to speak with "tongues," but I would much rather that you all preached the word of God. For the preacher of the word does a greater work than the speaker with "tongues," unless of course the latter interprets his words for the benefit of the Church.

Unless " tongues " are interpreted
do they help the Church ?   XIV : 6

For suppose I came to you, my brothers, speaking with " tongues," what good could I do you unless I could give you some revelation of Truth, some knowledge in spiritual things, some message from God, or some teaching about the Christian life ?

Even in the case of inanimate objects which are capable of making sound, such as a flute or harp, if their notes all sound alike, who can tell what tune is being played ? Unless the bugle-note is clear who will be called to arms ? So, in your case, unless you make intelligible sounds with your " tongue " how can anyone know what you are talking about ? You might just as well be addressing an empty room !

There are in the world a great variety of spoken sounds and each has a distinct meaning. But if the sounds of the speaker's voice mean nothing to me I am a foreigner to him, and he is a foreigner to me.

So, with yourselves, since you are so eager to possess spiritual gifts, concentrate your ambition upon receiving those which make for the real growth of your Church. And that means if one of your number speaks with a " tongue," he should pray that he may be able to interpret what he says.

If I pray in a " tongue " my spirit is praying but my mind is inactive. I am therefore determined to pray with my spirit *and* my mind, and if I sing I will sing with both spirit and mind. Otherwise, if you are blessing God with your spirit, how can those who are ungifted say Amen to your thanksgiving, since they do not know what you are talking about ? You may be thanking God splendidly, but it doesn't help the other man at all. I thank God that I have a greater gift of " tongues " than any of you, yet when I am in Church I would rather speak five words with my mind (which might teach something to other people) than ten thousand words in a " tongue " which nobody understands.

You must use your minds in this
matter of " tongues "   XIV : 20

My brothers, don't be like excitable children but use your intelligence ! By all means be innocent as babes as far as evil is concerned, but where your minds are concerned be full-grown men ! In the Law it is written :

By men of strange tongues and by the lips of strangers will
   I speak unto this people : and not even thus will they
   hear Me, saith the Lord.

That means that " tongues " are a sign of God's power, not for those who are unbelievers but to those who already believe.* Preaching the word of God, on the other hand, is a sign of God's power to those who do not believe rather than to believers. So that, if at a full church meeting you are all speaking with " tongues " and men come in who are both uninstructed and without faith, will they not say that you are insane ? But if you are preaching God's word and such a man should come in to your meeting, he is convicted and challenged by your united speaking of the truth. His secrets are exposed and he will fall on his knees acknowledging God and saying that God is truly among you !

Some practical regulations for the exercise
of spiritual gifts   XIV : 26

Well then, my brothers, whenever you meet let everyone be ready to contribute a psalm, a piece of teaching, a spiritual truth, or a " tongue " with an interpreter. Everything should be done to make your church strong in the faith.

If the question of speaking with a " tongue " arises, confine the speaking to two or three at the most and have someone to interpret what is said. If you have no interpreter then let the speaker with a " tongue " keep silent in the church and speak

---

* This is the sole instance of the translator's departing from the accepted text. He felt bound to conclude, from the sense of the next three verses, that we have here either a slip of the pen on the part of Paul, or, more probably, a copyist's error.

only to himself and God. Don't have more than two or three preachers either, while the others think over what has been said. But should a message of truth come to one who is seated, then the original speaker should stop talking. For in this way you can all have opportunity to give a message, one after the other, and everyone will learn something and everyone will have his faith stimulated. The spirit of a true preacher is under that preacher's control, for God is not a God of disorder but of harmony, as is plain in all the churches.

The speaking of women in church is forbidden
XIV : 34

Let women be silent in church; they are not to be allowed to speak. They must submit to this regulation, as the Law itself instructs. If they have questions to ask they must ask their husbands at home, for there is something indecorous about a woman's speaking in church.

You must accept the rules I have given by authority
XIV : 36

Do I see you questioning my instructions? Are you beginning to imagine that the Word of God originated in your Church, or that you have a monopoly of God's Truth? If any of your number think himself a true preacher and a spiritually-minded man, let him recognise that what I have written is by divine command! As for those who don't know it, well, we must just leave them in ignorance.

In conclusion, then, my brothers, set your heart on preaching the word of God, while not forbidding the use of "tongues." Let everything be done decently and in order.

A reminder of the Gospel Message: the Resurrection is an integral part of our faith
XV : 1

Now, my brothers, I want to speak about the Gospel which I have previously preached to you, which you accepted, in which you are at present standing, and by which, if you remain faithful to the message I gave you, your salvation is being worked out—unless, of course, your faith had no meaning behind it at all.

For I passed on to you Corinthians first of all the message I had myself received—that Christ died for our sins, as the Scriptures said He would ; that He was buried and rose again on the third day, again as the Scriptures foretold. He was seen by Cephas, then by the Twelve, and subsequently He was seen simultaneously by over five hundred Christians, of whom the majority are still alive, though some have since died. He was then seen by James, then by all the Messengers and last of all, as if to one born abnormally late, He appeared to me ! I am the least of the Messengers and indeed I do not deserve that title at all, because I persecuted the Church of God. But what I am now I am by the grace of God. The grace He gave me has not proved a barren gift. I have worked harder than any of the others— and yet it was not I but this same grace of God within me. In any event, whoever has done the work, whether I or they, this has been the Message and this has been the foundation of your faith.

If the Resurrection is the heart of the Gospel
how can any Christian deny life after death?   XV : 12

Now if the rising of Christ from the dead is the very heart of our Message, how can some of you deny that there is any resurrection ? If Christ is not risen then neither our preaching nor your faith has any meaning at all. Further it would mean that we are lying in our witness for God, for we have given our solemn testimony that He did raise up Christ— and that is utterly false if it should be true that the dead do not, in fact, rise again ! For if the dead do not rise neither did Christ rise, and if Christ did not rise your faith is futile and your sins have never been forgiven. Moreover those who have died believing in Christ are utterly dead and gone. Truly, if our faith in Christ were limited to this life only we should, of all mankind, be the most to be pitied !

But Christianity rests on a fact—
Christ did rise   XV : 20

But the glorious fact is that Christ *did* rise from the dead : He has become the very First to rise of all who sleep the sleep of death. As death entered the world through a man, so has rising from the dead come to us through a Man ! As members of a sinful race all men die ; as members of the Christ of God all men shall be raised to life, each in his proper order, with Christ the Very First and after Him all who belong to Him when He comes.

Then, and not till then, comes the End when Christ, having abolished all other rule, authority and power, hands over the Kingdom to God the Father. Christ's reign will and must continue until every enemy has been conquered. The last enemy of all to be destroyed is death itself. The Scripture says :

He hath put all things in subjection under His feet.

But in the term " all things " it is quite obvious that God, Who brings them all under subjection to Christ, is Himself excepted. Nevertheless, when everything created has been made obedient to God, then shall the Son acknowledge Himself subject to God the Father, Who gave the Son power over all things. Thus, in the End, shall God be wholly and absolutely God.

To refuse to believe in the Resurrection
is both foolish and wicked   XV : 29

Further, you should consider this, that if there is to be no Resurrection what is the point of some of you being baptised for the dead by proxy ? Why should you be baptised for *dead bodies* ? And why should I live a life of such hourly danger ? I assure you, by the certainty of Jesus Christ that we possess, that I face death every day of my life ! And if, to use the popular expression, I have " fought with wild beasts " here in Ephesus, what is the good of an ordeal like that if there is no life after this one? Let us rather eat, drink and be merry, for to-morrow we die!

Don't let yourselves be deceived. Talking about things that are not true is bound to be reflected in practical conduct. Come back to your senses, and don't dabble in sinful doubts. Remember that there are men who have plenty to say but have no knowledge of God. You should be ashamed that I have to write like this at all!

Parallels in nature help us to grasp
the truths of the Resurrection   XV : 35

But perhaps someone will ask, "How is the Resurrection achieved? With what sort of body do the dead arrive?" Now that is talking without using your minds! In your own experience you know that a seed does not germinate without itself "dying." When you sow a seed you do not sow the "body" that will eventually be produced, but bare grain, of wheat, for example, or one of the other seeds. God gives the seed a "body" according to His laws—a different "body" to each kind of seed.

Then again, even in this world, all flesh is not identical. The flesh of human beings, animals, fish and birds is different in each case. There are bodies which exist in this world, and bodies which exist in the heavens. These bodies are not, as it were, in competition; the splendour of an earthly body is quite a different thing from the splendour of a heavenly body. The sun, the moon and the stars all have their own particular splendour, while among the stars themselves there are different kinds of splendour.

There are illustrations here of the raising of the dead. The body is "sown" in dishonour; it is raised in splendour. It is sown in weakness; it is raised in power. It is sown a natural body; it is raised a spiritual body. As there is a natural body so will there be a spiritual body.

It is written, moreover, that:

The first man Adam became a living soul.

So the last Adam is a life-giving Spirit. But we should notice that the order is " natural " first and then " spiritual." The first man came out of the earth, a material creature. The second Man came from Heaven and was the Lord Himself. For the life of this world men are made like the material man ; but for the life that is to come they are made like the One from Heaven. So that just as we have been made like the material pattern, so we shall be made like the Heavenly Pattern. For I assure you, my brothers, it is utterly impossible for flesh and blood to possess the Kingdom of God. The transitory could never possess the Everlasting.

The dead and the living will be
fitted for immortality   XV : 51

Listen, and I will tell you a secret. We shall not all die, but suddenly, in the twinkling of an eye, every one of us will be changed as the trumpet sounds ! The trumpet will sound and the dead shall be raised beyond the reach of corruption, and we who are still alive shall suddenly be utterly changed. For this perishable nature of ours must be wrapped in imperishability, these bodies which are mortal must be wrapped in immortality. So when the perishable is lost in the imperishable, the mortal lost in the immortal, this saying will come true :

Death is swallowed up in Victory.

For where now, O Death, is your power to hurt us ? Where now, O Grave, is the victory you hoped to win ? It is sin which gives death its power, and it is the Law which gives sin its strength. All thanks to God, then, Who gives us the victory through our Lord Jesus Christ ; for He has delivered us from the fear of death, the power of sin and the condemnation of the Law !

And so, brothers of mine, stand firm ! Let nothing move you as you busy yourselves in the Lord's work. Be sure that nothing you do for Him is ever lost or ever wasted.

The matter of the fund : my own
immediate plans   XVI : 1

Now as far as the Fund for Christians in Need is concerned,
I should like you to follow the same rule that I gave to the
Galatian Church.

On the first day of the week let everyone put so much by
him, according to his financial ability, so that there will be
no need for collections when I come. Then, on my arrival, I
will send whomever you approve to take your gift, with my
recommendation, to Jerusalem. If it seems right for me to go
as well, we will make up a party together. I shall come to you
after my intended journey through Macedonia and I may stay
with you awhile or even spend the winter with you. Then you
can see me on my way—wherever it is that I go next. I don't
wish to see you now, for it would merely be in passing, and I
hope to spend some time with you, if it is God's Will. I shall
stay here in Ephesus until the feast of Pentecost, for there is a
great opportunity of doing useful work, and there are many
people against me.

News of Timothy and Apollos   XVI : 10

If Timothy comes to you, put him at his ease. He is as
genuine a worker for the Lord as I am, and there is therefore
no reason to look down on him. Send him on his way in
peace, for I am expecting him to come to me here with the
other Christian brothers. As for our brother Apollos I
pressed him strongly to go to you with the rest, but it was
definitely not God's Will for him to do so then. However, he
will come to you as soon as an opportunity occurs.

A little sermon in a nutshell !   XVI : 13

Be on your guard, stand firm in the faith, live like men, be
strong ! Let everything that you do be done in love.

A request, and final greetings   XVI : 15

You remember the household of Stephanas, the first men
of Achaia to be won for Christ ? Well, they have made up
their minds to devote their lives to looking after Christian

brothers. I do beg you to recognise them as Christ's ministers, and to extend your recognition to all their helpers and workers.

I am very glad that Stephanas, Fortunatus and Achaicus have arrived. They have made up for my not seeing you. They are a tonic to me and to you. You should appreciate having men like that !

Greetings from the Churches of Asia. Aquila and Prisca send you their warmest Christian greetings and so does the Church that meets in their house. All the Christians here send greetings. I should like you to shake hands all round as a sign of Christian love.

Here is my own greeting, written by me, Paul. If any man does not love the Lord, let him be accursed ; may the Lord soon come !

The grace of the Lord Jesus Christ be with you and my love be with you in Jesus Christ.

PAUL

THE SECOND LETTER TO
THE CHRISTIANS AT CORINTH

AUTHOR. *Paul, writing in Macedonia, probably as soon as Titus had arrived back from Corinth, bringing news of the reception of the " first letter." (Some think that Paul had paid a hurried personal visit to Corinth between the writing of these two letters.)*

DATE. *Possibly 57.*

DESTINATION. *The Church at Corinth, as in the " first letter."*

THEME. *There is a good deal of Paul's personal circumstances, feelings, activities, and attitude to his own ministry in this highly interesting letter. The Corinthian Church appears to have disciplined the guilty member referred to in the "first letter," and Paul recommends his restoration to the fellowship of the Church. Again in this letter Paul has to defend his own Divine com-*

*mission as Messenger, and even has to threaten strong action
against his traducers in a personal visit.*

*Throughout this letter the reader cannot help feeling how
"human" was Paul, and how genuine in his concern for the young
and struggling churches under his care.*

NOTE. *Many scholars believe that this letter contains parts of other
"lost" letters in the passages : VI, 14-VII, 1, and Chapters
X-XIII, which seem out of key with the rest. The first-named
passage may form part of the letter referred to by Paul in
1 Corinthians V, 9.*

THIS letter comes to you from Paul, God's Messenger for
Jesus Christ by the Will of God, and from brother Timothy,
and is addressed to the Church of God in Corinth and all
Christians throughout Achaia.

May grace and peace come to you from God our Father
and from the Lord Jesus Christ.

*God's encouragements are adequate
for all life's troubles*   1 : 3

Thank God, the Father of our Lord Jesus Christ, that He is
our Father and the Source of all mercy and comfort. For He
gives us comfort in our trials so that we in turn may be able
to give the same sort of strong sympathy to others in theirs.
Indeed, experience shows that the more we share Christ's
suffering the more we are able to give of His encouragement.
This means that if we experience trouble we can pass on to
you comfort and spiritual help ; for if we ourselves have
been comforted we know how to encourage you to endure
patiently the same sort of troubles that we have ourselves
endured. We are quite confident that if you have to suffer
troubles as we have done, then, like us, you will find the
comfort and encouragement of God.

Man's extremity is God's opportunity

We should like you, our brothers, to know somethi
what we went through in Asia. At that time we were
pletely overwhelmed, the burden was more than we
bear, in fact we told ourselves that this was the end. Y
believe now that we had this experience of coming to th
of our tether that we might learn to trust, not in ourse
but in God Who can raise the dead. It was God Who
served us from imminent death, and it is He Who
preserves us. Further, we trust Him to keep us safe i
future, and here you can join in and help by praying fo
so that the good that is done to us in answer to many pr
will mean eventually that many will thank God for
preservation.

Our dealings with you have always been straightforward

Now it is a matter of pride to us—endorsed by our
science—that our activities in this world, particularly
dealings with you, have been absolutely above-board
sincere and have not been marked by any " cleverness."
letters to you have no double meaning—they mean just
you understand them to mean when you read them. We
you will always understand these letters (as we believe
have already understood the purpose of our lives), and re
that you can be as honestly proud of us as we shall be of
on the day when Christ reveals all secrets.

Change of plan does not necessarily mean fickleness of heart

Trusting you, and believing that you trusted us,
original plan was to pay you a visit first, and give y
double " treat." We meant to come here to Macedonia
first visiting you, and then to visit you again on leaving
You could thus have helped us on our way towards Ju
Because we had to change this plan, does it mean that w
fickle ? Do you think I plan with my tongue in my ch
saying " yes " and meaning " no " ? We solemnly as

you that as certainly as God is faithful so we have never given you a message meaning "yes" and "no." Jesus Christ, the Son of God, whom Silvanus, Timothy and I have preached to you, is Himself no doubtful quantity, He is the Divine Yes. Every promise of God finds its affirmative in Him, and through Him can be said the final Amen, to the glory of God. We owe our position in Christ to this God of positive promise: it is He Who has consecrated us to this special work, He Who has given us the living guarantee of the Spirit in our hearts. Are we then the men to say one thing and mean another?

I have never wanted to hurt you I : 23

No, I declare before God that it was to avoid hurting you that I did not come to Corinth. For though I am not responsible for your faith—your standing in God is your own affair—yet I can add to your happiness. And I made up my mind that I would not pay you another painful visit. For what point is there in my depressing the very people who can give me such joy? The real purpose of my previous letter was in fact to save myself from being saddened by those whom I might reasonably expect to bring me joy. I have such confidence in you that my joy depends on all of you! I wrote to you in deep distress and out of a most unhappy heart (I don't mind telling you I shed tears over that letter), not, believe me, to cause you pain, but to show you how deep is my care for your welfare.

A word of explanation II : 5

There was a reason for my stern words; this is my advice now. If the behaviour of a certain person has caused distress, it does not mean so much that he has injured me, but that to some extent (I do not wish to exaggerate), he has injured all of you. But now I think that the punishment you have inflicted on him has been sufficient. Now is the time to offer him forgiveness and comfort, for it is possible for a man in his position to be completely overwhelmed by remorse. I ask you to show him plainly now that you love him. My previous letter was something of a test—I wanted to make sure that you would follow my orders implicitly. If you will forgive a certain person, rest assured that I forgive him too. Insofar as I had anything personally to forgive, I do forgive him, as before Christ. We don't want Satan to win any victory here, and well we know his methods !

And a further confidence   II : 12

Well, when I came to Troas to preach the gospel of Christ, although there was an obvious God-given opportunity, I must confess I was on edge the whole time because there was no sign of brother Titus. So I said good-bye and went from there to Macedonia. Thanks be to God Who leads us, wherever we are, on His own triumphant way and makes our knowledge of Him spread throughout the world like a lovely perfume ! We Christians have the unmistakable " scent " of Christ, discernible alike to those who are being saved and to those who are heading for death. To the latter it seems like the very smell of doom, to the former it has the fresh fragrance of life itself.

Who could think himself adequate for a responsibility like this ? Only the man who refuses to join that large class which trafficks in the Word of God—the man who speaks, as we do, in the Name of God, under the eyes of God, as Christ's chosen minister.

You yourselves are the proof of our ministry   III : 1

Is this going to be more self-advertisement in your eyes ? Do we need, as some apparently do, to exchange testimonials before we can be friends ? You yourselves are our testimonial, written in our hearts and yet open for anyone to inspect and read. You are an open letter about Christ which we ourselves have written, not with pen and ink but with the Spirit of the living God. Our message has been engraved not in stone, but in living men and women.

We dare to say such things because of the confidence we have in God through Christ, and not because we are confident of our own powers. It is God Who makes us competent administrators of the New Agreement, and we deal not in the letter but in the Spirit. The letter of the Law leads to the death of the soul; the Spirit of God alone can give life to the soul.

The splendour of our ministry outshines
that of Moses   III : 7

The administration of the Law which was engraved in stone (and which led in fact to spiritual death) was so magnificent that the Israelites were unable to look unflinchingly at Moses' face, for it was alight with heavenly splendour. Now if the old administration held such heavenly, even though transitory, splendour, can we not see what a much more glorious thing is the new administration of the Spirit of life? If to administer a system which is to end in condemning men was a splendid task, how infinitely more splendid is it to administer a system which ends in making men good! And while it is true that the former temporary glory has been completely eclipsed by the latter, we do well to remember that it is eclipsed simply because the present permanent plan is such a very much more glorious thing than the old.

Our ministry is an open and splendid thing   III : 12

With this hope in our hearts we are quite frank and open in our ministry. We are not like Moses, who veiled his face to prevent the Israelites from seeing its fading glory. But it was their minds really which were blinded, for even to-day when the Old Agreement is read to them there is still a veil over their minds—though the veil has actually been lifted by Christ. Yes, alas, even to this day there is still a veil over their hearts when the writings of Moses are read. Yet if they "turned to the Lord" the veil would disappear. For the Lord to Whom they could turn is the Spirit of the New Agreement, and wherever the Spirit of the Lord is, men's souls are set free.

But all of us who are Christians have no veils on our faces, but reflect like mirrors the glory of the Lord. We are transfigured by the Spirit of the Lord in ever-increasing splendour into His own image.

Ours is a straightforward ministry
bringing light into darkness
IV : 1

This is the ministry of the New Agreement which God in His mercy has given us and nothing can daunt us. We use no hocus-pocus, no clever tricks, no dishonest manipulation of the Word of God. We speak the plain truth and so commend ourselves to every man's conscience in the sight of God. If our gospel is " veiled," the veil must be in the minds of those who are spiritually dying. The spirit of this world has blinded the minds of those who do not believe, and prevents the light of the glorious gospel of Christ, the image of God, from shining on them. For it is Christ Jesus the Lord Whom we preach, not ourselves ; we are your servants for His sake. God, Who first ordered Light to shine in darkness has flooded our hearts with His Light. We now can enlighten men only because we can give them knowledge of the glory of God, as we see it in the face of Jesus Christ.

We experience death—we give life, by the
power of God
IV : 7

This priceless treasure we hold, so to speak, in a common earthenware jar—to show that the splendid power of it belongs to God and not to us. We are handicapped on all sides, but we are never frustrated ; we are puzzled, but never in despair. We are persecuted, but we never have to stand it alone : we may be knocked down but we are never knocked out ! Every day we experience something of the death of the Lord Jesus, so that we may also know the power of the life of Jesus in these bodies of ours. Yes, we who are living are always being exposed to death for Jesus' sake, so that the life of Jesus may be plainly seen in our mortal lives. We are always facing death, but this means that you know more and more of life. Our faith is like that mentioned in the Scripture :

I believed and therefore did I speak.

For we too speak because we believe, and we know for certain that He Who raised the Lord Jesus from death shall also by Him raise us. We shall all stand together before Him.

We live a transitory life with our
eyes on the life eternal   IV : 15

We wish you could see how all this is working out for your benefit, and how the more grace God gives, the more thanksgiving will redound to His glory. This is the reason why we never collapse. The outward man does indeed suffer wear and tear, but every day the inward man receives fresh strength. These little troubles (which are really so transitory) are winning for us a permanent and glorious reward out of all proportion to our pain. For we are looking all the time not at the visible things but at the invisible. The visible things are transitory : it is the invisible things that are really permanent.

We know, for instance, that if our earthly dwelling were taken down, like a tent, we have a permanent house in Heaven, made, not by man, but by God. In this present frame we sigh with deep longing for the heavenly house, for we do not want to face utter nakedness when death destroys our present dwelling—these bodies of ours. So long as we are clothed in this temporary dwelling we have a painful longing, not because we want just to get rid of these " clothes " but because we want to know the full cover of the permanent house that will be ours. We want our transitory life to be absorbed into the Life that is eternal.

Death can have no terrors, for it
means being with God   V : 5

Now the power that has planned this experience for us is God, and He has given us His Spirit as a guarantee of its truth. This makes us confident, whatever happens. We realise that being " at home " in the body means that to some extent we are " away " from the Lord, for we have to live by trusting Him without seeing Him. We are so sure of this that we would really rather be " away " from the body and be " at home " with the Lord.

It is our aim, therefore, to please Him, whether we are " at home " or " away." For every one of us will have to stand without pretence before Christ our Judge, and we shall be rewarded for what we did when we lived in our bodies, whether it was good or bad.

Our ministry is based on solemn convictions   V : 11

All our persuading of men, then, is with this solemn fear of God in our minds. What we are is utterly plain to God—and I hope to your consciences as well. (No, we are not recommending ourselves to you again, but we can give you grounds for legitimate pride in us—if that is what you need to meet those who are so proud of the outward rather than the inward qualification.) If we have been " mad " it was for God's glory ; if we are perfectly sane it is for your benefit. At any rate there has been no selfish motive. The very spring of our actions is the love of Christ. We look at it like this : if One died for all men then, in a sense, they all died, and His purpose in dying for them is that their lives should now be no longer lived for themselves but for Him Who died and rose again for them. This means that our knowledge of men can no longer be based on their outward lives (indeed, even though we knew Christ as a man we do not know Him like that any longer). For if a man is in Christ he becomes a new person altogether—the past is finished and gone, everything has become fresh and new. All this is God's doing, for He has reconciled us to Himself through Jesus Christ ; and He has made us agents of the reconciliation. God was in Christ personally reconciling the world to Himself—not counting their sins against them—and has commissioned us with the message of reconciliation. We are now Christ's ambassadors, as though God were appealing direct to you through us. As His personal representatives we say, " Make your peace with God." For God caused Christ, Who Himself knew nothing of sin, actually to *be* sin for our sakes, so that in Christ we might be made good with the goodness of God.

The hard but glorious life of God's ministers   VI : I

As co-operators with God Himself we beg you, then, not to fail to use the grace of God. For God's word is :

> At an acceptable time I hearkened unto thee,
> And in a day of salvation did I succour thee :
> Behold, now is the acceptable time ;
> Behold, now is the day of Salvation.

As far as we are concerned we do not wish to stand in any-one's way, nor do we wish to bring discredit on the ministry God has given us. Indeed we want to prove ourselves genuine ministers of God whatever we have to go through— patient endurance of troubles or even disasters, being flogged or imprisoned ; being mobbed, having to work like slaves, having to go without food or sleep. All this we want to meet with sincerity, with insight and patience ; by sheer kindness and the Holy Spirit ; with genuine love, speaking the plain truth, and living by the power of God. Our sole defence, our only weapon, is a life of integrity, whether we meet honour or dishonour, praise or blame. Called " impostors " we must be true, called " nobodies " we must be in the public eye. Never far from death, yet here we are alive, always " going through it " yet never " going under." We know sorrow, yet our joy is inextinguishable. We have " nothing to bless ourselves with " yet we bless many others with true riches. We are penniless, and yet in reality we have everything worth having.

We have used utter frankness,
won't you do the same ?   VI : II

Oh, our dear friends in Corinth, we are hiding nothing from you and our hearts are absolutely open to you. Any stiffness between us must be on your side, for we assure you there is none on ours. Do reward me (I talk to you as though you were my own children) with the same complete candour !

We must warn you against entanglement
with pagans   VI : 14

Don't link up with unbelievers and try to work with them. What common interest can there be between goodness and evil ? How can light and darkness share life together ? How can there be harmony between Christ and the Devil ? What business can a believer have with an unbeliever ? What common ground can idols hold with the temple of God ? For we, remember, are ourselves living temples of the living God, as God has said :

I will dwell in them and walk in them :
And I will be their God, and they shall be My people.

Wherefore

Come ye out from among them and be ye separate, saith
    the Lord,
And touch no unclean thing ;
And I will receive you,
And will be to you a Father,
And ye shall be to Me sons and daughters,
Saith the Lord Almighty.

With these promises ringing in our ears, dear friends, let us keep clear of anything that smirches body or soul. Let us prove our reverence for God by consecrating ourselves to Him completely.

Does " that letter " still rankle ?
Hear my explanation   VII : 2

Do make room in your hearts again for us ! Not one of you has ever been wronged or ruined or cheated by us. I don't say this to condemn your attitude, but simply because, as I said before, whether we live or die you live in our hearts. To your face I talk to you with utter frankness ; behind your back I talk about you with deepest pride. Whatever troubles I have gone through, the thought of you has filled me with comfort and deep happiness.

For even when we arrived in Macedonia we had a wretched time with trouble all round us—wrangling outside and anxiety within. Not but what God, Who cheers the depressed, gave us the comfort of the arrival of Titus. And it wasn't merely his coming that cheered us, but the comfort you had given him, for he could tell us of your eagerness to help, your deep sympathy and keen interest on my behalf. All that made me doubly glad to see him. For although my letter had hurt you I don't regret it now (as I did, I must confess, at one time). I can see that the letter did upset you, though only for a time, and now I am glad I sent it, not because I want to hurt you but because it made you grieve for things that were wrong. In other words, the result was to make you sorry as God would have had you sorry, and not merely to make you offended by what we said. The sorrow which God uses means a change of heart and leads to salvation—it is the world's sorrow that is such a deadly thing. You can look back now and see how the hand of God was in that sorrow. Look how seriously it made you think, how eager it made you to prove your innocence, how indignant it made you and, in some cases, how afraid ! Look how it made you long for my presence, how it stirred up your keenness for the faith, how ready it made you to punish the offender ! Yes, that letter cleared the air for you as nothing else would have done.

Now I did not write that letter really for the sake of the man who sinned, or even for the sake of the one who was sinned against, but to let you see for yourselves, in the sight of God, how deeply you really do care for us. That is why we now feel so deeply comforted, and our sense of joy was greatly enhanced by the satisfaction that your attitude had obviously given Titus. You see, I had told him of my pride in you, and you have not let me down. I have always spoken the truth *to* you, and this proves that my proud words *about* you were true as well. Titus himself has a much greater love for you, now that he has seen for himself the obedience you gave him and the respect and reverence with which you treated him. I am profoundly glad to have my confidence in you so fully proved.

The Macedonian churches have given
magnificently : will you not do so too ?   VIII : I

Now, my brothers, we must tell you about the grace that God has given to the Macedonian churches. Somehow, in most difficult circumstances, their joy and the fact of being down to their last penny themselves, produced a magnificent concern for other people. I can guarantee that they were willing to give to the limit of their means, yes and beyond their means, without the slightest urging from me or anyone else. In fact they simply begged us to accept their gifts and so let them share the honour of supporting their brothers in Christ. Nor was their gift, as I must confess I had expected, a mere cash payment. Instead they made a complete dedication of themselves first to the Lord and then to us, as God's appointed ministers.

Now this has made us ask Titus, who has already done so much among you, to complete his task by arranging for you too to share in this work of generosity. Already you are well to the fore in every good quality—you have faith, you can express that faith in words ; you have knowledge, enthusiasm and your love for us. Could you not add generosity to your virtues ? I don't want you to read this as an order. It is only my suggestion, prompted by what I have seen in others of eagerness to help, and here is a way to prove the reality of your love. Do you remember the generosity of Jesus Christ, the Lord of us all ? He was rich beyond our telling, yet He became poor for your sakes so that His poverty might make you rich.

I merely suggest that you finish your
original generous gesture   VIII : IO

Here is my opinion in the matter. I think it would be a good thing for you, who were the first a year ago to think of helping, as well as the first to give, to carry through what you then intended to do. Finish it, then, as well as you can, and show that you can complete what you set out to do with as much efficiency as you showed readiness to begin. After all, the important thing is to be willing to give as much as we can—that is what God accepts, and no one is asked to give what he has not got. Of course, I don't mean that others should be relieved to an extent that leaves you in distress. It is a matter of share and share alike. At present your plenty should supply their need, and then at some future date their plenty may supply your need. In that way we share with each other, as the Scripture says,

> He that gathered much had nothing over,
> And he that gathered little had no lack.

Titus is bringing you this letter personally   VIII : 16

Thank God Titus feels the same deep concern for you as we do ! He accepts the suggestion outlined above, and in his enthusiasm comes to you personally at his own request. We are sending with him that brother whose services to the Gospel are universally praised in the churches. He has been unanimously chosen to travel with us in this work of administering the gifts of others. It is a task that brings glory to God and demonstrates also the willingness of us Christians to help each other. Naturally we want to avoid the slightest breath of criticism in the distribution of their gifts, and to be absolutely above-board not only in the sight of God but in the eyes of men.

With these two we are also sending our brother, of whose keenness we have ample proof and whose interest is especially aroused on this occasion as he has such confidence in you. As for Titus, he is our colleague and partner in your affairs, and both the brothers are official messengers of the Church and shining examples of their faith. So do let them, and all the churches, see how genuine is your love, and justify all the nice things we have said about you !

A word in confidence about this
gift of yours   IX : 1

Of course I know it is really quite superfluous for me to be
writing to you about this matter of giving to fellow-Christians,
for I know how willing you are. Indeed I have told the
Macedonians with some pride that " Achaia was ready to
undertake this service twelve months ago." Your enthusiasm
has consequently been a stimulus to many of them. I am,
however, sending the brothers just to make sure that our pride
in you is not unjustified. For, between ourselves, it would
never do if some of the Macedonians were to accompany me
on my visit to you and find you unprepared for this act of
generosity ! We (not to speak of you) should be horribly
ashamed, just because we had been so proud and confident
of you. This is my reason, then, for urging the brothers
to visit you before I come myself, so that they can get your
promised gift ready in good time. But, having let you into
my confidence, I should like it to be a spontaneous gift, and
not money squeezed out of you by what I have said. All I
will say is that poor sowing means a poor harvest, and
generous sowing means a generous harvest.

Giving does not only help the one
who receives   IX : 7

Let everyone give as his heart tells him, neither grudgingly
nor under compulsion, for God loves the man who gives
cheerfully. After all, God can give you everything that you
need, so that you may always have sufficient both for yourselves and for giving away to other people. As the Scripture
says :

He hath scattered abroad, he hath given to the poor ;
His righteousness abideth for ever.

He Who gives the seed to the sower and turns that seed into
bread to eat, will give you the seed of generosity to sow and,
for harvest, the satisfying bread of good deeds done. The
more you are enriched by God the more scope will there be

for generous giving, and your gifts, administered through us, will mean that many will thank God. For your giving does not end in meeting the wants of your fellow-Christians. It also results in an overflowing tide of thanksgiving to God. Moreover, your very giving proves the reality of your faith, and that means that men thank God that you practise the gospel that you profess to believe in, as well as for the actual gifts you make to them and to others. And yet further, men will pray for you and feel drawn to you because you have obviously received a generous measure of the grace of God.

Thank God, then, for His indescribable generosity to you !

We are not merely human agents
but God-appointed ministers   x : 1

Now I am going to appeal to you personally, by the gentleness and sympathy of Christ Himself. Yes, I, Paul, the one who is " humble enough in our presence but outspoken when away from us," am begging you to make it unnecessary for me to be outspoken and stern in your presence. For I am afraid otherwise that I shall have to do some plain speaking to those of you who will persist in reckoning that our activities are on the purely human level. The truth is that, although of course we lead normal human lives, the battle we are fighting is on the spiritual level. The very weapons we use are not those of human warfare but powerful in God's warfare for the destruction of the enemy's strongholds. Our battle is to bring down every deceptive fantasy and every imposing defence that men erect against the true knowledge of God. We even fight to capture every thought until it acknowledges the authority of Christ. Once we are sure of your obedience we shall not shrink from dealing with those who refuse to obey.

I really am a Christian, you know !   x : 7

Do look at things which stare you in the face ! So-and-so considers himself to belong to Christ. All right ; but let him reflect that we belong to Christ every bit as much as he. You may think that I have boasted unduly of my authority (which the Lord gave me, remember, to build you up not to break you down), but I don't think I have done anything to be ashamed of. Yet I don't want you to think of me merely as the man who writes you terrifying letters. I know my critics say, "His letters are impressive and moving but his actual presence is feeble and his speaking beneath contempt." Let them realise that we can be just as "impressive and moving" in person as they say we are in our letters.

God's appointment means more than
self-recommendation   X : 12

Of course we shouldn't dare include ourselves in the same class as those who write their own testimonials, or even to compare ourselves with them ! All they are doing, of course, is to measure themselves by their own standards or by comparisons within their own circle, and that doesn't make for accurate estimation, you may be sure. No, we shall not make any wild claims, but simply judge ourselves by that line of duty which God has marked out for us, and that line includes our work on your behalf. We do not exceed our duty when we embrace your interests, for it was our preaching of the Gospel which brought us into contact with you. Our pride is not in matters beyond our proper sphere nor in the labours of other men. No, our hope is that your growing faith will mean the expansion of our sphere of action, so that before long we shall be preaching the Gospel in districts beyond you, instead of being proud of work that has already been done in someone else's province.

But,

He that glorieth let him glory in the Lord.

It is not self-commendation that matters, it is winning the approval of God.

*Why do you so readily accept the
false and reject the true?*   XI : I

I wish you could put up with a little of my foolishness—
please try! My jealousy over you is the right sort of jealousy,
for in my eyes you are like a fresh unspoiled girl whom I am
presenting as fiancée to your true husband, Christ Himself.
I am afraid that your minds may be seduced from a single-
hearted devotion to Him by the same subtle means that the
serpent used towards Eve. For apparently you cheerfully
accept a man who comes to you preaching a different Jesus
from the One we told you about, and you readily receive a
spirit and a gospel quite different from the ones you originally
accepted. Yet I cannot believe I am in the least inferior
to these extra-special Messengers. Perhaps I am not a
polished speaker, but I do know what I am talking about,
and both what I am and what I say is pretty familiar to you.
Perhaps I made a mistake in cheapening myself (though
I did it to help you) by preaching the Gospel without a fee?
As a matter of fact, I was only able to do this by "robbing"
other churches, for it was what they paid me that made it
possible to minister to you free of charge. Even when I was
with you and very hard up, I did not bother any of you. It
was the brothers who came from Macedonia who brought
me all that I needed. Yes, I kept myself from being a burden
to you then, and so I intend to do in the future. By the truth
of Christ within me, no one shall stop my being proud of this
independence through all Achaia!

Does this mean that I do not love you? God knows it
doesn't, but I am determined to maintain this boast, so as to
cut the ground from under the feet of those who profess to be
God's Messengers on the same terms as I am. Special
Messengers? They are counterfeits of the real thing, dishonest practitioners, "God's Messengers" only by their
own appointment. Nor do their tactics surprise me when I
consider how Satan himself masquerades as an angel of light.
It is only to be expected that his agents shall have the appearance of ministers of righteousness—but they will get their
deserts one day.

If you like self-commendations,
listen to mine !   XI : 16

Once more, let me advise you not to look upon me as a fool. Yet if you do, then listen to what this " fool " has to boast about.

I am not now speaking as the Lord commands me but as a fool who must be " in on " this business of boasting. Since all the others are so proud of themselves, let me do a little boasting as well. From your heights of superior wisdom I am sure you can smile tolerantly on a fool. Oh, you're tolerant all right ! You don't mind, do you, if a man takes away your liberty, spends your money, makes a fool of you or even smacks your face ? I am almost ashamed to say that I never did brave, strong things like that to you. Yet in whatever particular they enjoy such confidence I (speaking as a fool, remember) have just as much confidence.

Are they Hebrews ? So am I.

Are they Israelites ? So am I.

Are they descendants of Abraham ? So am I.

Are they ministers of Christ ? I have more claim to this title than they. This is a silly game but look at this list :

I have worked harder than any of them.

I have served more prison sentences !

I have been beaten times without number.

I have faced death again and again.

I have been beaten the regulation thirty-nine stripes by the Jews five times.

I have been beaten with rods three times.

I have been stoned once.

I have been shipwrecked three times.

I have been twenty-four hours in the open sea.

In my travels I have been in constant danger from rivers and floods, from bandits, from my own countrymen, and from pagans. I have faced danger, in city streets, danger in the desert, danger on the high seas, danger among false Christians. I have known exhaustion, pain, long vigils, hunger and thirst, doing without meals, cold and lack of clothing.

Apart from all external trials I have the daily burden of responsibility for all the churches. Do you think anyone is weak without my feeling his weakness? Does anyone have his faith upset without my longing to restore him?

Oh, if I am going to boast, let me boast of all the things I was not clever enough to dodge! The God and Father of our Lord Jesus Christ knows that I speak the simple truth.

In Damascus, the town governor, acting by King Aretas' order, had men out to arrest me. I escaped by climbing through a window and being let down the wall in a basket. That's the sort of dignified exit I can boast about.

I have real grounds for " boasting,"
but I will only hint at them   XII : I

No, I don't think it's really a good thing for me to boast at all, but I will just mention visions and revelations of the Lord Himself. I know a man in Christ who, fourteen years ago, had the experience of being caught up into the third heaven. I don't know whether it was an actual physical experience, only God knows that. All I know is that this man was caught up into Paradise. (I repeat, I do not know whether this was a physical happening or not, God alone knows.) This man heard words that cannot, and indeed must not, be translated into human speech. I am honestly proud of an experience like that, but I have made up my mind not to boast of anything personal, except of what may be called my weaknesses. If I should want to boast I should certainly be no fool to be proud of my experiences, and I should be speaking nothing but the sober truth. Yet I am not going to do so, for I don't want anyone to think more highly of me than his experience of me and what he hears of me should warrant. So tremendous, however, were the revelations that God gave me that, in order to prevent my becoming absurdly conceited, I was given a physical handicap—one of Satan's angels—to harass me and effectually stop any conceit. Three times I begged the Lord for it to leave me, but His reply has been, " My grace is enough for you : for where there is weakness, My power is shown the more completely." Therefore, I have cheerfully made up my mind to be proud of my weaknesses, because they mean a deeper experience of the power of Christ. I can even enjoy weaknesses, suffering, privations, persecutions and difficulties for Christ's sake. For my very weakness makes me strong in Him.

This boasting is silly, but you made
it necessary
XII : 11

I have made a fool of myself in this " boasting " business, but you forced me to do it. If only you had had a better opinion of me it would have been quite unnecessary. For I am not really in the least inferior, nobody as I am, to these extra-special Messengers. You have had an exhaustive demonstration of the power God gives to a genuine Messenger in the miracles, signs and works of spiritual power that you saw with your own eyes. What makes you feel so inferior to other churches ? Is it because I have not allowed you to support me financially ? My humblest apologies for this great wrong !

What can be your grounds for
suspicion of me ?
XII : 14

Now I am all ready to visit you for the third time, and I am still not going to be a burden to you. It is you I want—not your money. Children don't have to put by their savings for their parents ; parents do that for their children. Consequently I will most gladly spend and be spent for your good, even though it means that the more I love you the less you love me.

" All right then," I hear you say, " we agree that he himself had none of our money." But are you thinking that I nevertheless was rogue enough to catch you by some trick ? Just think. Did I make any profit out of the messengers I sent you ? I asked Titus to go, and sent a brother with him. You don't think Titus made anything out of you, do you ? Yet didn't I act in the same spirit as he, and take the same line as he did ?

Remember what I really am, and
whose authority I have   XII : 19

Are you thinking all this time that I am trying to justify
myself in your eyes ? Actually I am speaking in Christ
before God Himself, and my only reason for so doing is to
help you in your spiritual life.

For I must confess that I am afraid that when I come I
shall not perhaps find you as I should like to find you, and
that you will not find me coming quite as you would like me
to come. I am afraid of finding arguments, jealousy, ill-
feeling, divided loyalties, slander, whispering, pride and disharmony. When I come, will God make me feel ashamed of
you as I stand among you ? Shall I have to grieve over many
who have sinned already and are not yet sorry for the impurity, the immorality and the lustfulness of which they are
guilty ?

This third time I am really coming to you in person. Remember the ancient Law : "In the mouth of two or three
witnesses shall every word be established." My previous
warning, given on my second visit, still stands and, though
absent, I repeat it now as though I were present—my coming
will *not* mean leniency for those who had sinned before that
visit and those who have sinned since. It will in fact be a
proof that I speak by the power of Christ. The Christ you
have to deal with is not a weak person outside you, but a tremendous power inside you. He was "weak" enough to be
crucified, yes, but He lives now by the power of God. I am
weak as He was weak, but I am strong enough to deal with
you for I share His life by the power of God.

Why not test yourselves instead of me ?   XIII : 5

You should be looking at yourselves to make sure that you
are really Christ's. It is yourselves that you should be testing,
not me. You ought to know by this time that Christ is in you,
unless you are not real Christians at all. And when you have
applied your test, I am confident that you will soon find that
I myself am a genuine Christian. I pray God that you may
find the right answer to your test, not because I have any need

of your approval, but because I earnestly want you to find the right answer, even if that should make me no real Christian. For, after all, we can make no progress against the truth; we can only work for the truth.

We are glad to be weak if it means that you are strong. Our ambition for you is true Christian maturity. Hence the tone of this letter, so that when I do come I shall not be obliged to use that power of severity which God has given me —though even that is not meant to break you down but to build you up.

Finally, farewell   XIII : 11

Last of all then, my brothers, good-bye! Set your hearts on this maturity I have spoken of, consider my advice, live in harmony, be at peace with one another. So shall the God of love and peace be ever with you.

A handshake all round, please! All the Christians here send greetings.

The grace that comes through our Lord Jesus Christ, the love that is of God the Father, and the fellowship that is ours in the Holy Spirit be with you all!

                                              PAUL

THE LETTER TO
THE CHRISTIANS IN GALATIA

AUTHOR. *Paul, probably writing from Corinth, or possibly from Macedonia just before Titus returned from Corinth.*

DATE. *56 or 57.*

DESTINATION. *The meaning of " Galatia," to which this letter is addressed, has aroused some controversy, for it could mean the ancient district known by that name or the Roman province also called " Galatia," which included several other districts.*

THEME. *The Galatians appear to have been seduced from their first*

*faith by teachers who insisted that they must still keep the old
Jewish Law, including the rite of circumcision. In so doing they
impugned Paul's authority, which he feels called upon to justify in
this letter. Paul warns the Galatians that although they are free,
as Christians, from the Law, yet their lives must exhibit the
fruits of the inner law of love implanted by God's Spirit.*

I, Paul, who am appointed and commissioned a Messenger
not by man but by Jesus Christ and God the Father
(Who raised Him from the dead), I and all the brothers
with me send the churches in Galatia greeting. Grace and
peace to you from God the Father and from our Lord Jesus
Christ, Who according to the Father's Plan gave Himself for
our sins and thereby rescued us from the present evil world-
order. To Him be glory for ever and ever!

*The Gospel is God's Truth : men must
not dare to pervert it*   1 : 6

I am amazed that you have so quickly transferred your
allegiance from Him Who called you in the grace of Christ to
another "gospel"! Not, of course, that it is or ever could
be another gospel, but there are obviously men who are
upsetting your faith with a travesty of the Gospel of Christ.
Yet I say that if I, or an angel from Heaven, were to preach to
you any other gospel than the one you have heard, may he be
damned! You have heard me say it before and now I put it
down in black and white—may anybody who preaches any
other gospel than the one you have already heard be a
damned soul! (Does that make you think now that I am
serving man's interests or God's? If I were trying to win
human approval I should never be Christ's servant.)

The Gospel was given to me by Christ Himself,
and not by any human agency,
as my story will show I : II

The Gospel I preach to you is no human invention. No man gave it to me, no man taught it to me; it came to me as a direct revelation from Jesus Christ. For you have heard of my past career in the Jewish religion, how I persecuted the Church of God with fanatical zeal, and in fact, did my best to destroy it. I was ahead of most of my contemporaries in the Jewish religion and had a greater enthusiasm for the old traditions. But when the time came for God (Who was responsible both for my physical birth and for my being called by His grace), to reveal His Son within me so that I might proclaim Him to the non-Jewish world, I did not, as might have been expected, talk over the matter with any human being. I did not even go to Jerusalem to meet those who were God's Messengers before me—no, I went away to Arabia and later came back to Damascus. It was not until three years later that I went up to Jerusalem to see Peter, and I only stayed with him just over a fortnight. I did not meet any of the other Messengers, except James, the Lord's brother.

All this that I am telling you is, I assure you before God, the plain truth. Later, I visited districts in Syria and Cilicia, but I was still personally unknown to the churches of Judaea. All they knew of me, in fact, was the saying : "The man who used to persecute us is now preaching the faith he once tried to destroy." And they thanked God for what had happened to me.

Years later I met church leaders in Jerusalem :
no criticism of my Gospel was made II : I

Fourteen years later, I went up to Jerusalem again, this time with Barnabas, and we took Titus with us. My visit on this occasion was by Divine command, and I gave a full exposition of the Gospel which I preach among the Gentiles. I did this first in private conference with the Church leaders, to make sure that what I had done and proposed doing was acceptable to them. Not one of them intimated that Titus, because he was a Greek, ought to be circumcised. In fact, the suggestion would never have arisen but for the presence of some pseudo-Christians, who wormed their way into our meeting to spy on the liberty we enjoy in Jesus Christ, and then attempted to tie us up with rules and regulations. We did not give those men an inch, for the truth of the Gospel for you and all Gentiles was at stake. And as far as the leaders of the conference were concerned (I neither know nor care what their exact position was : God is not impressed with a man's office), they had nothing to add to my gospel. In fact they recognised that the Gospel for the uncircumcised was as much my commission as the Gospel for the circumcised was Peter's. For the God Who had done such great work in Peter's ministry for the Jews was plainly doing the same in my ministry for the Gentiles. When, therefore, James, Cephas and John (who were the recognised "pillars" of the Church there) saw how God had given me His grace, they held out to Barnabas and me the right hand of fellowship, in full agreement that our mission was to the Gentiles and theirs to the Jews. The only suggestion they made was that we should not forget the poor—and with this I was, of course, only too ready to agree.

I had once to defend the truth of the Gospel
even against a Church leader   II : 11

Later, however, when Peter came to Antioch I had to oppose him publicly, for he was then plainly in the wrong. It happened like this. Until the arrival of some of James' companions, he, Peter, was in the habit of eating his meals with the Gentiles. After they came, however, he withdrew and ate separately from the Gentiles—out of sheer fear of what the Jews might think. The other Jewish Christians carried out a similar piece of deception, and the force of their bad example was so great that even Barnabas was affected by it. But when I saw that this behaviour was a contradiction of the truth of the Gospel, I said to Peter so that everyone could hear, " If you, who are a Jew, do not live like a Jew but like a

Gentile, why on earth do you try to make Gentiles live like Jews ? " And then I went on to explain that we, who are Jews by birth and not Gentile sinners, know that a man is justified not by performing what the Law commands but by faith in Jesus Christ. We ourselves are justified by our faith and not by our obedience to the Law, for we have recognised that no one can achieve justification by doing the "works of the Law." Now if, as we seek the real truth about justification, we find we are as much sinners as the Gentiles, does that mean that Christ makes us sinners ? Of course not ! But if I attempt to build again the whole structure of justification by the Law then I do, in earnest, make myself a sinner. For under the Law I " died," and now I am dead to the Law's demands so that I may live for God. As far as the Law is concerned I may consider that I died on the Cross with Christ. And my present life is not that of the old " I," but with the living Christ within me. The bodily life I now live, I live believing in the Son of God, Who loved me and sacrificed Himself for me. Consequently I refuse to stultify the grace of God by reverting to the Law. For if righteousness were possible under the Law then Christ died for nothing !

What has happened to your life of faith?   III : 1

O you dear idiots of Galatia, who saw Jesus Christ the crucified so plainly, who has been casting a spell over you ? I will ask you one simple question : did you receive the Spirit of God by trying to keep the Law or by believing the message of the Gospel ? Surely you can't be so idiotic as to think that a man begins his spiritual life in the Spirit and then completes it by reverting to outward observances ? Has all your painful experience brought you nowhere ? I simply cannot believe it of you ! Does God, Who gives you His Spirit and works miracles among you, do these things because you have obeyed the Law or because you have believed the Gospel ? Ask yourselves that.

The futility of trying to be justified
by the Law : the promises to men of faith III : 6

You can go right back to Abraham to see the principle of faith in God. He, we are told, "believed God and it was counted unto him for righteousness." Can you not see, then, that all those who "believed God" are the real "sons of Abraham"? The Scripture, foreseeing that God would justify the Gentiles "by faith," really proclaimed the Gospel centuries ago in the words, "In thee shall all nations be blessed." All men of faith share the blessing of Abraham who "believed God."

Everyone, however, who is involved in trying to keep the Law's demands falls under a curse, for it is written :

Cursed is everyone which continueth not
In *all things* which are written in the book of the Law,
To do them.

It is made still plainer that no one is justified in God's sight by obeying the Law, for :

The righteous shall live by *faith*.

And the Law is not a matter of faith at all but of doing, as, for example, in the Scripture :

He that *doeth* them shall live in them.

Now Christ has redeemed us from the curse of the Law's condemnation, by Himself becoming a curse for us when He was crucified. For the Scripture is plain :

Cursed is every one that hangeth on a tree.

God's purpose is therefore plain : that the blessing promised to Abraham might reach the Gentiles through Jesus Christ, and the Spirit might become available to us all by faith.

The Law cannot interfere with
the original promise   III : 15

Let me give you an everyday illustration, my brothers. Once a contract has been properly drawn up and signed, it is honoured by both parties, and can neither be disregarded nor modified by a third party.

Now a Promise was made to Abraham and his seed. (Note in passing that the Scripture says not " seeds " but uses the singular " seed," meaning Christ.) I say then that the Law, which came into existence four hundred and thirty years later, cannot render null and void the original " contract " which God had made, and thus rob the Promise of its value. For if the receiving of the promised blessing were now made to depend on the Law, that would amount to a cancellation of the original " contract " which God made with Abraham as a Promise.

Where then lies the point of the Law ? It was an addition made to underline the existence and extent of sin until the arrival of the " Seed " to Whom the Promise referred. The Law was inaugurated in the presence of angels and by the hand of a human intermediary. The very fact that there was an intermediary is enough to show that this was not the fulfilling of the Promise. For the Promise of God needs neither angelic witness nor human intermediary but depends on Him alone.

Is the Law then to be looked upon as a contradiction of the Promise ? Certainly not, for if there could have been a law which gave men spiritual life then that law would have produced righteousness (which would have been, of course, in full harmony with the purpose of the Promise). But, as things are, the Scripture has all men " imprisoned," because they are found guilty by the Law, that to men in such condition the Promise might come to release all who believe in Jesus Christ.

By faith we are rescued from the
Law and become sons of God III : 23

Before the coming of faith we were all imprisoned under the power of the Law, with our only hope of deliverance the faith that was to be shown to us. Or, to change the metaphor, the Law was like a strict governess in charge of us until we went to the school of Christ and learned to be justified by faith in Him. Once we had that faith we were completely free from the governess's authority. For now that you have faith in Christ you are all sons of God. All of you who were baptised " into " Christ have put on the family likeness of Christ. Gone is the distinction between Jew and Greek, slave and free man, male and female—you are all one in Christ Jesus ! And if you belong to Christ, you are true descendants of Abraham, you are true heirs of his promise.

But you must realise that so long as an heir is a child, though he is destined to be master of everything, he is, in practice, no different from a servant. He has to obey a guardian or trustee until the time which his father has chosen for him to receive his inheritance. So is it with us : while we were " children " we lived under the authority of basic moral principles. But when the proper time came God sent His Son, born of a human mother and born under the jurisdiction of the Law, that He might redeem those who were under the authority of the Law and lead us into becoming, by adoption, true sons of God. It is because you really are His sons that God has sent the Spirit of His Son into your hearts to cry " Father, dear Father." You, my brother, are not a servant any longer ; you are a *son*. And, if you are a son, then you are certainly an heir of God through Christ.

Consider your own progress : do you
want to go backwards ? IV : 8

At one time when you had no knowledge of God, you were under the authority of gods who had no real existence. But now that you have come to know God or rather, are known by Him, how can you revert to dead and sterile principles and consent to be under their power all over again ?

Your religion is beginning to be a matter of observing certain days or months or years. Frankly, you stagger me; you make me wonder if all my efforts over you have been wasted!

I appeal to you by our past friendship,
don't be misled   IV : 12

I do beg you to follow me here, my brothers. I am a man like yourselves, and I have nothing against you personally. You know how handicapped I was by illness when I first preached the Gospel to you. You didn't shrink from me or let yourselves be revolted at the disease which was such a trial to me. No, you welcomed me as though I were an angel of God, or even as though I were Jesus Christ Himself! What has happened to that fine spirit of yours? I guarantee that in those days you would, if you could, have plucked out your eyes and given them to me. Have I now become your enemy because I continue to tell you the same truth? Oh, I know how keen these men are to win you over, but can't you see that it is for their own ends? They would like to see you and me separated altogether, and have you all to themselves. Don't think I'm jealous—it is a grand thing that men should be keen to win you, whether I'm there or not, provided it is for the truth. Oh, my dear children, I feel the pangs of childbirth all over again till Christ be formed within you, and how I long to be with you now! Perhaps I could then alter my tone to suit your mood. As it is, I honestly don't know how to deal with you.

Let us see what the Law itself has to say   IV : 21

Now tell me, you who want to be under the Law, have you heard what the Law says?

It is written that Abraham had two sons, one by the slave and the other by the free woman. The child of the slave was born in the ordinary course of nature, but the child of the free woman was born in accordance with God's promise. This can be regarded as an allegory. Here are the two Agreements represented by the two women: the one from Mount Sinai bearing children into slavery, typified by Hagar (Mount Sinai being in Arabia, the land of the descendants of Ishmael, Hagar's son), and corresponding to present-day Jerusalem—for the Jews are still, spiritually speaking, " slaves." But the free woman typifies the heavenly Jerusalem, which is the mother of us all, and is spiritually " free." It is written :

> Rejoice, thou barren that bearest not ;
> Break forth and cry, thou that travailest not :
> For more are the children of the desolate
> Than of her which hath the husband.

Now we, my brothers, are like Isaac, for we are children born " by promise." But just as in those far-off days the natural son persecuted the " spiritual " son, so it is to-day. Yet what is the scriptural instruction ?

> Cast out the handmaid and her son :
> For the son of the handmaid shall not inherit
> With the son of the free woman.

So then, my brothers, we are not to look upon ourselves as the sons of the slave woman but of the free, not sons of slavery under the Law but sons of freedom under grace.

Do not lose your freedom by giving in
to those who urge circumcision   V : I

Plant your feet firmly therefore within the freedom that Christ has won for us, and do not let yourselves be caught again in the shackles of slavery. Listen ! I, Paul, say this to you as solemnly as I can : if you consent to be circumcised then Christ will be of no use to you at all. I will say it again : every man who consents to be circumcised is bound to obey all the rest of the Law ! If you try to be justified by the Law you automatically cut yourself off from the power of Christ, you put yourself outside the range of His grace. For it is *by faith* that we await in His Spirit the righteousness we hope to see. In Jesus Christ there is no validity in either circumcision or uncircumcision; it is a matter of faith, faith which expresses itself in love.

You were making splendid progress; who put you off the course you had set for the truth? That sort of "persuasion" does not come from the One Who is calling you. Alas, it takes only a little leaven to affect the whole lump! I feel confident in the Lord that you will not take any fatal step. But whoever it is who is worrying you will have a serious charge to answer one day.

And as for me, my brothers, if I were still advocating circumcision (as some apparently allege!), why am I still suffering persecution? I suppose if only I would recommend this little rite all the hostility which the preaching of the Cross provokes would disappear! I wish those who are so eager to cut your bodies would cut themselves off from you altogether!

It is to freedom that you have been called, my brothers. Only be careful that freedom does not become mere opportunity for your lower nature. You should be free to serve each other in love. For after all, the whole Law towards others is comprised in this one command, "Thou shalt love thy neighbour as thyself."

But if freedom means merely that you are free to attack and tear each other to pieces, be careful that it doesn't mean that between you you destroy your fellowship altogether!

The way to live in freedom is by the Spirit   v : 16

Here is my advice. Live your whole life in the Spirit and you will not satisfy the desires of your lower nature. For the whole energy of the lower nature is set against the Spirit, while the whole power of the Spirit is contrary to the lower nature. Here is the conflict, and that is why you are not free to do what you want to do. But if you follow the leading of the Spirit, you stand clear of the Law.

The activities of the lower nature are obvious. Here is a list: sexual immorality, impurity of mind, sensuality, worship of false gods, witchcraft, hatred, quarrelling, jealousy, bad temper, rivalry, factions, party-spirit, envy, drunkenness, orgies and things like that. I solemnly assure you, as I did before, that those who indulge in such things will never inherit God's Kingdom. The Spirit, however, produces in human life fruits such as these: love, joy, peace, patience, kindness, generosity, fidelity, adaptability and self-control—and no law exists against any of them.

Those who belong to Christ have crucified their old nature with all that it loved and lusted for. If our lives are centred in the Spirit, let us be guided by the Spirit. Let us not be ambitious for our own reputations, for that only means making each other jealous.

Some practical wisdom   VI : 1

Even if a man should be detected in some sin, my brothers, the spiritual ones among you should quietly set him back on the right path, not with any feeling of superiority but being yourselves on guard against temptation. Carry each other's burdens and so live out the law of Christ.

If a man thinks he is " somebody," he is deceiving himself, for that very thought proves that he is nobody. Let every man learn to assess properly the value of his own work and he can then be glad when he has done something worth doing without depending on the approval of others. For every man must " shoulder his own pack."

The man under Christian instruction should be willing to contribute towards the livelihood of his teacher.

The inevitability of life's harvest   VI : 7

Don't be under any illusion: you cannot make a fool of God! A man's harvest in life will depend entirely on what he sows. If he sows for his own lower nature his harvest will be the decay and death of his own nature. But if he sows for the Spirit he will reap the harvest of everlasting life by that Spirit. Let us not grow tired of doing good, for, unless we throw in our hand, the ultimate harvest is assured. Let us then do good to all men as opportunity offers, especially to those who belong to the Christian household.

A final appeal, in my own hand-writing   VI : II

Look at these huge letters I am making in writing these words to you with my own hand ! *

These men who are always urging you to be circumcised—what are they after ? They want to present a pleasing front to the world and they want to avoid being persecuted for the Cross of Christ. For even those who have been circumcised do not themselves keep the Law. But they want you circumcised so that they may be able to boast about your submission to their ruling. Yet God forbid that I should boast about anything or anybody except the Cross of our Lord Jesus Christ, which means that the world is a dead thing to me and I am a dead man to the world. For in Christ it is not circumcision or uncircumcision that counts but the power of new birth. To all who live by this principle, to the true Israel of God, may there be peace and mercy !

Let no one interfere with me after this. I carry on my scarred body the marks of my Owner, the Lord Jesus.

The grace of our Lord Jesus Christ, my brothers, be with your spirit.

PAUL

THE LETTER TO
THE CHRISTIANS AT EPHESUS

AND IN OTHER PLACES

AUTHOR. *This letter was almost certainly written by Paul, although some argue from the style that it was drafted by another hand, possibly Timothy's, and then corrected and signed by Paul. It is very widely accepted that the letter was issued by him, during the same period as the letters to Colossae and Philippi and the*

---

*According to centuries-old Eastern usage this could easily mean, "Note how heavily I have pressed upon the pen in writing this." Thus it could be translated, "Notice how heavily I underline these words to you."

personal note to Philemon, while he was in prison. Almost certainly his imprisonment while he despatched these letters was at Rome (Acts XXVIII, 30).

DATE. *About 62.*

DESTINATION. *Probably not only Ephesus, for although Paul had spent two years there (Acts XIX, 9, 10), there are no personal references. For this and other good reasons it is generally believed that this is a circular letter meant to reach the churches in Asia. Tychicus, who took the letter in person, would probably reach Ephesus first. The letter would then be copied and taken on to the other churches. It is quite possible that the Letter to Laodicaea, mentioned in Colossians IV, 16, was this particular letter.*

THEME. *Paul is concerned first to establish in his readers' minds as great and wide and deep a conception of Christ as he can. He points out that He is not only the Saviour of the world, but also the Divinely appointed focal point of all activity and all knowledge, whether it is physical, mental or spiritual. Race distinctions cannot matter therefore for those who are " in Christ."*

He follows this by stressing the resultant responsibility of the Christian, and his own proper authority as the Special Messenger commissioned to deliver such news.

Then, as usual, Paul points out the practical outcome of being "members of Christ's Body," "new men," " children of God," etc., and begs his readers to see that their lives are lived on a level worthy of the staggering privileges that God has given them.

PAUL, Messenger of Jesus Christ by God's choice, to all faithful Christians at Ephesus (and other places where this letter is read): grace and peace be to you from God the Father and our Lord Jesus Christ.

*Praise God for what He has done
for us Christians !*   1 : 3

Praise be to God for giving us every possible spiritual benefit in Christ ! For consider what He has done—before

the foundation of the world He chose us to becom
Christ, His holy and blameless children living within
constant care. He planned, in His purpose of love, tha
should be adopted as His own children through Jesus C
—that we might learn to praise that glorious generosity o
which has made us welcome in the everlasting love He l
towards the Son. It is through the Son, at the cost of His
blood, that we are redeemed, freely forgiven through tha
and generous grace which has overflowed into our lives
opened our eyes to the truth. For God has allowed u
know the secret of His Plan, and it is this : He purpos
His sovereign Will that all human history shall be cons
mated in Christ, that everything that exists in Heaver
earth shall find its perfection and fulfilment in Him. And
is the staggering thing—that in all which will one day be
to Him we have been promised a share (since we were long
destined for this by the One Who achieves His purpose
His sovereign Will), so that we, as the first to put our
fidence in Christ, may bring praise to His glory ! And
too trusted Him, when you had heard the message of tr
the Gospel of your salvation. And after you gave your c
dence to Him you were, so to speak, stamped with the
mised Holy Spirit as a guarantee of purchase, until the
when God completes the redemption of what He has paic
as His own ; and that will again be to the praise of His g

I thank God for you, and pray for you   I

Since, then, I heard of this faith of yours in the Lord J
and the practical way in which you are expressing it tow
fellow-Christians, I thank God continually for you and I n
give up praying for you ; and this is my prayer. That (
the God of our Lord Jesus Christ and the all-glorious Fat
will give you spiritual wisdom and the insight to know r
of Him : that you may receive that inner illumination of
spirit which will make you realise how great is the hop
which He is calling you—the magnificence and splendou
the inheritance promised to Christians—and how tremend
is the power available to us who believe in God. That po

is the same Divine energy which was demonstrated in Christ when He raised Him from the dead and gave Him the place of supreme honour in Heaven—a place that is infinitely superior to any conceivable command, authority, power or control, and which carries with it a Name far beyond any name that could ever be used in this world or the world to come.

God has placed everything under the power of Christ and has set Him up as Head of everything for the Church. For the Church is His Body, and in that Body lives fully the One Who fills the whole wide universe.

We were all dead : God gave us life through Christ

II : I

To you, who were spiritually dead all the time that you drifted along on the stream of this world's ideas of living, and obeyed its unseen ruler (who is still operating in those who do not respond to the truth of God), to you Christ has given life! We all lived like that in the past, and followed the impulses and imaginations of our evil nature, being in fact under the wrath of God by nature, like everyone else. But even though we were dead in our sins God was so rich in mercy that He gave us the very life of Christ (for it is, remember, by grace and not by achievement that you are saved), and has lifted us right out of the old life to take our place with Him in Christ in the heavens. Thus He shows for all time the tremendous generosity of the grace and kindness He has expressed towards us in Christ Jesus. It was nothing you could or did achieve—it was God's gift to you. No one can pride himself that he earned the love of God. The fact is that what we are we owe to the Hand of God upon us. We are born afresh in Christ, and born to do those good deeds which God planned for us to do.

You were Gentiles : we were Jews. God has made us fellow-Christians

II : II

Do not lose sight of the fact that you were born " Gentiles," known by those whose bodies were circumcised as " the Uncircumcised." You were without Christ, you were utter strangers to God's chosen community, the Jews, and you had no knowledge of, or right to, the promised Agreements. You had nothing to look forward to and no God to Whom you could turn. But now, through the blood of Christ, you who were once outside the pale are with us inside the circle of God's love and purpose. For Christ is our living Peace. He has made a unity of the conflicting elements of Jew and Gentile by breaking down the barrier which lay between us. By His sacrifice He removed the hostility of the Law, with all its commandments and rules, and made in Himself out of the two, Jew and Gentile, One New Man, thus producing peace. For He reconciled both to God by the sacrifice of one Body on the Cross, and by this act made utterly irrelevant the antagonism between them. Then He came and told both you who were far from God and us who were near that the war was over. And it is through Him that both of us now can approach the Father in the one Spirit.

So you are no longer outsiders or aliens, but fellow-citizens with every other Christian—you belong now to the household of God. Firmly beneath you is the foundation. God's Messengers and Prophets, the actual Foundation-stone being Jesus Christ Himself. In Him each separate piece of building, properly fitting into its neighbour, grows together into a temple consecrated to God. You are all part of this building in which God Himself lives by His Spirit.

God has made me minister to you Gentiles   III : I

It is in this great cause that I, Paul, have become Christ's prisoner for you Gentiles. For you must have heard how God gave me grace to become your minister, and how He allowed me to understand His Secret by giving me a direct revelation. (What I have written briefly of this above will explain to you my knowledge of the mystery of Christ.) This Secret was hidden to past generations of mankind, but it has now, by the Spirit, been made plain to God's consecrated Messengers and Prophets. It is simply this : that the Gentiles, who were previously excluded from God's Agreements, are to be equal

heirs with His chosen people, equal members and equal
partners in God's Promise given by Christ through the
Gospel. And I was made a minister of that Gospel by the
grace He gave me, and by the power with which He equipped
me. Yes, to me, less than the least of all Christians, has God
given this grace, to enable me to proclaim to the Gentiles the
incalculable riches of Christ, and to make plain to all men the
meaning of that Secret which He Who created everything in
Christ has kept hidden from the Creation until now. The
purpose is that all the angelic powers should now see the
complex wisdom of God's plan being worked out through
the Church, in conformity to that timeless Purpose which He
centred in Jesus, our Lord. It is in this same Jesus, because
we have faith in Him, that we dare, even with confidence, to
approach God. In view of these tremendous issues, I beg you
not to lose heart because I am now suffering for my part in
bringing you the Gospel. Indeed, you should be honoured.

I pray that you may know God's
power in practice   III : 14

When I think of the greatness of this great Plan I fall on my
knees before God the Father (from Whom all Fatherhood,
earthly or heavenly, derives its name), and I pray that out of
the glorious richness of His resources He will enable you to
know the strength of the Spirit's inner reinforcement—that
Christ may actually live in your hearts by your faith. And I
pray that you, firmly fixed in love yourselves, may be able to
grasp (with all Christians) how wide and deep and long and
high is the love of Christ—and to know that love for yourselves. May you be filled through all your being with God
Himself !

Now to Him Who by His power within us is able to do far
more than we ever dare to ask or imagine—to Him be glory
in the Church through Jesus Christ for ever and ever, Amen !

Christians should be at one, as God is one   IV : 1

As God's prisoner, then, I beg you to live lives worthy of
your high calling. Accept life with humility and patience,

making allowances for each other because you love each o
Make it your aim to be at one in the Spirit, and you wi
evitably be at peace with one another. You all belong to
Body, of which there is one Spirit, just as you all experie
one calling to one hope. There is one Lord, one faith
baptism, one God, one Father of us all, Who is the One
all, the One working through all and the One living in a

God's gifts vary, but it is the
same God Who gives   I

Naturally there are different gifts and functions ;
vidually grace is given to us in different ways out of the
diversity of Christ's giving. As the Scripture says :

When He ascended on high, He led captivity capti
and gave gifts unto men.

(Note the implication here—to say that Christ " ascen
means that He must previously have " descended," th
from the height of Heaven to the depth of this world.
One Who made this descent is identically the same Pers
He Who has now ascended high above the very heave
that the whole universe from lowest to highest might l
His Presence.)

His " gifts unto men " were varied. Some He made
Messengers, some prophets, some preachers of the Go
to some He gave the power to guide and teach His pe
His gifts were made that Christians might be pro
equipped for their service, that the whole Body might be
up until the time comes when, in the unity of common
and common knowledge of the Son of God, we arrive a
maturity—that measure of development which is mean
" the fullness of Christ."

True maturity means growing up " into " Christ   IV

We are not meant to remain as children at the mer
every chance wind of teaching and the jockeying of men
are expert in the crafty presentation of lies. But we are r

to hold firmly to the truth in love, and to grow up in every way into Christ, the Head. For it is from the Head that the whole Body, as a harmonious structure knit together by the joints with which it is provided, grows by the proper functioning of individual parts to its full maturity in love.

Have no more to do with the old life !
Learn the new   IV : 17

This is my instruction, then, which I give you from God. Do not live any longer as the Gentiles live. For they live blindfold in a world of illusion, and are cut off from the life of God through ignorance and insensitiveness. They have stifled their consciences and then surrendered themselves to sensuality, practising any form of impurity which lust can suggest. But you have learned nothing like that from Christ, if you have really heard His voice and understood the truth that He has taught you. No, what you learned was to fling off the dirty clothes of the old way of living, which were rotted through and through with lust's illusions, and, with yourselves mentally and spiritually re-made, to put on the clean fresh clothes of the new life which was made by God's design for righteousness and the holiness which is no illusion.

Finish, then, with lying and tell your neighbour the truth. For we are not separate units but intimately related to each other in Christ. If you are angry, be sure that it is not out of wounded pride or bad temper. Never go to bed angry—don't give the Devil that sort of foothold.

The new life means positive good   IV : 28

If you used to be a thief you must not only give up stealing, but you must learn to make an honest living, so that you may be able to give to those in need.

Let there be no more foul language, but good words instead —words suitable for the occasion, which God can use to help other people. Never hurt the Holy Spirit. He is, remember, the Personal pledge of your eventual full redemption.

Let there be no more resentment, no more anger or temper, no more violent self-assertiveness, no more slander and no more malicious remarks. Be kind to each other, be understanding. Be as ready to forgive others as God for Christ's sake has forgiven you.

As children copy their fathers you, as God's children, are to copy Him. Live your lives in love—the same sort of love which Christ gave us and which He perfectly expressed when He gave Himself up for us in sacrifice to God. But as for sexual immorality in all its forms, and the itch to get your hands on what belongs to other people—don't even talk about such things; they are no fit subjects for Christians to talk about. The key-note of your conversation should not be nastiness or silliness or flippancy, but a sense of all that we owe to God.

Evil is as utterly different from good
as light from darkness   v : 5

For of this much you can be quite certain : that neither the immoral nor the dirty-minded nor the covetous man (which latter is, in effect, worshipping a false god) has any inheritance in the Kingdom of Christ and of God. Don't let anyone fool you on this point, however plausible his argument. It is these very things which bring down the wrath of God upon the disobedient. Have nothing to do with men like that—once you were " darkness " but now you are " light." Live then as children of the Light. The Light produces in men quite the opposite of sins like these—everything that is wholesome and good and true. Let your lives be living proofs of the things which please God. Steer clear of the activities of darkness ; let your lives show by contrast how dreary and futile these things are. (You know the sort of things I mean—to detail their secret doings is really too shameful.) For light is capable of " showing up " everything for what it really is. It is even possible (after all, it happened with you !) for light to turn the thing it shines upon into light also. Thus God speaks through the Scriptures :

Awake thou that sleepest, and arise from the dead,
And Christ shall shine upon thee.

You know the truth—let your life show it !   V : 15

Live life, then, with a due sense of responsibility, not as men who do not know the meaning and purpose of life but as *those who do.* Make the best use of your time, despite all the difficulties of these days. Don't be vague but firmly grasp what you know to be the Will of God. Don't get your stimulus from wine (for there is always the danger of excessive drinking) but let the Spirit stimulate your souls. Express your joy in singing among yourselves psalms and hymns and spiritual songs making music in your hearts for the ears of God ! Thank God at all times for everything, in the name of our Lord Jesus Christ. And " fit in with " each other, just because you all recognise that God is the Supreme Power over all.

Christ and the Church the pattern relationship
for husband and wife   V : 22

You wives must learn to adapt yourselves to your husbands, for the husband is the " head " of the wife in the same way that Christ is Head of the Church. The willing subjection of the Church to Christ should be reproduced in the submission of wives to their husbands. But, remember, this means that the husband must give his wife the same sort of love that Christ gave to the Church, when He sacrificed Himself for her. Christ gave Himself to make her holy, having cleansed her through the baptism of his Word—to make her an altogether glorious Church in his eyes. She is to be free from spots, wrinkles or any other disfigurements—a Church holy and perfect.

Men ought to give their wives the love they naturally have for their own bodies. The love a man gives his wife is the extending of his love for himself to enfold her. Nobody ever hates or neglects his own body : he feeds it and looks after it. And that is what Christ does for His Body, the Church. And we are all members of that Body, we are His flesh and blood !

For this cause shall a man leave his father and mother,

And shall cleave to his wife ; and the twain shall bec
one flesh.

The marriage relationship is doubtless a great mystery,
I am speaking of something deeper still—the marriag
Christ and His Church.

In practice what I have said amounts to this : let every
of you who is a husband love his wife as he loves himself,
let the wife reverence her husband.

Children and parents : servants and masters   VI

Children, the right thing for you to do is to obey y
parents as those whom God has set over you. The
commandment to contain a promise was :

Honour thy father and thy mother
That it may be well with thee, and that thou mayest
    long on the earth.

Fathers, don't over-correct your children or make it c
cult for them to obey the commandment. Bring them up
Christian teaching in Christian discipline.

Slaves, obey your human masters sincerely with a pro
sense of respect and responsibility, as service rendered
Christ Himself ; not with the idea of currying favour
men, but as the servants of Christ conscientiously doing v
you believe to be the will of God for you. You may be
that God will reward a man for good work, irrespectivel
whether the man be slave or free. And as for you employ
be as conscientious and responsible towards those who se
you as you expect them to be towards you, neither misu
the power over others that has been put in your hands,
forgetting that you are responsible yourselves to a Heav
Employer Who makes no distinction between master and n

Be forewarned and forearmed in your
spiritual conflict
VI : 10

In conclusion, be strong—not in yourselves but in the Lord, in the power of His boundless resource. Put on God's complete armour so that you can successfully resist all the Devil's methods of attack. For, as I expect you have learned by now, our fight is not against any physical enemy : it is against organisations and powers that are spiritual. We are up against the unseen power that controls this dark world, and spiritual agents from the very headquarters of evil. Therefore you must wear the whole armour of God that you may be able to resist evil in its day of power, and that even when you have fought to a standstill you may still stand your ground. Take your stand then with Truth as your belt, Righteousness your breastplate, the Gospel of Peace firmly on your feet, Salvation as your helmet and in your hand the Sword of the Spirit, the Word of God. Above all be sure that you take Faith as your shield, for it can quench every burning missile the enemy hurls at you. Pray at all times with every kind of spiritual prayer, keeping alert and persistent as you pray for all Christ's men and women. And pray for me, too, that I may be able to speak freely here to make known the secret of that Gospel for which I am, so to speak, an ambassador in chains. Pray that I may speak out about it, as is my plain and obvious duty.

Tychicus, beloved brother and faithful Christian minister, will tell you personally what I am doing and how I am getting on. I am sending him to you bringing this letter for that purpose, so that you will know exactly how we are and may take fresh heart.

Peace be to all Christian brothers, and love with faith from God the Father and the Lord Jesus Christ !

Grace be with all those who sincerely love our Lord Jesus Christ. Amen.

PAUL

THE LETTER TO
THE CHRISTIANS AT PHILIPPI

AUTHOR. *Paul, writing from prison, possibly in Rome (Acts XXVIII, 30).*

DATE. *About 62.*

DESTINATION. *The Church at Philippi, where Paul had been beaten and imprisoned but had seen his gaoler converted (Acts XVI, 25-34). It was also at Philippi that Lydia, a business woman selling purple-dyed cloth, became one of the first Christians.*

THEME. *The first purpose of the letter is to acknowledge a gift sent to Paul in prison by Epaphroditus from the Christians at Philippi. Possibly this letter was delayed by the serious illness of Epaphroditus while with Paul (II, 27) and Paul is evidently by now himself expecting early release from prison (II, 24). Except possibly for the letter to Philemon, this is the most personal example of Paul's correspondence, and he is obviously very fond of the little church at Philippi. It expresses his high hopes for their unity, faithfulness and progress in the faith. It also contains a warning, like that in the letter to the Galatians, against false teachers who wanted to bring these inexperienced Christians under the Jewish Law.*

PAUL and Timothy, true servants of Jesus Christ, to the bishops, deacons and all true Christians at Philippi, grace and peace from God our Father and Jesus Christ the Lord!

I have the most pleasant memories of you all   1 : 3

I thank God for you Christians at Philippi whenever I think of you. My constant prayers for you are a real joy, for they bring back to my mind how we have worked together for the Gospel from the earliest days until now. I feel sure that the One Who has begun His good work in you will go on developing it until the Day of Jesus Christ.

It is only natural that I should feel like this about you all, for during the time I was in prison as well as when I was out defending and demonstrating the power of the Gospel we shared together the grace of God. God knows how much I long, with the deepest Christian love and affection, for your companionship. My prayer for you is that you may have still more love—a love that is full of knowledge and wise insight. I want you to be able always to recognise the highest and the best, and to live sincere and blameless lives until the Day of Jesus Christ. I want to see your lives full of true goodness, produced by the power that Jesus Christ gives you to the praise and glory of God.

My imprisonment has turned out to
be no bad thing   I : 12

Now, concerning myself, I want you to know, my brothers, that what has happened to me has, in effect, turned out to the advantage of the Gospel. For, first of all, my imprisonment means a personal witness for Christ before the Palace guards, not to mention others who come and go. Then, it means that most of our brothers, somehow taking fresh heart in the Lord from the very fact that I am a prisoner for Christ's sake, have shown far more courage in boldly proclaiming the Word of God. I know that some are preaching Christ out of jealousy, in order to annoy me, but some are preaching Him in good faith. The motive of the former is questionable— they preach in a partisan spirit, hoping to make my chains even more galling than they would otherwise be. But what does it matter? However they may look at it, the fact remains that Christ *is* being preached, whether sincerely or not, and that fact makes me very happy. Yes, and I shall go on being very happy, for I know that what is happening will be for the good of my own soul, thanks to your prayers and the resources of the Spirit of Jesus Christ. It all accords with my own earnest wishes and hopes, which are that I should never be in any way ashamed, but that now, as always, I should honour Christ with the utmost boldness by the way I live, whether that means I am to face death or to go on living.

living to me means simply "Christ," and if I die I sh
merely gain more of Him. I realise, of course, that the v
which I have started may make it necessary for me to g
living in this world. I should find it very hard to ma
choice. I am torn in two directions—on the one hand I
to leave this world and live with Christ, and that is obvio
the best thing for me. Yet, on the other hand, it is prob
more necessary for you that I should stay here on earth.
is why I feel pretty well convinced that I shall not leave
world yet, but shall be able to stand by you, to help you
ward in Christian living and to find increasing joy in
faith. So you can look forward to making much of me as
minister in Christ when I come to see you again !

But whatever happens, make sure that your everyday li
worthy of the Gospel of Christ. So that whether I do c
and see you, or merely hear about you from a distance, I
know that you are standing fast in a united spirit, bat
with a single mind for the faith of the Gospel and not ca
two straws for your enemies. The very fact that they
your enemies is plain proof that they are lost to God, whil
fact that you have such men as enemies is plain proof
you yourselves are being saved by God. You are given, in
battle, the privilege not merely of believing in Christ but
of suffering for His sake. It is now your turn to take pa
that battle you once saw me engaged in, and which, in p
of fact, I am still fighting.

Above all things be loving, humble, united   II

Now if your experience of Christ's encouragement
love means anything to you, if you have known somethin
the fellowship of His Spirit, and all that it means in kind
and deep sympathy, do make my best hopes for you c
true ! Live together in harmony, live together in love
though you had only one mind and one spirit between
Never act from motives of rivalry or personal vanity, bu
humility think more of each other than you do of yoursel
None of you should think only of his own affairs, but sho
learn to see things from other people's point of view.

Let Christ be your example of humility   II : 5

Let Christ Himself be your example as to what your attitude should be. For He, Who had always been God by nature, did not cling to His prerogatives as God's Equal, but stripped Himself of all privilege by consenting to be a slave by nature and being born as mortal man. And, having become man, He humbled Himself by living a life of utter obedience, even to the extent of dying, *and the death he died was the death of a common criminal.* That is why God has now lifted Him so high, and has given Him the Name beyond all names, so that at the Name of Jesus " every knee shall bow," whether in Heaven or Earth or under the earth. And that is why, in the end, " every tongue shall confess " that Jesus Christ is the Lord, to the glory of God the Father.

God is Himself at work within you   II : 12

So then, my dearest friends, as you have always followed my advice—and that not only when I was present to give it— so now that I am far away be keener than ever to work out the salvation that God has given you with a proper sense of awe and responsibility. For it is God Who is at work within you, giving you the will and the power to achieve His purpose.

Do all you have to do without grumbling or arguing, so that you may be God's children, blameless, sincere and whole-some, living in a warped and diseased world, and shining there like lights in a dark place. For you hold in your hands the very word of life. Thus can you give me something to be proud of in the day of Christ, for I shall know then that I did not spend my energy in vain. Yes, and if it should happen that my life-blood is, so to speak, poured out upon the sacrifice and offer-ing which your faith means to God, then I can still be very happy, and I can share my happiness with you all. I should like to feel that you could be glad about this too, and could share with me the happiness I speak of.

I am sending Epaphroditus with this
letter, and Timothy later   II : 19

But I hope in Jesus Christ that it will not be long before I
can send Timothy to you, and then I shall be cheered by a
first-hand account of you and your doings. I have nobody
else with a genuine interest in your well-being. All the others
seem to be wrapped up in their own affairs and do not really
care for the business of Jesus Christ. But you know how
Timothy has proved his worth, working with me for the
Gospel like a son with his father. I hope to send him to you
as soon as I can tell how things will work out for me, but
God gives me some hope that it will not be long before I am
able to come myself as well. I have considered it desirable,
however, to send you Epaphroditus. He has been to me
brother, fellow-worker and comrade-in-arms, as well as being
the messenger you sent to see to my wants. He has been
home-sick for you, and was worried because he knew that
you had heard that he was ill. Indeed he was ill, very danger-
ously ill, but God had mercy on him—and incidentally on me
as well, so that I did not have the sorrow of losing him to add
to my sufferings. I am particularly anxious, therefore, to send
him to you so that when you see him again you may be glad,
and to know of your joy will lighten my own sorrows.
Welcome him in the Lord with great joy ! You should hold
men like him in highest honour, for his loyalty to Christ
brought him very near death—he risked his life to do for me
in person what distance prevented you all from doing.

In conclusion, my brothers, delight yourselves in the Lord !
It doesn't bore me to repeat a piece of advice like this, and if
you follow it you will find it a great safeguard to your souls.

The " circumcision " party are the enemies
of your faith and freedom   III : 2

Be on your guard against these curs, these wicked work-
men, these would-be mutilators of your bodies ! We are,
remember, truly circumcised when we worship God by the
Spirit, when we find our joy in Christ Jesus and put no
confidence in what we are in the flesh.

I was even more of a Jew than these Jews,
yet knowing Christ has changed my whole life   III : 4

If it were right to have such confidence, I could certainly
have it, and if any of these men thinks he has grounds for
such confidence I can assure him I have more. I was born a
true Jew, I was circumcised on the eighth day, I was a
member of the tribe of Benjamin, I was in fact a full-blooded
Jew. As far as keeping the Law is concerned I was a Pharisee,
and you can judge my enthusiasm for the Jewish faith by my
active persecution of the Church. As far as the Law's
righteousness is concerned, I don't think anyone could have
found fault with me. Yet every advantage that I had gained I
considered lost for Christ's sake. Yes, and I look upon everything as loss compared with the overwhelming gain of knowing Christ Jesus my Lord. For His sake I did in actual fact
suffer the loss of everything, but I considered it useless
rubbish compared with being able to win Christ. For now my
place is in Him, and I am not dependent upon any of the self-
achieved righteousness of the Law. God has given me that
genuine righteousness which comes from faith in Christ.
How changed are my ambitions ! Now I long to know Christ
and the power shown by His Resurrection : now I long to
share His sufferings, even to die as He died, so that I may
perhaps attain, as He did, the Resurrection from the dead. Yet,
my brothers, I do not consider myself to have " arrived,"
spiritually, nor do I consider myself already perfect. But I
keep going on, grasping ever more firmly that purpose for
which Christ grasped me. My brothers, I do not consider
myself to have fully grasped it even now. But I do concentrate on this : I leave the past behind and with hands out-
stretched to whatever lies ahead I go straight for the goal—
my reward the honour of being called by God in Christ.

My ambition is the true goal of the spiritually
adult : make it yours too   III : 15

All of us who are spiritually adult should set ourselves this
sort of ambition, and if at present you cannot see this, yet you
will find that this is the attitude which God is leading you to

adopt. It is important that we go forward in the light of such truth as we have ourselves attained to.

Let me be your example here, my brothers : let my example be the standard by which you can tell who are the genuine Christians among those about you. For there are many, of whom I have told you before and tell you again now, even with tears, that they are the enemies of the Cross of Christ. These men are heading for utter destruction—their god is their own appetite, their pride is in what they should be ashamed of, and this world is the limit of their horizon. But we are citizens of Heaven ; our outlook goes beyond this world to the hopeful expectation of the Saviour Who will come from Heaven, the Lord Jesus Christ. He will re-make these wretched bodies of ours to resemble his own glorious Body, by that power of His which makes Him the Master of everything that is.

So, my brothers whom I love and long for, my joy and my crown, do stand firmly in the Lord, and remember how much I love you.

Be united, be joyful, be at peace   IV : 2

Euodias and Syntyche, I beg you by name to make up your differences as Christians should ! And you, my true fellow-worker, I ask you to help these women. They both worked hard with me for the Gospel, as did Clement and all my other fellow-workers whose names are in the Book of Life.

Delight yourselves in God, yes, find you joy in Him at all times. Have a reputation for gentleness, and never forget the nearness of your Lord.

Don't worry over anything whatever ; tell God every detail of your needs in earnest and thankful prayer, and the peace of God, which transcends human understanding, will keep constant guard over your hearts and minds as they rest in Christ Jesus.

Here is a last piece of advice. If you believe in goodness and if you value the approval of God, fix your minds on the things which are holy and right and pure and beautiful and good. Model your conduct on what you have learned from me, on what I have told you and shown you, and you will find that the God of peace will be with you.

The memory of your generosity is an abiding joy to me

IV : 10

It has been a great joy to me that after all this time you have shown such interest in my welfare. I don't mean that you had forgotten me, but up till now you had no opportunity of expressing your concern. Nor do I mean that I have been in actual need, for I have learned to be content, whatever the circumstances may be. I know now how to live when things are difficult and I know how to live when things are prosperous. In general and in particular I have learned the secret of facing either poverty or plenty. I am ready for anything through the strength of the One Who lives within me. Nevertheless I am not disparaging the way in which you were willing to share my troubles. You Philippians will remember that in the early days of the Gospel when I left Macedonia, you were the only church who shared with me the fellowship of giving and receiving. Even in Thessalonica you twice sent me help when I was in need. It isn't the value of the gift that I am keen on, it is the reward that will come to you because of these gifts that you have made.

Now I have everything I want—in fact I am rich. Yes, I am quite content, thanks to your gifts received through Epaphroditus. Your generosity is like a lovely fragrance, a sacrifice that pleases the very heart of God. My God will supply all that you need from His glorious resources in Christ Jesus. And may glory be to our God and our Father for ever and ever, Amen!

Farewell messages

IV : 21

Greetings to every true Christian, from me and all the brothers here with me. All the Christians here would like to send their best wishes, particularly those who belong to the Emperor's household.

The grace of the Lord Jesus Christ be with your spirit.

PAUL

THE LETTER TO THE
CHRISTIANS AT COLOSSAE

AUTHOR. *Paul, writing probably at the same time as he wrote the letters to Ephesus, Philippi and Philemon while in prison at Rome.*

DATE. *About 62.*

DESTINATION. *The church at Colossae, a town in Asia Minor about a hundred miles inland from Ephesus. Paul had never himself been there, and it appears that the church was founded by Epaphras. The latter was apparently imprisoned in Rome after his arrival from Colossae, and this letter was sent back by the hand of Tychicus.*

THEME. *This letter is plainly written to refute the false teaching which was poisoning the church life at Colossae. This false teaching was propagating two errors : first, that the universe contained a number of beings of various degrees of power and importance ranging from man to God, and that Christ was to be thought of as merely one of the superior powers. Paul combats this by his unequivocal declaration that Christ is God's "Son," the First Principle and Upholding Principle of the whole creation. The second false tendency was the attempt to force on the Colossian Christians a system of purely arbitrary observances and angel-worship, coupled with an extreme asceticism. Paul meets this by pointing out that the Christian's position in God is far beyond the petty observance of man-made rules. The true asceticism, moreover, is to abstain from evil passion and evil thoughts, not to cut oneself off from the normal use of God's good gifts.*

Although writing to those he had never seen, Paul writes with obvious love and interest and is sincerely pleased with the genuine Christianity which has taken root at Colossae.

PAUL, Messenger of Jesus Christ by God's Will, and

brother Timothy send this greeting to all faithful Christians
at Colossae : grace and peace be to you from God our
Father and the Lord Jesus Christ !

We thank God for you and pray
constantly for you   1 : 3

I want you to know by this letter that we here are constantly praying for you, and whenever we do we thank God
the Father because you believe in Christ and because you are
showing true Christian love towards other Christians. We
know that you are showing these qualities because you have
grasped what we call " the heavenly hope "—that hope which
first became yours when the Truth was brought to you. It is,
of course, part of the Gospel itself, which has reached you as it
spreads all over the world. Wherever that Gospel goes, it
produces Christian character, and develops it, as it has done
in your own case from the time you first heard and realised the
amazing fact of God's grace.

You learned these things, we understand, from Epaphras,
who is in the same service as we are. He is a most well-loved
minister of Christ, and has your well-being very much at
heart. As a matter of fact, it was from him that we heard
about your growth in Christian love, so you will understand
that since we heard about you we have never missed you in
our prayers. We are asking God that you may see things, as it
were, from His point of view by being given spiritual insight
and understanding. We also pray that your outward lives,
which men see, may bring credit to your Master's Name, and
that you may bring joy to His heart by bearing genuine
Christian fruit, and that your knowledge of God may grow yet
deeper.

We pray for you to have real
Christian experience   1 : 11

As you live this new life, we pray that you will be strengthened from God's boundless resources, so that you will
find yourselves able to pass through any experience and
endure it with courage. You will even be able to thank

God in the midst of pain and distress because you are privileged to share the lot of those who are living in the Light. For we must never forget that He rescued us from the power of darkness, and re-established us in the Kingdom of His beloved Son, that is, in the Kingdom of Light. For it is by His Son alone that we have been redeemed and have had our sins forgiven.

Who Christ is, and what He has done   1 : 15

Now Christ is the visible expression of the invisible God. He existed before creation began, for it was through Him that everything was made, whether spiritual or material, seen or unseen. Through Him and for Him, also, were created power and dominion, ownership and authority. In fact, every single thing was created through, and for, Him. He is both the First Principle and the Upholding Principle of the whole scheme of creation. And now He is the Head of the Body which is composed of all Christian people. Life from nothing began through Him, and life from the dead began through Him, and He is, therefore, justly called the Lord of all. It was in Him that the full nature of God chose to live, and through Him God planned to reconcile in His own Person, as it were, everything on earth and everything in Heaven by virtue of the sacrifice of the Cross.

And you yourselves, who were strangers to God, and, in fact, through the evil things you had done, His spiritual enemies, He has now reconciled through the death of His Body on the Cross, so that He might welcome you to His presence clean and pure, without blame or reproach. This reconciliation assumes, of course, that you maintain a firm position in the faith, and do not allow yourselves to be shifted away from the hope of the Gospel, which you have heard, and which, indeed, the whole world is now having an opportunity of hearing.

My Divine commission   1 : 23b

I myself have been made a minister of this same Gospel, and though it is true at this moment that I am suffering on behalf of you who have heard the Gospel, yet I am far from sorry about it. Indeed, I am glad, because it gives me a chance to complete in my own sufferings something of the untold pains which Christ suffers on behalf of His Body, the Church. For I am a minister of the Church by Divine commission, a commission granted to me for your benefit and for a special purpose : that I might fully declare God's Word —that sacred mystery which up till now has been hidden in every age and every generation, but which is now as clear as daylight to those who love God. They are those to whom God has planned to give a vision of the full wonder and splendour of His secret plan for the sons of men. And this secret is simply this : Christ *in you* ! Yes, Christ *in you* bringing with Him the hope of all the glorious things to come.

To preach and teach Christ is
everything to us   I : 28

So, naturally, we proclaim Christ ! We warn everyone we meet, and we teach everyone we can, all that we know about Him, so that, if possible, we may bring every man up to his full maturity in Christ. This is what I am working at all the time, with all the strength that God gives me.

I wish you could understand how deep is my anxiety for you, and for those at Laodicea, and for all who have never met me. How I long that you may be encouraged, and find out more and more how strong are the bonds of Christian love. How I long for you to grow more certain in your knowledge and more sure in your grasp of God Himself. May your spiritual experience become richer as you see more and more fully God's great secret, Christ Himself ! For it is *in Him*, and in Him alone, that men will find all the treasures of wisdom and knowledge.

Let me warn you against " intellectuals "   II : 4

I write like this to prevent you from being led astray by someone or other's attractive arguments. For though I am a long way away from you in body, in spirit I am by your side, watching like a proud father the solid steadfastness of your faith in Christ. Just as you received Christ, so go on living in Him—in simple faith. Grow out of Him as a plant grows out of the soil it is planted in, becoming more and more sure of your " ground," and your lives will overflow with joy and thankfulness.

Be careful that nobody spoils your faith through intellectualism or high-sounding nonsense. Such stuff is at best founded on men's ideas of the nature of the world and disregards Christ ! Yet it is in Him that God gives a full and complete expression of Himself (within the physical limits that He set Himself in Christ). Moreover, your own completeness is only realised in Him, Who is the Authority over all authorities, and the Supreme Power over all powers.

The old Law can't condemn you now   II : 11

In Christ you were circumcised, not by any physical act, but by being set free from the sins of the flesh by virtue of Christ's circumcision. You, so to speak, shared in that, just as in baptism you shared in His death, and in Him are sharing the miracle of rising again to new life—and all this because you have faith in the tremendous power of God, Who raised Christ from the dead. You, who were spiritually dead because of your sins and your uncircumcision (i.e. your disobedience to the Law of God), God has now made to share in the very life of Christ ! He has forgiven you all your sins : Christ has utterly wiped out the damning evidence of broken laws and commandments which always hung over our heads, and has completely annulled it by nailing it over His own Head on the Cross. And then, having drawn the sting of all the powers ranged against us, He exposed them, shattered, empty and defeated, in His final, glorious triumphant act !

It is the spiritual, not the material,
attitude which matters   II : 16

In view of these tremendous facts, don't let anyone worry you by criticising what you eat or drink, or what holy days you ought to observe, or bothering you over new moons or sabbaths. All these things have at most only a symbolical value : the solid fact is Christ. Nor let any man cheat you of your joy in Christ by persuading you to make yourselves " humble " and fall down and worship angels. Such a man, inflated by an unspiritual imagination, is pushing his way into matters he knows nothing about, and in his cleverness forgetting the Head. It is from the Head alone that the body, by natural channels, is nourished and built up and grows according to God's laws of growth.

So, if, through your faith in Christ, you are dead to the principles of this world's life, why, as if you were still part and parcel of this world-wide system, do you take the slightest notice of these purely human prohibitions—"Don't touch this," " Don't taste that " and " Don't handle the other " ? " This," " that " and " the other " will all pass away after use ! I know that these regulations look wise with their self-inspired efforts at worship, their policy of self-humbling, and their studied neglect of the body. But in actual practice they do honour, not to God, but to man's own pride.

Live a new life by the power of
the risen Christ

III : 1

If you are then " risen " with Christ, reach out for the highest gifts of Heaven, where your Master reigns in power. Give your heart to the heavenly things, not to the passing things of earth. For, as far as this world is concerned, you are already dead, and your true life is a hidden one in Christ. One day, Christ, the secret centre of our lives, will show Himself openly, and you will all share in that magnificent dénouement.

In so far, then, as you have to live upon this earth, consider yourselves dead to worldly contacts : have nothing to do with sexual immorality, dirty-mindedness, uncontrolled passion, evil desire, and the lust for other people's goods, which last, remember, is as serious a sin as idolatry. It is because of these very things that the holy anger of God falls upon those who refuse to obey Him. And never forget that you had your part in those dreadful things when you lived that old life.

But now, put all these things behind you. No more evil temper or furious rage : no more evil thoughts or words about others, no more evil thoughts or words about God, and no more filthy conversation. Don't tell each other lies any more, for you have finished with the old man and all he did and have begun life as a new man, who is out to learn what he ought to be, according to the plan of God. In this new man of God's design there is no distinction between Greek and Hebrew, Jew or Gentile, foreigner or savage, slave or free man. Christ is all that matters, for Christ lives in them all.

The expression of the new life (i)   III : 12

As, therefore, God's picked representatives of the new humanity, purified and beloved of God Himself, be merciful in action, kindly in heart, humble in mind. Accept life, and be most patient and tolerant with one another, always ready to forgive if you have a difference with anyone. Forgive as freely as has the Lord forgiven you. And, above everything else, be truly loving, for love is the golden chain of all the virtues. Let the harmony of God reign in your hearts, remembering that as members of the same body you are called to live in harmony, and never forget to be thankful for what God has done for you.

Let Christ's teaching live in your hearts, making you rich in the true wisdom. Teach and help one another along the right road with your psalms and hymns and Christian songs, singing God's praises with joyful hearts. And whatever work you may have to do, do everything in the Name of the Lord Jesus, thanking God the Father through Him.

The expression of the new life (ii)   III : 18

Wives, adapt yourselves to your husbands, that your marriage may be a Christian unity. Husbands, be sure you give your wives much love and sympathy ; don't let bitterness or resentment spoil your marriage. As for you children, your duty is to obey your parents, for at your age this is one of the best things you can do to show your love for God. Fathers, don't over-correct your children, or they will grow up feeling inferior and frustrated. Slaves, your job is to obey your masters, not with the idea of currying favour, but as a sincere expression of your devotion to God. Whatever you do, put your whole heart and soul into it, as into work done for God, and not merely for men—knowing that your real reward, a heavenly one, will come from God, since you are actually employed by Christ, and not just by your earthly master.

But the slacker and the thief will be judged by God Himself, Who naturally has no distinction to make between master and man. Remember, then, you employers, that your responsibility is to be fair and just towards those whom you employ, never forgetting that you yourselves have a Heavenly Employer.

Some simple, practical advice   IV : 2

Always maintain the habit of prayer : be both alert and thankful as you pray. Include us in your prayers, please, that God may open for us a door for the entrance of the Gospel. Pray that we may talk freely of the mystery of Christ (for which talking I am at present in chains), and that I may make that mystery plain to men, which I know is my duty.

Be wise in your behaviour towards non-Christians, and make the best possible use of your time. Speak pleasantly to them, but never sentimentally, and learn how to give a proper answer to every questioner.

Greetings and farewell   IV : 7

Tychicus (a well-loved brother, a faithful minister and a fellow-servant) will tell you all about my present circumstances. This is partly why I am sending him to you. The other reasons are that he may find out for me how you are all getting on, and that he may give you courage. With him is Onesimus, one of your own congregation (well-loved and faithful, too). Between them they will tell you of conditions and activities here.

Aristarchus, who is also in prison here, sends greetings, and so does Barnabas' cousin, Mark. I believe I told you before about him ; if he comes to you, make him welcome. Jesus Justus, another Hebrew Christian, is here too. Only

these few are working with me for the Kingdom, but what a
help they have been!

Epaphras, another member of your Church, and a real servant of Christ, sends his greetings. He works hard for you
even here, for he prays constantly and earnestly for you, that
you may become mature Christians, and may fulfil God's
plans for you. From my own observation I can tell you that
he has a real passion for your welfare, and for that of the
churches at Laodicea and Hierapolis.

Luke, our beloved doctor, and Demas send their best
wishes. My own greetings to the Christians in Laodicea, and
to Nymphas and the congregation who meet in his house.

When you have had this letter read in your church, see that
the Laodiceans have it read in their church too; and see that
you read the letter I have written to them.

A brief message to Archippus: God ordained you to your
work—see that you don't fail Him!

My personal greetings to you written by myself.

Don't forget I'm in prison. Grace be with you.

PAUL

THE FIRST LETTER TO
THE CHRISTIANS IN THESSALONICA

AUTHOR. *Paul, writing from Corinth.*

DATE. *About 50. The earliest Pauline letter in our possession.*

DESTINATION. *The Christian church in Thessalonica (now Salonika)
which was founded by Paul (Acts XVII, 1-10). There were
evidently many Jews in the town, many of whom were bitterly
opposed to the Christian message.*

THEME. *This letter is an encouragement to the young church to stand
firm under persecution. It contains a defence of Paul's own
position as Divinely appointed Messenger, in view of the bitter
and malicious attacks that were being made upon him. Then*

follows a plea for sexual purity on the grounds that the sex instinct is part of God's design and is not meant to be despised or exploited.

The closing section gives some definite teaching about the Second Coming of Christ, which the Thessalonian Christians were expecting at any moment.

To the church of the Thessalonians, founded on God the Father and Jesus Christ the Lord, grace and peace from Paul, Silvanus and Timothy.

*Your faith cheers us and encourages
many others*   I : 2

We are always thankful as we pray for you all, for we never forget that your faith has meant solid achievement, your love has meant hard work, and the hope that you have in our Lord Jesus Christ means sheer dogged endurance in the life that you live before God, the Father of us all.

We know that God not only loves you but has selected you for a special purpose. For we remember how our Gospel came to you not as mere words, but as a message with power behind it—the effectual power, in fact, of the Holy Spirit. You know how we lived among you. You remember how you set yourselves to copy us, and through us, Christ Himself. You remember how, although accepting the message meant bitter persecution, yet you experienced the joy of the Holy Spirit. You thus became examples to all who believe in Macedonia and Achaia. You have become a sort of sounding-board from which the Word of the Lord has rung out, not only in Macedonia and Achaia but everywhere where the story of your faith in God has become known. We find we don't have to tell people about it. They tell *us* the story of our coming to you : how you turned from idols to serve the true living God, and how your whole lives now look forward to the coming of His Son from Heaven—the Son Jesus, Whom God raised from the dead, and Who personally delivered us from the judgment which hung over our heads.

The spirit of our visit to you is
well known to you all   II : I

My brothers, you know from your own experience that our visit to you was no failure. We had, as you also know, been treated abominably at Philippi, and we came on to you only because God gave us courage. We came to tell you the Gospel, whatever the opposition might be.

Our message to you is true, our motives are pure, our conduct is absolutely above board. We speak under the solemn sense of being entrusted by God with the Gospel. We do not aim to please men, but to please God Who knows us through and through. No one could ever say, as again you know, that we used flattery to conceal greedy motives, and God Himself is witness to our honesty. We made no attempt to win honour from men, either from you or from anybody else, though I suppose as Christ's own Messengers we might have done so. Our attitude among you was one of tenderness, rather like that of a devoted nurse among her babies. Because we loved you, it was a joy to us to give you not only the Gospel of God but our very hearts—so dear did you become to us. Our struggles and hard work, my brothers, must be still fresh in your minds. Day and night we worked so that our preaching of the Gospel to you might not cost you a penny. You are witnesses, as is God Himself, that our life among you believers was honest, straightforward and above criticism. You will remember how we dealt with each one of you personally, like a father with his own children, stimulating your faith and courage and giving you instruction. Our only object was to help you to live lives worthy of the God Who has called you to share the splendour of His Kingdom.

And so we are continually thankful that when you heard us preach the Word of God you accepted it, not as a mere human message, but as it really is, God's Word, a power in the lives of you who believe.

You have experienced persecution
like your Jewish brothers   II : 14

When you suffered at the hands of your fellow-countrymen you were sharing the experience of the Judaean Christian churches, who suffered persecution by the Jews. It was the Jews who killed their own prophets, the Jews who killed the Lord Jesus, and the Jews who drove out us, His messengers. Their present attitude is in opposition to both God and man. They refused to let us speak to those who were not Jews, to tell them the news of salvation. Alas, I fear they are completing the full tale of their sins and the wrath of God is over their heads.

Absence has indeed made our hearts grow fonder   II : 17

Since we have been physically separated from you, my brothers (though never for a moment separated in heart), we have longed all the more to see you. Yes, I Paul, have longed to come and see you more than once—but somehow Satan prevented our coming.

Yet who could take your place as our hope and joy and pride when Jesus comes ? Who but you, as you will stand before Him at His coming ? Yes, you are indeed our pride and our joy !

And so at length, when the separation became intolerable, we thought the best plan was for me to stay at Athens alone, while Timothy, our brother and fellow-worker in the Gospel of Christ, was sent to strengthen and encourage you in your faith. We did not want any of you to lose heart at the troubles you were going through, but to realise that we Christians must expect such things. Actually we did warn you what to expect, when we were with you, and our words have come true, as you know. You will understand that, when the suspense became unbearable, I sent someone to find out how your faith was standing the strain, and to make sure that the tempter's activities had not destroyed our work.

The good news about you is a tonic to us   III : 6

But now that Timothy has just come straight from you to us—with a glowing account of your faith and love, and definite news that you cherish happy memories of us and long to see us as much as we to see you—how these things have cheered us in all the miseries and troubles we ourselves are going through. To know that you are standing fast in the Lord is indeed a breath of life to us. How can we thank our God enough for all the joy you give us as we serve Him, praying earnestly day and night to see you again, and to complete whatever is imperfect in your faith?

This is our prayer for you   III : 11

So may God our Father Himself and our Lord Jesus Christ guide our steps to you. May the Lord give you the same increasing and overflowing love for each other and towards all men as we have towards you. May He establish you, holy and blameless in heart and soul, before Himself, the Father of us all, when our Lord Jesus Christ comes with all who belong to Him.

Purity, love and hard work are good
rules for life   IV : I

To sum up, my brothers, we beg and pray you by the Lord Jesus, that you continue to learn more and more of the life that pleases God, the sort of life we told you about before. You will remember the instructions we gave you then in the Name of the Lord Jesus. God's plan is to make you holy, and that entails first of all a clean cut with sexual immorality. Every one of you should learn to control his body, keeping it pure and treating it with respect, and never regarding it as an instrument for self-gratification, as do pagans with no knowledge of God. You cannot break this rule without in some way cheating your fellow-men. And you must remember that God will punish all who do offend in this matter, and we have warned you how we have seen this work out in our experience of life. The calling of God is not to impurity but to the most thorough purity, and anyone who makes light of the matter is not making light of a man's ruling but of God's command. It is not for nothing that the Spirit God gives us is called the *Holy* Spirit.

Next, as regards brotherly love, you don't need any written instructions. God Himself is teaching you to love each other, and you are already extending your love to all the Macedonians. Yet we urge you to have more and more of this love, and to make it your ambition to have no ambition! Be busy with your own affairs and do your work yourselves. The result will be a reputation for honesty in the world outside and an honourable independence.

God's message regarding those who have died   IV : 13

Now we don't want you, my brothers, to be in any doubt about those who " fall asleep " in death, or to grieve over them like men who have no hope. After all, if we believe that Jesus died and rose again from death, then we can believe that God will just as surely bring with Jesus all who are "asleep" in Him. Here we have a definite message from the Lord. It is that those who are still living when He comes will not in any way precede those who have previously fallen asleep. One word of command, one shout from the Archangel, one blast from the trumpet of God and God in Person will come down from Heaven! Those who have died in Christ will be the first to rise, and then we who are still living on the earth will be swept up with them into the clouds to meet the Lord in the air. And after that we shall be with Him for ever.

God has given me this message on the matter, so by all means use it to encourage one another.

We must keep awake for His sudden coming   V : 1

But as far as times and seasons go, my brothers, you don't need written instructions. You are well aware that the day of the Lord will come as unexpectedly as a burglary to a householder. When men are saying " Peace and security " catastrophe will sweep down upon them as suddenly and inescapably as birth-pangs to a pregnant woman.

But because you, my brothers, are not living in darkness

the Day cannot take you completely by surprise. After all, burglary only takes place at night ! You are all sons of light, sons of the day, and none of us belongs to darkness or the night. Let us then never fall into the sleep that stupefies the rest of the world : let us keep awake, with our wits about us. Night is the time for sleep and the time when men get drunk, but we men of the daylight should be alert, with faith and love as our breastplate and the hope of our salvation as our helmet. For God did not choose us to condemn us, but that we might secure His salvation through Jesus Christ our Lord. He died for us, so that whether we are "awake" or "asleep" we share His life. So go on cheering and strengthening each other with thoughts like these, as I have no doubt you have been doing.

Reverence your ministers : regulate
the conduct of Church members   v : 12

We ask you too, my brothers, to get to know those who work so hard among you. They are your spiritual leaders to keep you on the right path. Because of this high task of theirs, hold them in highest honour.

Live together in peace, and our instruction to this end is to reprimand the unruly, encourage the timid, help the weak and be very patient with all men. Be sure that no one repays a bad turn by a bad turn ; good should be your objective always, among yourselves and in the world at large.

Be happy in your faith at all times. Never stop praying. Be thankful, whatever the circumstances may be.

If you follow this advice you will be working out the Will of God expressed to you in Jesus Christ.

Final advice and farewell   v : 19

Never damp the fire of the Spirit, and never despise what is spoken in the Name of the Lord. By all means use your judgment, and hold on to whatever is really good. Steer clear of evil in any form.

May the God of peace make you holy through and through. May you be kept in soul and mind and body in spotless integrity until the coming of our Lord Jesus Christ. He Who calls you is utterly faithful and He will finish what He has set out to do.

Pray for us, my brothers. Give a handshake all round among the brotherhood. God's command, which I give you now, is that this letter should be read to all the brothers.

The grace of our Lord Jesus Christ be with you all.

PAUL

THE SECOND LETTER TO
THE CHRISTIANS IN THESSALONICA

AUTHOR. *Paul, writing from Corinth.*

DATE. *Possibly 51.*

DESTINATION. *The Christian church in Thessalonica.*

THEME. *Since the first letter was written to this church, Paul had evidently heard that the idea of Christ's Second Coming had become such an obsession with the Thessalonians that some of them had given up working for their living and were thereby bringing the faith into disrepute. He tells them quite plainly that the Coming is not to be immediate ; and in the meantime it is part of a Christian's duty to work hard and conscientiously.*

To the church of the Thessalonians, founded on God our Father and Jesus Christ the Lord, from Paul, Silvanus and Timothy ; grace to you and peace from God the Father and the Lord Jesus Christ !

Your sufferings are a guarantee of
great joy one day   1 : 3
My brothers, nowadays I thank God for you not only in common fairness but as a moral obligation ! Your faith has made such strides, and (without any individual exceptions) your love towards each other has reached such proportions

that we actually boast about you in the churches, because you have shown such endurance and faith in all the trials and persecutions you have gone through.

These qualities show how justly the judgment of God works out in your case. Without doubt He intends to use your suffering to make you worthy of His Kingdom, yet His justice will one day repay troubles to those who have troubled you, and peace to all of us who, like you, have suffered. This judgment will issue eventually in the terrific dénouement of Christ's personal coming from Heaven with the angels of His power. It will bring full justice in dazzling flame upon those who have refused to know God or to obey the Gospel of our Lord Jesus Christ. Their punishment will be eternal exclusion from the radiance of the Face of the Lord, and the glorious majesty of His power. But to those whom He has made holy His coming will mean splendour unimaginable. It will be a breath-taking wonder to all who believe—including you, for you have believed the message that we have given you.

In view of this great prospect, we pray for you constantly, that God will think you worthy of this calling, and that He will effect in you all that His goodness desires to do, and that your faith makes possible. We pray that the Name of our Lord Jesus Christ may become more glorious through you, and that you may share something of His glory—all through the grace of our God and Jesus Christ the Lord.

*Before Christ's Coming there will
be certain signs*   II : I

₡ Now we do implore you, by the very certainty of Christ's coming and of our meeting Him together, to keep your heads and not be thrown off balance by any prediction or message or letter purporting to come from us, and saying that the day of Christ is almost here. Don't let anyone deceive you by any means whatsoever. That day will not come before there arises a definite rejection of God and the appearance of the Lawless Man. He is the product of all that leads to death, and he sets himself up in opposition to every religion. He himself takes his seat in the Temple of God, to show that he really claims to be God.

I expect you remember now how I talked about this when I was with you. You will probably also remember how I used to talk about a " restraining power " which would operate until the time should come for the emergence of this Man. Evil is already insidiously at work but its activities are restricted until what I have called the " restraining power " is removed. When that happens the Lawless Man will be plainly seen—though the truth of the Lord Jesus spells his doom, and the radiance of the coming of the Lord Jesus will be his utter destruction. The Lawless Man is produced by the spirit of evil and armed with all the force, wonders and signs that falsehood can devise. To those involved in this dying world he will come with evil's undiluted power to deceive, for they have refused to love the truth which could have saved them. God sends upon them, therefore, the full force of evil's delusion, so that they put their faith in an utter fraud and meet the inevitable judgment of all who have refused to believe the truth and who have made evil their play-fellow.

You, thank God, belong to those who
believe the truth   II : 13

But we can thank God continually for you, brothers, whom the Lord loves. He has chosen you from the beginning to save you, to make you holy by the work of His Spirit and your own belief in the truth. It was His call that you followed when we preached the Gospel to you, and He has set before you the prospect of sharing the glory of our Lord Jesus Christ. So stand firm, and hold on ! Be loyal to the teachings we passed on to you, whether by word of mouth or in our writings.

May the Lord Jesus Christ and God our Father (Who has loved us and given us unending encouragement and unfailing hope by His grace) inspire you with courage and confidence in every good thing you say or do.

We ask your prayers for God's work here   III : I

Finally, my brothers, do pray for us here. Pray that the
Lord's message may go forward unhindered and may bring
Him glory, as it has done with you. Pray too, that we may
not be embroiled with bigoted and wicked men ; for all men,
alas, have not faith. Yet the Lord is utterly to be depended
upon by all who have faith in Him, and He will give you
stability and protection against all that is evil. It is He Who
makes us feel confident about you, that you are acting and will
act in accordance with our commands. May He guide your
hearts into ever deeper understanding of His love and of the
patient suffering of Christ.

Remember our example : everyone should do
his fair share of work   III : 6

One further order we must give you in the Name of our
Lord Jesus Christ : don't associate with the brother whose
life is undisciplined, and who despises the teaching we gave
him. You know well that we ourselves are your examples
here, and that our lives among you were never undisciplined.
We did not eat anyone's food without paying for it. In fact
we toiled and laboured night and day to avoid being the
slightest expense to any of you. This was not because we had
no right to ask our necessities of you, but because we wanted
to set you an example. When we were actually with you we
gave you this principle to work on : " If a man will not work,
he shall not eat." Now we hear that you have some among
you living quite undisciplined lives, never doing a stroke of
work, and busy only in other people's affairs. Our order to
such men, indeed our appeal by the Lord Jesus Christ, is to
settle down to work and eat the food they have earned themselves.

And the rest of you—don't get tired of honest work ! If
anyone refuses to obey the command given above, mark that
man, do not associate with him until he is ashamed of himself.
I don't mean, of course, treat him as an enemy, but reprimand
him as a brother.

My blessing on you all!

Now may the Lord of peace personally give you His peace at all times and in all ways. The Lord be with you all.

This is the farewell message of PAUL, written in my own writing—my "mark" on all my letters.

The grace of our Lord Jesus Christ be with you all.

THE FIRST LETTER TO
TIMOTHY

AUTHOR. *Probably Paul, writing from Rome during a second term of imprisonment which ended in his martyrdom. Many scholars do not accept the Pauline authorship of the two letters to Timothy or the letter to Titus.*

DATE. *About 66, but possibly 90-115 and post-Pauline.*

DESTINATION. *This is a personal letter to Timothy, son of a Greek father and a Jewish mother. He was converted during Paul's visit to Lystra (Acts XVI, 1). He became Paul's special protégé, and, though evidently diffident and nervous in temperament, was his loyal assistant. He accompanied Paul on various missions and has now been left in charge of the Church at Ephesus.*

THEME. *Paul reminds Timothy of his responsibility as a minister ordained for the preaching of the Gospel and warns him of the dangers of false teaching. He then gives him some interesting details for the ordering of the life of the church, the choosing of church officers and the administration of charitable funds. The letter closes with an earnest plea to Timothy to remain loyal to the true Gospel.*

PAUL, Jesus Christ's Messenger by command of God our Saviour and Christ our Hope, to Timothy my true son in the faith : grace, mercy and peace be to you from God our Father and Jesus Christ our Master.

A reminder   I : 3

I am repeating in this letter the advice I gave you just before I went to Macedonia and urged you to stay at Ephesus. I wanted you to do this so that you could order certain persons to stop inventing new doctrines and to leave hoary old myths and interminable genealogies alone. They only raise queries in men's minds without leading them to faith in God. The ultimate aim of the Christian minister, after all, is to produce the love which springs from a pure heart, a good conscience and a genuine faith. Some seem to have forgotten this and to have lost themselves in endless words. They want a reputation as teachers of the Law, yet they fail to realise the meaning of their own words, still less of the subject they are so dogmatic about. We know, of course, that the Law is good in itself and has a legitimate function. Yet we also know that the Law is not really meant for the good man, but for the man who has neither principles nor self-control, for the man who is really wicked, who has neither scruples nor reverence. Yes, the Law is directed against the sort of people who attack their own parents, who kill their fellows, who are sexually uncontrolled or perverted, or who traffic in the bodies of others. It is against liars and perjurers—in fact it is against any and every action which contradicts the wholesome teaching of the glorious Gospel which our blessed God has given and entrusted to me.

My debt to Jesus Christ   I : 12

I am deeply grateful to our Lord Jesus Christ (to Whom I owe all that I have accomplished) for trusting me enough to appoint me His minister, despite the fact that I had previously blasphemed His name, persecuted His Church and damaged His cause. I believe He was merciful to me because what I did was done in the ignorance of a man without faith, and then He poured out His grace upon me, giving me tremendous faith in, and love for, Himself. This statement is completely reliable and should be universally accepted :—*Christ Jesus entered the world to rescue sinners.* I realise that I was the worst of them all, and that because of this very fact God was particularly merciful to me. It was a kind of demonstration of the extent of Christ's patience towards the worst of men, to serve as an example to all who in the future should trust Him for eternal life.

So to the King of all the Ages, the Immortal, Invisible, and only God, be honour and glory for ever and ever!

My personal charge to you   I : 18

Timothy my son, I give you the following charge. (And may I say, before I give it to you, that it is in full accord with those prophecies made at your ordination, which sent you out to battle for the right armed only with your faith and a clear conscience. Some, alas, have laid these simple weapons contemptuously aside and, as far as their faith is concerned, have run their ships on the rocks. Hymenaeus and Alexander are men of this sort, and as a matter of fact I had to expel them from the Church to teach them not to blaspheme.) Here then is my charge:

First, supplications, prayers, intercessions and thanks-givings should be made on behalf of all men: for kings and rulers in positions of responsibility, so that our common life may be lived in peace and quiet, with a proper sense of God and of our responsibility to Him for what we do with our lives. In the sight of God our Saviour this is undoubtedly the right thing to pray for; for His purpose is that all men should be saved and come to realise the truth. And that is, that there is only one God, and only one Intermediary between God and men, Jesus Christ the Man. He gave Himself as a ransom for us all—an act of Redemption which happened once, but which stands for all time as a witness to what He is. I was appointed Proclaimer and Messenger of this great Act of His, to teach (incredible as it may sound) the Gentile world to believe and know the truth.

My views on men and women in the Church   II : 8

Therefore, I want the men to pray in all the churches with sincerity, without resentment or doubt in their minds. The women should be dressed quietly, and their demeanour should be modest and serious. The adornment of a Christian woman is not a matter of an elaborate coiffure, expensive clothes or valuable jewellery, but the living of a good life. A woman should learn quietly and humbly. Personally, I don't allow women to teach, nor do I ever put them in positions of authority over men—I believe their role is to be receptive. (My reasons are that Man was created before Woman. Further, it was Eve and not Adam who was first deceived and fell into sin. Nevertheless, in spite of the curse upon Eve, I believe that women will come safely through child-birth if they maintain a life of faith, love, holiness and gravity.)

The sort of men to bear office : Bishops III : 1

It is quite true to say that a man who sets his heart on holding office has laudable ambition. Well, for the office of a Bishop a man must be of blameless reputation, he must be married to one wife only, and be a man of self-control and discretion. He must be a man of disciplined life ; he must be hospitable and have the gift of teaching. He must be neither intemperate nor violent, but gentle. He must not be a controversialist nor must he be fond of money-grabbing. He must have proper authority in his own household, and be able to control and command the respect of his children. (For if a man cannot rule in his own house how can he look after the Church of God ?) He must not be a beginner in the faith, for fear of his becoming conceited and sharing Satan's downfall. He should, in addition to the above qualifications, have a good reputation with the outside world, in case his good name is attacked and he is caught by the Devil that way.

Deacons III : 8

Deacons, similarly, should be men of serious outlook and sincere conviction. They too should be temperate and not greedy for money. They should hold the faith as a sacred trust, with complete sincerity.

Let them serve a period of probation first, and only serve as deacons if they prove satisfactory. Their wives should share their serious outlook, and must be women of discretion and self-control—women who can be trusted. Deacons should be

men with only one wife, able to control their children and
manage their own households properly. Those who do well as
deacons earn for themselves a certain legitimate standing, as
well as gaining confidence and freedom in the Christian faith.

The tremendous responsibility of
being God's minister   III : 14

At the moment of writing I hope to be with you soon, but
if there should be any considerable delay then what I have
written will show you the sort of character men of God's
household ought to have. It is, remember, the Church of the
living God, the pillar and the foundation of the Truth. No
one can deny that this religion of ours is a tremendous mystery,
resting as it does on the One Who showed Himself as a human
being, and met, as such, every demand of the Spirit in the
sight of angels as well as of men. Then, after His restoration
to the Heaven from whence He came, He has been proclaimed
among men of different nationalities and believed in in all
parts of the world

Beware of false teachers : warn your people   IV : I

God's Spirit specifically tells us that in later days there will
be men who abandon the true faith and allow themselves to
be spiritually seduced by teachings of the Devil, teachings
given by men who are lying hypocrites, whose consciences are
as dead as seared flesh. These men forbid marriage and command abstinence from food—good things which, in fact, God
intends to be thankfully enjoyed by those who believe in Him
and know the truth. Everything God made is good, and is
meant to be gratefully used, not despised. The holiness or
otherwise of a certain food, for instance, depends not on its
nature but on whether it is eaten thankfully or not.

You will be doing your duty as Christ's minister if you
remind your Church members of these things, and you will
show yourself as one who owes his strength to the truth of the
faith he has absorbed and the sound teaching he has followed.
But steer clear of all these stupid Godless fictions.

Take time and trouble to keep yourself spiritually fit. Bodily fitness has a certain value, but spiritual fitness is essential, both for this present life and for the life to come. There is no doubt about this at all, and Christians should remember it. It is because we realise the paramount importance of the spiritual that we labour and struggle. We place our whole confidence in the living God, the Saviour of all men, and particularly of those who believe in Him.

A little personal advice   IV : 12

Don't let people look down on you because you are young ; see that they look up to you because you are an example to them in your speech and behaviour, in your love and faith and sincerity. Concentrate until my arrival on your reading and on your preaching and teaching. Never forget that you received the gift of proclaiming God's Word when the assembled elders laid their hands on you. Give your whole attention, all your energies, to these things, so that your progress is plain for all to see. Keep a critical eye both upon your own life and on the teaching you give, and if you continue to follow the line I have indicated you will not only save your own soul but the souls of many of your hearers as well.

Don't reprimand a senior member of your Church, appeal to him as a father. Treat the young men as brothers, and the older women as mothers. Treat the younger women as sisters, and no more.

How to deal with widows in the church   V : 3

You should treat with great consideration widows who are really alone in the world. But remember that if a widow has children or grandchildren it is primarily their duty to show the genuineness of their religion in their own homes by repaying their parents for what has been done for them, and God readily accepts such service.

But the widow who is really alone and desolate can only hope in God, and she will pray to Him day and night. The widow who plunges into all the pleasure that the world can give her is killing her own soul.

You should therefore make the following rules for the widows, to avoid abuses :

i. You should make it clear that for a man to refuse to look after his own relations, especially those actually living in his house, is a denial of the faith he professes. He is far worse than a man who makes no profession.

ii. Widows for your Church list should be at least sixty years of age, should have had only one husband and have a well-founded reputation for having lived a good life. Some such questions as these should be asked :—has she brought up her children well, has she been hospitable to strangers, has she been willing to serve fellow-Christians in menial ways, has she relieved those in distress, has she, in a word, conscientiously done all the good she can ?

iii. Don't put the younger widows on your list. My experience is that when their natural desires grow stronger than their spiritual devotion to Christ they want to marry again, thus proving themselves unfaithful to their first loyalty. Moreover, they get into habits of slackness by being so much in and out of other people's houses. In fact they easily become worse than lazy, and degenerate into gossips and busybodies with dangerous tongues.

iv. My advice is that the younger widows should, normally, marry again, bear children and run their own households. They should certainly not be the means of lowering the reputation of the Church, although some, alas, have already played into the enemy's hands.

v. As a general rule it should be taken for granted that any Christian, man or woman, who has a widow in the family should do everything possible for her, and not allow her to become the Church's responsibility. The Church will then be free to look after those widows who are alone in the world.

You and your Elders   v : 17

Elders with a gift of leadership should be considered worthy of respect, and of adequate salary, particularly if they work hard at their preaching and teaching. Remember the Scriptural principle :

Thou shalt not muzzle the ox when he treadeth out the corn,

and

The labourer is worthy of his hire.

Take no notice of charges brought against an elder unless they can be substantiated by proper witnesses. If sin is actually proved, then the offenders should be publicly rebuked as a salutary warning to others.

Timothy, I solemnly charge you in the sight of God and Christ Jesus and the holy angels to follow these orders with the strictest impartiality and to have no favourites.

Never be in a hurry to ordain a man, or you may be making yourself responsible for his sins. Be careful that your own life is pure. (By the way, I should advise you to drink wine in moderation, instead of water. It will do your stomach good and help you to get over your frequent spells of illness.) Remember that some men's sins are obvious, and are equally obviously bringing them to judgment. The sins of other men are not apparent, but are dogging them, nevertheless, under the surface. Similarly some virtues are plain to see, while others, though not at all conspicuous, will eventually make themselves felt.

The behaviour of slaves in the church   VI : 1

Christian slaves should treat their masters with respect, and avoid causing dishonour to the Name of God and our teaching. If they have Christian masters they should not despise them because they work for brothers in the Faith. Indeed they should serve them all the better because they are thereby benefiting those who have the same faith and love as themselves.

The dangers of false doctrines and
the love of money   VI : 3

This is the sort of thing you should teach, and if anyone
tries to teach some doctrinal novelty which is not compatible
with sound teaching (which we base on Christ's own words
and which leads to Christ-like living), then he is a conceited
idiot ! His mind is a morbid jumble of disputation and argument, things which lead to nothing but jealousy, quarrelling,
insults and malicious innuendoes—continual wrangling, in
fact, among men of warped minds who have lost their real
hold on the truth but hope to make some profit out of the
Christian religion. There is a real profit, of course, but it
comes only to those who live contentedly as God would have
them live. We brought absolutely nothing with us when we
entered this world and we can be sure we shall take absolutely
nothing with us when we leave it. Surely then, as far as
physical things are concerned, it is sufficient for us to keep our
bodies fed and clothed. For men who set their hearts on being
wealthy expose themselves to temptation. They fall into one
of the world's traps, and lay themselves open to all sorts of
silly and wicked desires, which are quite capable of utterly
ruining and destroying their souls. For loving money leads
to all kinds of evil, and some men in the struggle to be rich
have lost their faith and caused themselves untold agonies of
mind.

Maintain a fearless witness until
the last day   VI : 11

But you, the man of God, keep clear of such things. Set
your heart not on riches, but on goodness, Christ-likeness,
faith, love, patience, and humility. Fight the worth-while
battle of the Faith, keep your grip on that life eternal to which
you have been called, and to which you boldly professed your
loyalty before many witnesses. I charge you in the sight of
God Who gives us life, and Jesus Christ Who fearlessly
witnessed to the truth before Pontius Pilate, to keep your
commission clean and above reproach until the final coming
of Christ. This will be, in His own time, the Final Dénoue-

ment of God, Who is the blessed Controller of all things, the King over all kings and the Master of all masters, the only Source of Immortality, the One Who lives in unapproachable Light, the One Whom no mortal eye has ever seen or ever can see. To Him be acknowledged all honour and power for ever, Amen !

Have a word for the rich   VI : 17

Tell those who are rich in this present world not to be contemptuous of others, and not to rest the weight of their confidence on the transitory power of wealth but on the living God, Who generously gives us everything for our enjoyment. Tell them to do good, to be rich in kindly actions, to be ready to give to others and to sympathise with those in distress. Their security should be invested in the life to come, so that they may be sure of holding a share in the Life which is permanent.

My final appeal   VI : 20

O Timothy, guard most carefully your Divine commission. Avoid the Godless mixture of contradictory notions which is falsely known as " knowledge "—some have followed it *and lost their faith*.

Grace be with you.

PAUL

THE SECOND LETTER TO

TIMOTHY

AUTHOR. *Paul, almost certainly writing from Rome, where he is awaiting sentence of death. (But see note on 1 Timothy.)*

DATE. *About 67.*

DESTINATION. *Timothy, still at Ephesus.*

THEME. *This second letter also aims at stimulating Timothy's faith and courage, and renews its plea for faithfulness to sound teaching and loyalty to what he, Timothy, knows to be true.*

The personal requests which end this letter are peculiarly touching since we realise that Paul knew that it was only a question of time before he was executed.

PAUL, Messenger by God's appointment in the promised life of Christ Jesus, to Timothy, my own dearly loved son : grace, mercy and peace be to you from God the Father and Christ Jesus, our Lord.

I thank God for your faith : guard it well   1 : 3

I thank the God of my forefathers, Whom I serve with a clear conscience, as I remember you in my prayers. Every day and every night I have been longing to see you, for I can't forget how moved you were when I left you, and to have you with me again would be the greatest possible joy. I often think of that genuine faith of yours—a faith that first appeared in your grandmother Lois, then in Eunice your mother, and is now, I am convinced, in you as well. Because you have this faith, I now remind you to stir up that inner fire which God gave you at your ordination. For God has not given us a spirit of fear, but a spirit of power and love and a sound mind. So never be ashamed of bearing witness to our Lord, nor of me, His prisoner. Accept, as I do, all the hardship that faithfulness to the Gospel entails in the strength that God gives you. For He has rescued us from all that is really evil and called us to a life of holiness—not because of any of our achievements but for His own purpose. Before time began He planned to give us in Christ the grace to achieve this purpose, but it is only since our Saviour Jesus Christ has been revealed that the method has become apparent. For Christ has completely abolished death, and has now, through the Gospel, opened to us men the shining possibilities of the life that is eternal. It is this Gospel that I am commissioned to proclaim ; it is of this Gospel that I am appointed both

Messenger and Teacher, and it is for this Gospel that I am now suffering these things. Yet I am not in the least ashamed. For I know the One in Whom I have placed my confidence, and I am perfectly certain that the work He has committed to me is safe in His Hands until that Day.

So keep my words in your mind as the pattern of sound teaching, given to you in the faith and love of Jesus Christ. Take the greatest care of the good things which were entrusted to you by the Holy Spirit Who lives within you.

Deserters—and a friend　　　　　　　　　　　I : 15

You will know, I expect, that all those who are in Asia have turned against me, Phygelus and Hermogenes among them. But may the Lord have mercy on the household of Onesiphorus. Many times did that man put fresh heart into me, and he was not in the least ashamed of my being a prisoner in chains. Indeed, when he was in Rome he went to a great deal of trouble to find me—may the Lord grant he finds His mercy in that Day !—and you well know in how many ways he helped me at Ephesus as well.

Above all things be faithful　　　　　　　　　II : I

So, my son, be strong in the grace that Jesus Christ gives. Everything that you have heard me teach in public you should in turn entrust to reliable men, who will be able to pass it on to others.

Put up with your share of hardship as a loyal soldier in Christ's army. Remember : 1. That no soldier on active service gets himself entangled in business, or he will not please his commanding officer. 2. A man who enters an athletic contest wins no prize unless he keeps the rules laid down. 3. Only the man who works on the land has the right to the first share of its produce. Consider these three illustrations of mine and the Lord will help you to understand all that I mean.

Remember always, as the centre of everything, Jesus Christ, a Man of human ancestry, yet raised by God from the dead according to my Gospel. For preaching this I am having to endure being chained in prison as if I were some sort of a criminal. But they cannot chain the Word of God, and I can endure all these things for the sake of those whom God is calling, so that they too may receive the salvation of Jesus Christ, and its complement of glory after the world of time. I rely on this saying : *If we died with Him we shall also live with Him : if we suffer with Him we shall also reign with Him. If we deny Him He will also deny us : yet if we are faithless He always remains faithful. He cannot deny His own nature.*

Hold fast to the true : avoid dangerous error   II : 14

Remind your people of things like this, and tell them as before God not to fight wordy battles, which help no one and may undermine the faith of some who hear them.

For yourself, concentrate on winning God's approval, on being a workman with nothing to be ashamed of, and who knows how to use the word of truth to the best advantage. But steer clear of these unchristian babblings, which in practice lead farther and farther away from Christian living. False teachings are as dangerous as blood-poisoning to the body, and spread like sepsis from a wound. Hymenaeus and Philetus are responsible for this sort of thing, and they are men who are palpable traitors to the truth, for they say that the Resurrection has already occurred and, of course, badly upset some people's faith.

God's solid foundation still stands, however, with this double inscription : *The Lord knows those who belong to Him*, and *Let every true Christian have no dealings with evil.*

In any big household there are naturally not only gold and silver vessels but wooden and earthenware ones as well. Some are used for the highest purposes and some for the lowest. If a man keeps himself clean from the contaminations of evil he will be a vessel used for honourable purposes, clean and serviceable for the use of the Master of the Household, all ready, in fact, for any good purpose.

Be positively good—and patient   II :

Turn your back on the turbulent desires of youth and g
your positive attention to goodness, faith, love and peace
company with all those who approach God in sincerity.
have nothing to do with silly and ill-informed controver
which lead inevitably, as you know, to strife. And the Lo
servant must not be a man of strife : he must be kind to
ready and able to teach : he must have patience and
ability gently to correct those who oppose his message.
must always bear in mind the possibility that God will g
them a different outlook, and that they may come to know
truth. They may come to their senses and be rescued fr
the power of the Devil by the servant of the Lord and se
work for God's purposes.

A warning of what to expect   III

But you must realise that in the last days the times will
full of danger. Men will become utterly self-centred, gre
for money, full of big words. They will be proud and c
temptuous, without any regard for what their parents tau
them. They will be utterly lacking in gratitude, purity
normal human affections. They will be men of unscrupul
speech and have no control of themselves. They will
passionate and unprincipled, treacherous, self-willed
conceited, loving all the time what gives them pleas
instead of loving God. They will maintain a façade
"religion," but their conduct will deny its validity. Y
must keep clear of people like this.

From their number come those creatures who worm th
way into people's houses, and find easy prey in silly wor
with an exaggerated sense of sin and morbid cravings—w
are always learning and yet never able to grasp the tru
These men are as much enemies to the truth as Jannes
Jambres were to Moses. Their minds are distorted, and t
are traitors to the faith. But in the long run they won't
very far. Their folly will become as obvious to everybod
did that of Moses' opponents.

Your knowledge of the truth should
be your safeguard   III : 10

But you, Timothy, have known intimately both what I
have taught and how I have lived. My purpose and my faith
are no secrets to you. You saw my endurance and love and
patience as I met all those persecutions and difficulties at
Antioch, Iconium and Lystra. And you know how the
Lord brought me safely through them all. Persecution is
inevitable for those who are determined to live really Christian
lives, while wicked and deceitful men will go from bad to
worse, deluding others and deluding themselves.

Yet you must go on steadily in those things that you have
learned and which you know are true. Remember from what
sort of people your knowledge has come, and how from early
childhood your mind has been familiar with the holy Scriptures, which can open the mind to the salvation which comes
through believing in Christ Jesus. All Scripture is inspired by
God and is useful for teaching the faith and correcting error,
for re-setting the direction of a man's life and training him in
good living. The Scriptures are the comprehensive equip-
ment of the man of God, and fit him fully for all branches of
his work.

My time is nearly over : you must carry on   IV : 1

I urge you, Timothy, as we live in the sight of God and of
Christ Jesus (Whose coming in power will judge the living
and the dead), to preach the Word of God. Never lose your
sense of urgency, in season or out of season. Prove, correct,
and encourage, using the utmost patience in your teaching.
For the time is coming when men will not tolerate wholesome teaching. They will want something to tickle their own
fancies, and they will collect teachers who will pander to their
own desires. They will no longer listen to the Truth, but will
wander off after man-made fictions.

For yourself, stand fast in all that you are doing, meeting
whatever suffering this may involve. Go on steadily preaching
the Gospel and carry out to the full the commission that God
gave you.

As for me, I feel that the last drops of my life are being poured out for God. The glorious fight that God gave me I have fought, the course that I was set I have finished, and I have kept the faith. The future for me holds the crown of righteousness which God, the True Judge, will give to me in that Day—and not, of course, only to me but to all those who have loved what they have seen of Him.

Personal messages   IV : 9

Do your best to come to me as soon as you can. Demas, loving this present world, I fear, has left me and gone to Thessalonica. Crescens has gone to Galatia, and Titus is away in Dalmatia. Only Luke is with me now.

When you come, pick up Mark and bring him with you. I can certainly find a job for him here. (I had to send Tychicus off to Ephesus.) And please bring with you the cloak I left with Carpus at Troas, and the books, especially the manuscripts. Alexander the coppersmith did me a great deal of harm—the Lord reward him for what he did—and I should be very careful of him if I were you. He has been an obstinate opponent of our teaching.

The first time I had to defend myself no one was on my side—they all deserted me, God forgive them ! Yet the Lord Himself stood by me and gave me the strength to proclaim the message clearly and fully, so that the Gentiles could hear it, and I was rescued " from the lion's mouth." I am sure the Lord will rescue me from every evil plot, and will keep me safe until I reach His heavenly Kingdom. Glory be to Him for ever and ever !

Closing greetings   IV : 19

Give my love to Prisca and Aquila and Onesiphorus and his family. Erastus is still staying on at Corinth, and Trophimus I had to leave sick at Miletus.

Do your best to get here before the winter. Eubulus, Pudens, Linus, Claudia and all here send their greetings to you. The Lord be with your spirit. Grace be with you.

                                                    PAUL

THE LETTER TO TITUS

AUTHOR. *Paul wrote this letter towards the end of his life, possibly from Rome at roughly the same time as the second letter to Timothy, if it is true that he was released from his first imprisonment mentioned in Acts XXVIII, 30, and was imprisoned again later.*

DATE. *About 66.*

DESTINATION. *This is a letter of guidance and instruction to Titus, a pagan convert of Paul. He is believed by some to have been Luke's brother. He apparently helped Paul to found a church in Crete, where he now receives this letter.*

THEME. *This letter contains directions as to the type of church officer Titus should appoint in Crete, and the sort of Christian character he is trying to develop in the Cretan Church.*

PAUL, servant of God and Messenger of Jesus Christ in the faith God gives to His chosen, in the knowledge that comes from a God-fearing life, and in the hope of the everlasting life which God, Who cannot lie, promised before the beginning of time—(at the right moment He made His Word known in the declaration which has been entrusted to me by His command)—to Titus, my true son in our common faith, be grace, mercy and peace from God the Father and the Lord Jesus Christ our Saviour.

Men who are appointed to the ministry
must be of the highest character   I : 5

I left you in Crete to set right matters which needed attention, and gave you instructions to appoint elders in every city. They were to be men of unquestioned integrity with only one wife, and with children brought up as Christians and not likely to be accused of loose living or law-

breaking. To exercise spiritual oversight a man must be
unimpeachable virtue, for he is God's agent in the affair
His household. He must not be aggressive or hot-tempe
or over-fond of wine ; nor must he be violent or greedy
financial gain. On the contrary, he must be hospitable
genuine lover of what is good, a man who is discreet,
minded, holy and self-controlled : a man who takes his st
on the orthodox faith, so that he can by sound teaching b
stimulate faith and confute opposition.

Be on your guard against counterfeit Christians   I :

For there are many, especially among the Jews, who will
recognise authority, who talk nonsense and yet in so do
have managed to deceive men's minds. They must be silen
for they upset the faith of whole households, teaching v
they have no business to teach for the sake of what they
get. One of them, yes, one of their prophets, has s
" Men of Crete are always liars, evil and beastly, lazy
greedy." There is truth in this testimonial of theirs ! D
hesitate to reprimand them sharply, for you want them t
sound and healthy Christians, with a proper contempt
Jewish fairy tales and orders issued by men who have
saken the path of truth. Everything is wholesome to th
who are themselves wholesome. But nothing is wholes
to those who are themselves unwholesome and who have
faith in God—their very minds and consciences are disea
They profess to know God, but their actual behaviour de
their profession, for they are obviously vile and rebellious
when it comes to doing any real good they are palpable fra

Good character should follow good teaching   II

Now you must tell them the sort of character which sh
spring from sound teaching. The old men should be t
perate, serious, wise—spiritually healthy through their f
and love and patience. Similarly the old women shoul
reverent in their behaviour, should not make unfoun
complaints and should not be over-fond of wine. They sh
be examples of the good life, so that the younger women

learn to love their husbands and their children, to be sensible and chaste, home-lovers, kind-hearted and willing to adapt themselves to their husbands—a good advertisement for the Christian faith. The young men, too, you should urge to take life seriously, letting your own life stand as a pattern of good living. In all your teaching show the strictest regard for truth, and show that you appreciate the seriousness of the matters you are dealing with. Your speech should be un-affected and logical so that your opponent may feel ashamed at finding nothing in which to pick holes.

The duty of slaves—and of us all   II : 9

Slaves should be told that it is their duty as Christians to obey their masters and to give them satisfactory service in every way. They are not to "answer back" or to be light-fingered, but they are to show themselves utterly trust-worthy, a living testimonial to the teaching of God our Saviour. For the grace of God, which can save every man, has now become known, and it teaches us to have no more to do with godlessness or the desires of this world but to live, here and now, responsible, honourable and God-fearing lives. And while we live this life we hope and wait for the glorious dénouement of the great God and of Jesus Christ our Saviour. For he gave Himself for us all, that He might rescue us from all our evil ways and make for Himself a people of His own, clean and pure, with our hearts set upon living a life that is good.

Tell men of these things, Titus. Urge them to action, using a reprimand where necessary with all the authority of God's minister—and as such let no one treat you with contempt.

Instructions for the Christians of Crete   III : 1

Remind your people to recognise the power of those who rule and bear authority. They must obey the laws of the State and be prepared to render whatever good service they can. They are not to speak evil of any man, they must not be argumentative but gentle, showing themselves agreeable to everybody. For we ourselves have known what it is to be

ignorant, disobedient and deceived, the slaves of v:
desires and pleasant feelings, while our lives were sp
malice and jealousy—we were hateful and we hated
other. But when the kindness of God our Saviour an
love towards man appeared, He saved us—not by vir
any moral achievements of ours, but by the cleansing
of a new birth and the moral renewal of the Holy Spirit,
He gave us so generously through Jesus Christ our Sa
The result is that we are acquitted by His grace, and ca
forward to inheriting Life for evermore. This is solid
I want you to speak about these matters with ab
certainty, so that those who have believed in God
concentrate upon a life of goodness.

Subjects like this are always good and useful but min
steer clear of stupid arguments, genealogies, controversi
quarrels over the Law. They settle nothing and lead nov
If a man is still argumentative after the second warnin
should reject him. You can be sure that he has a moral
and he knows it.

Final messages   II

As soon as I send Artemas to you (or perhaps it w
Tychicus), do your best to come to me at Nicopolis,
have made up my mind to spend the winter there. Se
Zenas the lawyer and Apollos have what they requir
give them a good send-off. And our people should le
earn what they require by leading an honest life and so b
supporting.

All those here with me send you greetings. Please gi
greetings to all who love us in the faith. Grace be wit
all.

THE LETTER TO PHILEMON

AUTHOR. *Paul, who wrote this letter when in prison at the same time as those to Ephesus, Colossae and Philippi, probably in Rome.*

DATE. *About 62.*

DESTINATION. *This is a personal letter to Philemon, a rich leading member of the church at Colossae.*

THEME. *Here we have a charming intimate letter written by Paul to a dear friend. Philemon's slave, Onesimus (which means " useful " and explains the untranslatable pun in verse 11 !), had run away from him and come under Paul's influence in Rome. He not only became a Christian but became very dear to Paul. They both realise, however, that he must return to his master and Paul sends him back with this " covering " letter.*

PAUL, prisoner for the sake of Jesus Christ, and brother Timothy to Philemon our fellow-worker, Apphia our sister and Archippus who is with us in the fight; to the Church that meets in your house—grace and peace be to you from God our Father and from the Lord Jesus Christ.

A personal appeal 4

I always thank God for you, Philemon, in my constant prayers for you all, for I have heard how you love and trust both the Lord Jesus Himself and those who believe in Him. And I pray that those who share your faith may also share your knowledge of all the good things that believing in Jesus Christ can mean to us. It is your love that gives us such comfort and happiness, for it cheers the hearts of your fellow-Christians. And although I could rely on my authority in Christ and dare to *order* you to do what I consider right, I am not doing that. No I, am appealing to that love of yours, a

simple personal appeal from Paul the old man, in priso[n]
Jesus Christ's sake. I am appealing for my child. Yes, I
become a father though I have been under lock and key
the child's name is—Onesimus! Oh, I know you have f[ound]
him pretty useless in the past but he is going to be useful
to both of us. I am sending him back to you: *will you*
him as my son, part of me? I should have dearly loved to
kept him with me: he could have done what you would
done—looked after me here in prison for the Gospel's
But I would do nothing without consulting you first,
you have a favour to give me, let it be spontaneous an[d]
forced from you by circumstances!

It occurs to me that there has been a purpose in your l[osing]
him. You lost him, a slave, for a time; now you are h[aving]
him back for good, not merely as a slave, but as a bro[ther]
Christian. He is already especially loved by me—how r[much]
more will you be able to love him, both as a man and
fellow-Christian! You and I have so much in com[mon,]
haven't we? Then do welcome him as you would wel[come]
me. If you feel he has wronged or cheated you put it do[wn to]
my account. I've written this with my own hand: I,
hereby promise to repay you. (Of course I'm not stressin[g the]
fact that you might be said to owe me your very soul!)
do grant me this favour, my brother—such an act of love
do my old heart good. As I send you this letter I know y[ou'll]
do what I ask—I believe, in fact, you'll do more.

Will you do something else? Get the guest-room read[y for]
me, for I have great hopes that through your prayers I m[yself]
will be returned to you as well!

Epaphras, here in prison with me, sends his greetings
do Mark, Aristarchus, Demas and Luke, all fellow-wo[rkers]
for God. The grace of our Lord Jesus Christ be with
spirit, Amen.

THE LETTER TO
JEWISH CHRISTIANS

AUTHOR. *Although the Authorised Version calls this letter " the Epistle of Paul the Apostle " it is almost universally agreed that he did not write it. The style is very unlike Paul's, and every other letter of his is plainly stated to be by him. Various fascinating speculations have been made as to its authorship, including the names of Barnabas, Luke, Silas, Apollos and Priscilla.*

DATE. *Probably before the fall of Jerusalem. Possibly 67.*

DESTINATION. *Christian Jews probably living in some large town. Rome is favoured by some scholars.*

THEME. *The general idea of this letter is to demonstrate that Jesus amply fulfils all the highest conceptions of the Jewish religion, and is infinitely superior to any predecessors. Christian Jews must realise that Christ has fulfilled and surpassed all their old ideas, and they must not therefore relapse into the old Jewish religion. Because the New Agreement was established by God's visiting the earth in Person, it is infinitely more important than the Old Agreement of the Law. There is, therefore, for those who belong to Christ far greater privilege in knowing God, but far greater responsibility in serving Him loyally.*

GOD, Who gave to our forefathers many different glimpses of the truth in the words of the prophets, has now, at the end of the present age, given us the Truth in the Son. Through the Son God made the whole universe, and to the Son He has ordained that all creation shall ultimately belong. This Son, Radiance of the glory of God, flawless Expression of the nature of God, Himself the Upholding Principle of all that is, effected in person the reconciliation between God and Man and then took His seat at the right hand of the Majesty on high—thus proving Himself, by the more glorious Name that He has won, far greater than all the angels of God.

Scripture endorses this superiority   1 : 5
     For to which of the angels did He ever say such words as these :

> Thou art my Son,
> This day have I begotten Thee ?

Or, again :

> I will be to Him a Father,
> And He shall be to Me a Son ?

Further, when He brings His first-born into this world of men, He says :

> Let all the angels of God worship Him.

This is what He says of the angels :

> Who maketh His angels winds
> And His ministers a flame of fire.

But when He speaks of the Son, He says :

> Thy throne, O *God*, is for ever and ever ;
> And the sceptre of uprightness is the sceptre of Thy
>   Kingdom.
> Thou hast loved righteousness and hated iniquity ;
> Therefore God, Thy God, hath anointed Thee
> With the oil of gladness above Thy fellows.

He also says :

> Thou, *Lord*, in the beginning has laid the foundation of
>   the earth,

And the heavens are the work of Thy hands :
They shall perish, but Thou continuest :
And they all shall wax old as doth a garment ;
And as a mantle shalt Thou roll them up,
As a garment, and they shall be changed :
But Thou art the same,
And Thy years shall not fail.

But does He ever say this of any of the angels :

Sit Thou on My right hand,
Till I make Thine enemies the footstool of Thy feet ?

Surely the angels are no more than spirits in the service of God, commissioned to serve the heirs of God's salvation.

The angels had authority in past ages :
to-day the Son is the authority   II : I

We ought, therefore, to pay the greatest attention to the truth that we have heard and not allow ourselves to drift away from it. For if the message given through angels proved authentic, so that defiance of it and disobedience to it received appropriate retribution, how shall we escape if we refuse to pay proper attention to the salvation that is offered us to-day ? For this salvation came first through the words of the Lord Himself : it was confirmed for our hearing by men who had heard Him speak, and God moreover has plainly endorsed their witness by signs and miracles, by all kinds of spiritual power, and by gifts of the Holy Spirit, all working to the Divine Plan.

For though in past ages God did grant authority to angels, yet He did not put the future world of men under their control, and it is this world that we are now talking about.

But someone has said :

What is man, that Thou art mindful of him ?
Or the Son of man, that Thou visitest him ?
Thou madest him a little lower than the angels ;

Thou crownest him with glory and honour,
And didst set him over the works of Thy hands :
Thou didst put all things in subjection under his feet.

Notice that the writer puts " all things " under the sovereignty of man : he left nothing outside his control. But we do not yet see " all things " under his control.

Christ became man, not angel, to save mankind   II : 9

What we actually see is Jesus, after being made temporarily inferior to the angels (and so subject to pain and death), in order that He should, in God's grace, taste death for every man, now crowned with glory and honour. It was right and proper that in bringing many sons to glory, God (from Whom and by Whom everything exists) should make the Leader of their salvation a Perfect Leader through the fact that He suffered. For the One Who makes men holy and the men who are made holy share a common humanity. So that He is not ashamed to call them His brothers, for He says :

I will declare Thy name unto My brethren,
In the midst of the congregation will I sing Thy praise.

And again, speaking as a man, He says :

I will put my trust in Him.

And, one more instance, in these words :

Behold, I and the children which God hath given Me. . . .

Since, then, " the children " have a common physical nature as human beings, He also became a human being, so that by going through death as a man He might destroy him who had the power of death, that is, the Devil ; and might also set free those who lived their whole lives a prey to the fear of death. It is plain that for this purpose He did not become an angel ; He became a *man*, in actual fact a descendant of Abraham. It

was imperative that He should be made like His brothers in
nature, if He were to become a High Priest both compassion-
ate and faithful in the things of God, and at the same time
able to make atonement for the sins of the people. For by
virtue of His own suffering under temptation He is able to
help those who are exposed to temptation.

Moses was a faithful servant .
Christ a faithful Son   III : 1

So then, my brothers in holiness who share the highest of
all callings, I want you to think of the Messenger and
High Priest of our faith, Christ Jesus. See Him as faithful to
the charge God gave Him, and compare Him with Moses who
also faithfully discharged his duty in the household of God.
For this Man has been considered worthy of greater honour
than Moses, just as the founder of a house may be truly said
to have more honour than the house itself. Every house is
founded by someone, but the Founder of everything is God
Himself. Moses was certainly faithful in all his duties in God's
household, but he was faithful as a servant and his work was
only a foreshadowing of the truth that would be known later.
But Christ was faithful as a loyal son in the household of the
Founder, His own Father. And we are members of this
household if we maintain our trust and joyful hope steadfast
to the end.

Let us be on our guard that unbelief
does not creep in   III : 7

We ought to take note of these words which the Holy
Spirit says :

> To-day if ye shall hear His voice,
> Harden not your hearts, as in the provocation,
> Like as in the day of the temptation in the wilderness,
> Wherewith your fathers tempted Me by proving Me,
> And saw My works forty years.
> Wherefore I was displeased with this generation,
> And said, They do alway err in their heart :

> But they did not know My ways;
> As I sware in My wrath,
> They shall not enter into My rest.

You should therefore be most careful, my brothers, that there should not be in any of you that wickedness of heart which refuses to trust, and deserts the cause of the living God. Help each other to stand firm in the faith every day, while it is still called " to-day," and beware that none of you becomes deaf and blind to God through the delusive glamour of sin. For we continue to share in all that Christ has for us so long as we steadily maintain until the end the trust with which we began. These words are still being said for our ears to hear:

> To-day if ye shall hear His voice,
> Harden not your hearts, as in the provocation.

For who was it who heard the Word of God and yet provoked His indignation? Was it not all who were rescued from slavery in Egypt under the leadership of Moses? And who was it with whom God was displeased for forty long years? Was it not those who, after all their hearing of God's Word, fell into sin, and left their bones in the desert? And to whom did God swear that they should never enter into His Rest? Was it not these very men who refused to trust Him?

Yes, it is all too plain that it was refusal to trust God that prevented those men from entering His Rest.

Men failed in the past to find God's
Rest : let us not fail !   IV : X

Now since the same promise of Rest is offered to us to-day, let us be continually on our guard that none of us even looks like failing to attain it. For we too have had a Gospel preached to us, as those men had. Yet the message proclaimed to them did them no good, because they only heard and did not believe as well. It is only as a result of our faith and trust that we experience that Rest. For He said :

As I sware in My wrath,
They shall not enter into My Rest:

not because the Rest was not prepared—it had been ready since the work of Creation was completed, as He says elsewhere in the Scriptures, speaking of the Seventh Day of Creation,

And God rested on the seventh day from all His works.

And in the passage above He refers to "My Rest" as something already in existence. No, it is clear that some were

intended to experience this Rest and, since the previous hearers of the message failed to attain to it because they would not believe God, He proclaims a further opportunity when He says through David, many years later, "To-day," just as He had said "To-day" before.

To-day if ye shall hear His voice,
Harden not your hearts.

For if Joshua had given them the Rest, we should not find God saying, at a much later date, "To-day." There still exists, therefore, a full and complete Rest for the people of God. And he who experiences this real Rest is resting from his own work as fully as God from His.

Let us then be eager to know this Rest for ourselves, and let us beware that no one misses it through falling into the same kind of unbelief as those we have mentioned. For the Word that God speaks is alive and active : it cuts more keenly than any two-edged sword : it strikes through to the place where soul and spirit meet, to the innermost intimacies of a man's being : it exposes the very thoughts and motives of a man's heart. No creature has any cover from the sight of God ; everything lies naked and exposed before the eyes of Him with Whom we have to do.

G

For our help and comfort—Jesus the
great High Priest   IV : 14

Seeing that we have a great High Priest Who has entered the inmost Heaven, Jesus the Son of God, let us hold firmly to our faith. For we have no super-human High Priest to whom our weaknesses are unintelligible—He Himself has shared fully in all our experience of temptation, except that He never sinned.

Let us therefore approach the Throne of grace with fullest confidence, that we may receive mercy for our failures and grace to help in the hour of need.

A high priest must be duly qualified
and Divinely appointed   V : 1

Note that when a man is chosen as high priest he is appointed on men's behalf as their representative in the things of God—he offers gifts to God and makes the necessary sacrifices for sins on behalf of his fellowmen. He must be able to deal sympathetically with the ignorant and foolish because he realises that he is himself prone to human weakness. This naturally means that the offering which he makes for sin is made on his own personal behalf as well as on behalf of those whom he represents.

Note also that nobody chooses for himself the honour of being a high priest, but he is called by God to the work, as was Aaron, the first high priest in ancient times.

Thus we see that the Christ did not choose for Himself the glory of being High Priest, but He was honoured by the One Who said :

> Thou art My Son,
> This day have I begotten Thee.

And He says in another passage :

> Thou art a priest for ever
> After the order of Melchizedek.

Christ the perfect High Priest, was
the perfect Son   V : 7

Christ, in the days when He was man, appealed to the One
Who could save Him from death in desperate prayer and the
agony of tears. His prayers were heard; He was freed from
His shrinking from death, but, Son though He was, He had
to prove the meaning of obedience through all that He
suffered. Then, when He had been proved the Perfect Son,
He became the source of eternal salvation to all who should
obey Him, being now recognised by God Himself as High
Priest " after the order of Melchizedek."

There is much food for thought here—
but only for the mature Christian   V : 11

There is a great deal that we should like to say about this
high priesthood, but it is not easy to explain to you since you
seem so slow to grasp spiritual truth. At a time when you
should be teaching others, you need teachers yourselves to
repeat to you the ABC of God's revelation to men! For
anyone who continues to live on " milk " is obviously
immature—he simply has not grown up. " Solid food " is
only for the adult, that is, for the man who has developed by
experience his power to discriminate between what is good
and bad for him.

Can we not leave spiritual babyhood
behind—and go on to maturity?   VI : 1

Let us leave behind the elementary teaching about Christ
and go forward to adult understanding. Let us not lay over
and over again the foundation truths—repentance from the
deeds which led to death, believing in God, baptism and lay-
ing-on of hands, belief in the life to come and the final
Judgment. No, if God allows, let us go on.

Going back to the foundations will not help those
who have deliberately turned away from God   VI : 4

When you find men who have been enlightened, who have
experienced salvation and received the Holy Spirit, who

have known the wholesome nourishment of the Word of God and touched the spiritual resources of the eternal world and who then fall away, it proves impossible to make them repent as they did at first. For they are re-crucifying the Son of God in their own souls, and by their conduct exposing Him to shame and contempt. Ground which absorbs the rain that is constantly falling upon it and produces plants which are useful to those who cultivate it, is ground which has the blessing of God. But ground which produces nothing but thorns and thistles is of no value and is bound sooner or later to be condemned—the only thing to do is to burn it clean.

We want you to make God's promises real
through your faith, hope and patience   VI : 9

But although we give these words of warning we feel sure that you, whom we love, are capable of better things and will enjoy the full experience of salvation. God is not unfair: He will not lose sight of all that you have done nor of the loving labour which you have shown for His sake in looking after fellow-Christians (as you are still doing). It is our earnest wish that every one of you should show a similar keenness in fully grasping the hope that is within you. We do not want any of you to grow slack, but to follow the example of those who through sheer patient faith came to possess the promises.

When God made His promise to Abraham He swore by Himself, for there was no one greater by whom He could swear, and He said:

> Surely blessing I will bless thee
> And multiplying I will multiply thee.

And then Abraham, after patient endurance, found the promise true.

Among men it is customary to swear by something greater than themselves. And if a statement is confirmed by an oath, that is the end of all quibbling. So in this matter, God, wishing to show beyond doubt that His Plan was unchangeable, confirmed it with an oath. So that by two utterly immutable things, the Word of God and the Oath of God, Who cannot lie, we who are refugees from this dying world might have a source of strength, and might grasp the hope that He holds out to us. This hope we hold as the utterly reliable anchor for our souls, fixed in the very certainty of God Himself in Heaven, where Jesus has already entered on our behalf, having become, as we have seen, " High Priest for ever after the order of Melchizedek."

The mysterious Melchizedek : his superiority to Abraham and the Levites

VII : 1

Now this Melchizedek was, we know, King of Salem and priest of God Most High. He met Abraham when the latter was returning from the defeat of the kings, and blessed him. Abraham gave him a tribute of a tenth part of all the spoils of battle.

(Melchizedek means "King of Righteousness," and his other title is "King of Peace " (for Salem means Peace). He had no father or mother and no family tree. He was not born nor did he die, but, being like the Son of God, is a perpetual priest.)

Now notice the greatness of this man. Even Abraham the patriarch pays him a tribute of a tenth part of the spoils. Further, we know that, according to the Law, the descendants of Levi who accepted the office of priest have the right to demand a " tenth " from the people, that is from their brothers, despite the fact that the latter are descendants of Abraham. But here we have one who is quite independent of Levitic ancestry taking a " tenth " from Abraham, and giving a blessing to Abraham, the holder of God's Promises ! And no one can deny that the receiver of a blessing is inferior to the one who gives it. Again, in the one case it is mortal men who receive the " tenths," and in the other it is one who, we are assured, is alive. One might say that even Levi, the proper receiver of " tenths," has paid his tenth to this man, for in a sense he already existed in the body of his father Abraham when Melchizedek met him.

The revival of the Melchizedek priesthood means
that the Levitical priesthood is superseded   VII : 11

We may go further. If it be possible to bring men to
spiritual maturity through the Levitical priestly system (for
that is the system under which the people were given the
Law), why does the necessity arise for another priest to make
his appearance *after the order of Melchizedek*, instead of following the normal priestly calling of Aaron? For if there is a
transference of priestly powers, there will necessarily follow
an alteration of the Law regarding priesthood. He Who is
described as our High Priest belongs to another tribe, no
member of which had ever attended the altar! For it is a
matter of history that our Lord was a descendant of Judah,
and Moses made no mention of priesthood in connection with
that tribe.

How fundamental is this change becomes all the more
apparent when we see this other Priest appearing according to
the Melchizedek pattern, and deriving His Priesthood not by
virtue of a command imposed from outside, but from the
power of indestructible Life within. For the witness to Him,
as we have seen, is:

> Thou art a priest for ever
> After the order of Melchizedek.

Quite plainly, then, there is a definite cancellation of the
previous commandment because of its ineffectiveness and
uselessness—the Law was incapable of bringing anyone to
real maturity—followed by the introduction of a better Hope,
through which we approach our God.

The High Priesthood of Christ rests
upon the Oath of God   VII : 20

This means a "better" Hope for us because Jesus has
become our Priest by the Oath of God. Other men have been
priests without any sworn guarantee, but Jesus has the Oath
of Him that said of Him:

> The Lord sware and will not repent Himself,
> Thou art a priest for ever.

And He is, by virtue of this fact, Himself the living guarantee of a " better " agreement. Human high priests have always been changing, for death made a permanent appointment impossible. But Christ, because He lives for ever, possesses a priesthood that needs no successor. This means that He can save fully and completely those who approach God through Him, for He is always living to intercede on their behalf.

Christ the perfect High Priest,
Who meets our need   VII : 26

Here is the High Priest we need. A Man Who is holy, faultless, unstained, beyond the very reach of sin and lifted to the very heavens. There is no need for Him, like the high priests we know, to offer up sacrifice, first for His own sins and then for the people's. He made one sacrifice, once for all, when He offered up Himself.

The Law makes for its priests men of human weakness. But the word of the Oath makes for Priest the Son, Who is Perfect for ever !

Christ our High Priest in Heaven is
High Priest of a New Agreement   VIII : I

Now to sum up—we have an ideal High Priest such as has been described above. He has taken His seat on the right hand of the Heavenly Majesty. He is the Minister of the Sanctuary and of the real Tabernacle—that is the one God has set up and not man. Every high priest is appointed to offer gifts and make sacrifices. It follows, therefore, that in these Holy Places this Man has something that He is offering.

Now if He were still living on earth He would not be a priest at all, for there are already priests offering the gifts prescribed by the Law. These men are serving what is only a pattern or reproduction of things that exist in Heaven. (Moses, you will remember, when he was going to construct the tabernacle, was cautioned by God in these words :

See that thou make all things
According to the pattern that was showed thee in the
mount.)

But Christ has been given a far higher ministry for He medi-
ates a higher Agreement, which in turn rests upon higher
promises. If the first Agreement had proved satisfactory there
would have been no need for the second.

Actually, however, God does show Himself dissatisfied for
He says to those under the first Agreement:

Behold, the days come, saith the Lord,
That I will make a new covenant with the house of Israel
    and with the house of Judah;
Not according to the covenant that I made with their
    fathers
In the day that I took them by the hand to lead them forth
    out of the land of Egypt;
For they continued not in my covenant,
And I regarded them not, saith the Lord.
For this is the covenant that I will make with the house of
    Israel
After those days, saith the Lord;
I will put my laws into their mind,
And on their heart also will I write them:
And I will be to them a God,
And they shall be to me a people:
And they shall not teach every man his fellow-citizen,
And every man his brother saying, Know the Lord:
For all shall know me,
From the least to the greatest of them.
For I will be merciful to their iniquities,
And their sins will I remember no more.

The mere fact that God speaks of a new Covenant or Agreement makes the old one out of date. And when a thing grows
weak and out of date it is obviously soon going to be dis-
pensed with altogether.

The sanctuary under the Old Agreement   IX : I

Now the first Agreement had certain rules for the service of
God, and it had a Sanctuary, a holy place in this world for the
eternal God. A tent was erected : in the outer compartment
were placed the lamp-standard, the table and the sacred loaves.
Inside, beyond the curtain, was the inner tent called the
Holy of Holies, in which were the golden incense-altar and
the gold inlaid ark of the Agreement, containing the golden
jar of manna, Aaron's budding staff and the stone tablets
inscribed with the words of the actual Agreement. Above
these things were fixed representations of the cherubim of
glory, casting their shadow over the ark's covering, known as
the mercy seat. (All this is full of meaning but we cannot
enter now into a detailed explanation.)

Under this arrangement the outer tent was habitually used
by the priests in the regular discharge of their religious duties.
But the inner tent was entered once a year only, by the High
Priest, alone, bearing a sacrifice of shed blood to be offered for
his own sins and those of the people.

The old arrangements stood as symbols
until Christ, the Truth, came   IX : 8

By these things the Holy Spirit means us to understand
that the way to the Holy of Holies was not yet open, that is,
so long as the first tent and all that it stands for still exist. For
in this outer tent we see a picture of the present time, in which
both gifts and sacrifices are offered and yet are incapable of
cleansing the soul of the worshipper. The ceremonies are
concerned with food and drink, various washings and rules
for bodily conduct, and were only intended to be valid until
the time when Christ should establish the truth. For now
Christ has come among us, the High Priest of the good
things which were to come, and has passed through a greater
and more perfect Tent which no human hand had made (for
it was no part of this world of ours). It was not with goats'
or calves' blood but with His own blood that He entered
once and for all into the Holy of Holies, having won for us
men eternal reconciliation with God. And if the blood of

bulls and goats and the ashes of a burnt heifer were, when sprinkled on the unholy, sufficient to make the body pure, then how much more will the blood of Christ Himself, Who in His eternal spirit offered Himself to God as the Perfect Sacrifice, purifying your souls from the deeds of death, that you may serve the living God !

The death of Christ gives Him power
to administer the New Agreement   IX : 15

Christ is consequently the administrator of an entirely new Agreement, having the power, by virtue of His death, to redeem transgressions committed under the first Agreement : to enable those who obey God's call to enjoy the promises of the eternal inheritance. For, as in the case of a will, the Agreement is only valid after death. While the testator lives, a will has no legal power. And indeed we find that even the first Agreement of God's Will was not put into force without the shedding of blood. For when Moses had told the people every command of the Law he took calves' and goats' blood with water and scarlet wool, and sprinkled both the book and all the people with a sprig of hyssop, saying : " This is the blood of the Agreement God makes with you." Moses also sprinkled with blood the Tent itself and all the sacred vessels. And you will find that in the Law almost all cleansing is made by means of blood—as the common saying has it : " No shedding of blood, no remission of sin."

Christ has achieved the real appearance
before God for us   IX : 23

It was necessary for the earthly reproduction of heavenly realities to be purified by such methods, but the actual heavenly things could only be made pure in God's sight by higher sacrifices than these. Christ did not therefore enter into any holy places made by human hands (however truly these may represent heavenly realities), but He entered Heaven itself to make His appearance before God as High Priest on our behalf. There is no intention that He should offer Himself regularly, like the High Priest entering the Holy of Holies every year with the blood of another creature. For that would mean that He would have to suffer death every time He entered Heaven from the beginning of the world! No, the fact is that now, at this point in time, the end of the present age, He has appeared once and for all to abolish sin by the sacrifice of Himself. And just as surely as it is appointed for all men to die and after that pass to their judgment, so is it certain that Christ was offered once to bear the sins of many and after that, to those who look for Him, He will appear a second time, not this time to deal with sin, but to bring them to full salvation.

Sacrifices under the Law were " typical," not final   x : 1

The Law possessed only a dim outline of the benefits Christ would bring and did not actually reproduce them. Consequently it was incapable of perfecting the souls of those who offered their regular annual sacrifices. For if it had, surely the sacrifices would have been discontinued—on the grounds that the worshippers, having been really cleansed, would have had no further consciousness of sin. In practice, however, the sacrifices amounted to an annual reminder of sins ; for the blood of bulls and goats cannot really remove the guilt of sin.

Christ, however, makes the old order obsolete
and makes the perfect Sacrifice   x : 5

Therefore, when Christ enters the world, He says :

Sacrifice and offering Thou wouldest not,
But a body didst Thou prepare for Me ;
In whole burnt offerings and sacrifices for sin Thou hadst
    no pleasure :
Then said I, Lo, I am come
(In the roll of the book it is written of me)
To do Thy will, O God.

After saying that God has " no pleasure in sacrifice, offering and burnt-offering " (which are made according to the Law),

Christ then says, " Lo, I am come to do Thy will." That means that He is dispensing with the old order of sacrifices, and establishing a new order of obedience to the Will of God, and in that Will we have been made holy by the single unique offering of the body of Christ.

Every human priest stands day by day performing his religious duties and offering time after time the same sacrifices —which can never actually remove sins. But this Man, after offering one Sacrifice for sins for ever, took His seat at God's right hand, from that time offering no more sacrifice, but waiting until " His enemies be made His footstool". For by virtue of that one Offering He has perfected for all time every one whom He makes holy. The Holy Spirit Himself endorses this truth for us, when He says, first :

> This is the covenant that I will make with them
> After those days, saith the Lord ;
> I will put My laws on their heart,
> And upon their mind also will I write them.

And then, He adds :

And their sins and their iniquities will I remember no more.

Where God grants remission of sin there can be no question of making further atonement.

Through Christ we can confidently approach God   x : 19

So by virtue of the blood of Jesus, you and I, my brothers, may now have courage to enter the Holy of Holies by way of the One Who died and is yet alive, Who has made for us a holy means of entry by Himself passing through the Curtain, that is, His own human nature. Further, since we have a great High Priest set over the household of God, let us draw near with true hearts and fullest confidence, knowing that our inmost souls have been purified by the sprinkling of His blood just as our bodies are cleansed by the washing of clean water. In this confidence let us hold on to the hope that we profess without the slightest hesitation—for He is utterly dependable—and let us think of one another and how we can encourage each other to love and do good deeds. And let us not hold aloof from our church meetings, as some do. Let us do all we can to help one another's faith, and this the more earnestly as we see the Final Day drawing ever nearer.

A warning: let us not abuse the Great Sacrifice   x : 26

Now if we sin deliberately after we have known and accepted the Truth, there can be no further sacrifice for sin for us but only a terrifying expectation of judgment and the fire of God's indignation, which will one day consume all that sets itself against Him. The man who showed contempt for Moses' Law died without hope of appeal on the evidence of two or three of his fellows. How much more dreadful a punishment will he be thought to deserve who has poured scorn on the Son of God, treated like dirt the blood of the Agreement which had once made him holy, and insulted the very Spirit of grace ? For we know the One Who said :

Vengeance belongeth unto Me, I will recompense.

And, again :

The Lord shall judge His people.

Truly it is a terrible thing for a man who has done this to fall into the hands of the living God !

Recollect your former faith, and
stand firm to-day !   x : 32

You must never forget those past days when you had received the Light and went through such a great and painful struggle. It was partly because everyone's eye was on you as you endured harsh words and hard experiences, partly because you threw in your lot with those who suffered much the same. You sympathised with those who were put in prison and you were cheerful when your own goods were confiscated, for you knew that you had a much more solid and lasting treasure in Heaven. Don't throw away your trust now—it carries with it a rich reward in the world to come. Patient endurance is what you need if, after doing God's Will, you are to receive what He has promised.

> For yet a very little while,
> He that cometh shall come, and shall not tarry.
> But my righteous one shall live by faith ;
> And if he shrink back, my soul hath no pleasure in him.

Surely we are not going to be men who cower back and are lost, but men who maintain their faith until the salvation of their souls is complete !

Now faith means putting our full confidence in the things we hope for, it means being certain of things we cannot see. It was this kind of faith that won their reputation for the saints of old. And it is after all only by faith that our minds accept as fact that the whole scheme of time and space was designed by God—that the world which we can see is operating on principles which are invisible.

Faith is the distinctive mark of the
saints of the Old Agreement   XI : 4

ABEL

It was because of his faith that Abel made a better sacrifice to God than Cain, and he had evidence that God looked upon him as a righteous man, whose gifts He could accept. And though Cain killed him, yet by his faith he still speaks to us to-day.

ENOCH

It was because of his faith that Enoch was promoted to the eternal world without experiencing death. He disappeared from this world because God promoted him, and before that happened his reputation was that " he pleased God". And without faith it is impossible to please Him. The man who approaches God must have faith in two things, first that God exists and secondly that it is worth a man's while to try to find God.

NOAH

It was through his faith that Noah, on receiving God's warning of impending disaster, reverently constructed an ark to save his household. This action of faith condemned the unbelief of the rest of the world, and won for Noah the righteousness before God which follows such a faith.

ABRAHAM

It was by faith that Abraham obeyed the summons to go out to a place which he would eventually possess, and he set out in complete ignorance of his destination. It was faith that kept him journeying like a foreigner through the land of promise, with no more home than the tents which he shared with Isaac and Jacob, co-heirs with him of the promise. For Abraham's eyes were looking forward to that City with solid foundations of which God Himself is both Architect and Builder.

SARAH

It was by faith that even Sarah gained the physical vitality to become a mother despite her great age, and she gave birth to a child when far beyond the normal years of child-bearing. She could do this because she believed that the One Who had given the promise was utterly trustworthy. So it happened that from one man, who as a potential father was already considered dead, there arose a race "as numerous as the stars," as "countless as the sands of the sea-shore."

All the heroes of faith looked forward
to their true country   XI : 13

All these whom we have mentioned maintained their faith but died without actually receiving God's promises, though they had seen them in the distance, had hailed them as true

and were quite convinced of their reality. They freely admitted
that they lived on this earth as exiles and foreigners. Men who
say that mean, of course, that their eyes are fixed upon their
true Home-land. If they had meant the particular country
they had left behind, they had ample opportunity to return.
No, the fact is that they longed for a better country altogether,
nothing less than a heavenly one. And because of this faith
of theirs, God is not ashamed to be called their God for in
sober truth He has prepared for them a City in Heaven.

Abraham's faith once more   XI : 17
    It was by faith that Abraham, when put to the test, made
a sacrifice of Isaac. Yes, the man who had heard God's
promises was prepared to offer up his only son of whom it
had been said, "In Isaac shall thy seed be called." He
believed that God could raise his son up, even if he were dead.
And he did, in a manner of speaking, receive him back from
death.

The faith of Isaac, Jacob and Joseph   XI : 20
    It was by faith that Isaac gave Jacob and Esau his blessing,
for his words dealt with what should happen in the future. It
was by faith that the dying Jacob blessed each of Joseph's sons
as he bowed in prayer over his staff. It was by faith that Joseph
on his death-bed spoke of the exodus of the Israelites, and
gave confident orders about the disposal of his own mortal
remains.

Moses   XI : 23
    It was by faith that Moses was hidden by his parents for
three months after his birth, for they saw that he was an
exceptional child and refused to be daunted by the king's
decree that all male children should be drowned. It was also
by faith that Moses himself when grown up refused to be
called the son of Pharoah's daughter. He preferred sharing
the burden of God's people to enjoying the temporary
advantages of alliance with a sinful nation. He considered the

" reproach of Christ " more precious than all the wealth of Egypt, for he looked steadily at the ultimate, not the immediate, reward.

By faith he led the Exodus from Egypt ; he defied the king's anger with the strength that came from obedience to the Invisible King.

By faith Moses kept the first Passover and made the blood-sprinkling, so that the Angel of Death which killed the first-born should not touch his people.

By faith the people walked through the Red Sea as though it were dry land, and the Egyptians who tried to do the same thing were drowned.

Rahab   XI : 30

It was by faith that the walls of Jericho collapsed, for the people had obeyed God's command to encircle them for seven days.

It was because of her faith that Rahab the prostitute did not share the fate of the disobedient, for she showed her faith in the true God when she welcomed the Israelites sent out to reconnoitre.

The Old Testament is full of examples of faith   XI : 32

And what other examples shall I give ? There is simply not time to continue by telling the stories of Gideon, Barak, Samson and Jephtha ; of David, Samuel and the prophets. Through their faith these men conquered kingdoms, ruled in justice and proved the truth of God's promises. They shut the mouths of lions, they quenched the furious blaze of fire, they escaped from death itself. From being weaklings they became strong men and mighty warriors ; they routed whole armies of foreigners. Some returned to their women-folk from certain death, while others were tortured and refused to be ransomed, because they wanted to deserve a more honourable resurrection in the world to come. Others were exposed to the test of public mockery and flogging, and to the torture of being left bound in prison. They were killed by stoning, by being sawn in two ; they were tempted by specious promises of release and then were killed with the sword. Many became refugees with nothing but sheepskins or goatskins to cover them. They lost everything and yet were spurned and ill-treated by a world that was too evil to see their worth. They lived as vagrants in the desert, on the mountains, or in caves or holes in the ground.

All these won a glowing testimony to their faith, but they did not then and there receive the fulfilment of the promise. God had something better planned for our day, and it was not His Plan that they should reach perfection without us.

We should consider these examples
and Christ the perfect example   XII : 1

Surrounded then as we are by these serried ranks of witnesses, let us strip off everything that hinders us, as well as the sin which dogs our feet, and let us run the race that we have to run with patience, our eyes fixed on Jesus the Source and the Goal of our faith. For He Himself endured a cross and thought nothing of its shame because of the joy He had in doing His Father's Will; and He is now seated at the right hand of God's Throne. Think constantly of Him enduring all that sinful men could say against Him, and you will not lose your purpose or your courage.

Look upon suffering as Heavenly discipline   XII : 4

After all, your fight against sin has not yet meant the shedding of blood, and you have perhaps lost sight of that piece of advice which reminds you of your sonship in God :

My son, regard not lightly the chastening of the Lord,
Nor faint when thou art reproved of Him ;
For whom the Lord loveth He chasteneth,
And scourgeth every son whom He receiveth.

Bear what you have to bear as " chastening "—as God's dealing with you as sons. No true son ever grows up uncorrected by his father. For if you had no experience of the correction which all sons have to bear you might well doubt the legitimacy of your sonship. After all, when we were children we had fathers who corrected us, and we respected them for it. Can we not much more readily submit to a Heavenly Father's discipline, and learn how to live?

For our fathers used to correct us according to their own ideas during the brief days of childhood. But God corrects us all our days for our own benefit, to teach us His holiness. Now obviously no " chastening " seems pleasant at the time : it is in fact most unpleasant. Yet when it is all over we can see that it has quietly produced the fruit of real goodness in the character of those who have accepted it in the right spirit. So take a fresh grip on life and brace your trembling limbs. Don't wander away from the path but forge steadily onward. On the right path the limping foot recovers strength and does not collapse.

In times of testing be especially on
your guard against certain sins   XII : 14

Let it be your ambition to live at peace with all men and to achieve holiness " without which no man shall see the Lord ". Be careful that none of you fails to respond to the grace which God gives, for if he does there can very easily spring up in him a bitter spirit which is not only bad in itself but can also poison the lives of many others. Be careful, too, that none of you falls into impurity or loses his reverence for the things of God and then, like Esau, is ready to sell his birthright to satisfy the momentary hunger of his body. Remember how afterwards, when he wanted to have the blessing which was his birthright, he was refused. He never afterwards found the way of repentance though he sought it desperately and with tears.

Your experience is not that of the
Old Agreement but of the New   XII : 18

You have not had to approach things which your senses could experience as they did in the old days—flaming fire, black darkness, shrieking storm and out of it a trumpet-blast, a Voice speaking human words. So terrible was that Voice that those who heard it begged and prayed that it might stop speaking, for what it had already commanded was more than they could bear—that " if even a beast touch this Mountain it must be stoned or killed with a spear." So fearful was the spectacle that Moses cried out, " I am terrified and trembled at this sight ! "

No, you have been allowed to approach the true Mount Zion, the City of the living God, the heavenly Jerusalem. You have drawn near to the countless angelic army, the Great Assembly of Heaven and the Church of the First-born whose names are written above. You have drawn near to God, the Judge of All, to the souls of good men made perfect, and to Jesus, mediator of a New Agreement, to the cleansing of Blood which tells a better story than the age-old sacrifice of Abel.

So be sure you do not refuse to hear the Voice of God ! For if they who refused to hear those who spoke to them on earth did not escape, how little chance of escape is there for us if we refuse to hear the One Who speaks from Heaven.

Now He has made a promise, saying :

Yet once more will I make to tremble
Not the earth only, but also the heaven.

This means that in this final " shaking " all that is impermanent will be removed, that is, everything that is merely " made," and only the unshakable things will remain. Since then we have been given a kingdom that is " unshakable," let us serve God with thankfulness in the ways which please Him, but always with reverence and holy fear. For it is perfectly true that our God is a burning Fire.

Some practical instructions for Christian Living   XIII : I
Never let your brotherly love fail, nor refuse to extend your hospitality to strangers—sometimes men have entertained angels unawares. Think constantly of those in prison as if you were prisoners at their side. Think too of all who suffer as if you shared their pain.

Both honourable marriage and chastity should be honoured by all of you. God Himself will judge those who traffic in the bodies of others or defile the relationship of marriage. Keep your lives free from the lust for money : be content with what you have.

God has said :

> I will in no wise fail thee,
> Neither will I in any wise forsake thee.

We, therefore, can confidently say :

> The Lord is my helper ; I will not fear :
> What shall man do unto me ?

Be loyal to your leaders and, above all, to Christ   XIII : 7

Never forget your leaders, who first spoke to you the Word of God. Remember how they lived, and imitate their faith.

Jesus Christ is always the same, yesterday, to-day and for ever. Do not be swept off your feet by various peculiar teachings. Spiritual stability depends on the grace of God, and not on rules of diet—which after all have not spiritually benefited those who have made a speciality of that kind of thing. We have an Altar from which those who still serve the Tabernacle have no right to eat.

When the blood of animals was presented as a sin-offering by the High Priest in the sanctuary, their bodies were burned outside the precincts of the camp. That is why Jesus, when He sanctified men by the shedding of His own blood, suffered and died outside the city gates. Let us go out to Him, then, beyond the boundaries of the camp, proudly bearing His " disgrace." For we have no permanent city here on earth, we are looking for one in the world to come. Our constant sacrifice to God should be the praise of lips that give thanks to His Name. Yet we should not forget to do good and to share our good things with others, for these too are the sort of sacrifices God will accept.

Obey your rulers and recognise their authority. They are

like men standing guard over your spiritual good, and they have great responsibility. Try to make their work a pleasure and not a burden—by so doing you will help not only them but yourselves.

Personal : our blessing and our greetings   XIII : 18

Pray for us. Our conscience is clear before God, and our great desire is to lead a life that is completely honest. Please pray earnestly, that I may be restored to you the sooner.

Now the God of peace, Who brought back from the dead that great Shepherd of the sheep, our Lord Jesus, by the blood of the Everlasting Agreement, equip you thoroughly for the doing of His Will! May He effect in you everything that pleases Him through Jesus Christ, to Whom be glory for ever and ever.

All I have said, my brothers, I ask you to accept as though it were an appeal in person, although I have compressed it into a short letter.

You will be glad to know that brother Timothy is now at liberty. If he comes here soon, he and I will perhaps visit you together.

Greetings to all your leaders and all your Church members. The Christians of Italy send their greeting.

Grace be with you all.

THE LETTER OF JAMES

AUTHOR. *Quite probably James, brother or step-brother of Jesus. He had a high reputation and was known as " the Just." Paul calls him a Messenger (Galatians 1, 19).*
Some think he was the first bishop of Jerusalem, and he was certainly the head of the church there at Paul's last visit (Acts XXI, 18).

DATE. *Possibly early, about 50, making it the earliest letter of the New Testament. Some suggest a date as late as " after 100." If this is so it cannot be the work of James, who died about 62.*

DESTINATION. *The Displaced Jews, or the "Dispersion," i.e.*
Christian Jews who had been scattered by persecution or force of
circumstance.

THEME. *The teaching closely follows that of Jesus' Sermon on the*
Mount and reads like a collection of short homilies. It deals
particularly with the dangers of an uncontrolled tongue, snobbery,
belief in God unaccompanied by Christian conduct, and trusting in
material prosperity. The emphasis in this letter on behaviour has
sometimes been supposed to contradict Paul's teaching on "justifica-
tion by faith." In fact it does not contradict but complement. Paul
says that a man is "justified" before God not by achievement but
by a real faith : James says that the test of a real faith is whether
it issues in appropriate behaviour.

JAMES, Servant of God and of the Lord Jesus Christ, sends
greeting to the Twelve Dispersed Tribes.

The Christian can even welcome trouble   1 : 2

When all kinds of trials and temptations crowd into your
lives, my brothers, don't resent them as intruders, but welcome them as friends ! Realise that they come to test your
faith and to produce in you the quality of endurance. But let
the process go on until that endurance is fully developed, and
you will find you have become men of mature character with
the right sort of independence. And if, in the process, any
of you does not know how to meet any particular problem he
has only to ask God—Who gives generously to all men without making them feel foolish or guilty—and he may be quite
sure that the necessary wisdom will be given him. But he
must ask in sincere faith without secret doubts as to whether
he really wants God's help or not. The man who trusts God,
but with inward reservations, is like a wave of the sea, carried
forward by the wind one moment and driven back the next.
That sort of man cannot hope to receive anything from God,
and the life of a man of divided loyalty will reveal instability
at every turn.

Rich and poor can be glad—for different reasons ! 1 : 9

The brother who is poor may be glad because God has called him to the true riches. The rich may be glad that God has shown him his spiritual poverty. For the rich man, as such, will wither away as surely as summer flowers. One day the sunrise brings a scorching wind ; the grass withers at once and so do all the flowers—all that lovely sight is destroyed. Just as surely will the rich man and all his expensive ways fall into the blight of decay.

No temptation comes from God, only highest good 1 : 12

The man who patiently endures the temptations and trials that come to him is the truly happy man. For once his testing is complete he will receive the crown of life which the Lord has promised to all who love Him.

A man must not say when he is tempted, " God is tempting me." For God has no dealings with evil, and does not Himself tempt anyone. No, a man's temptation is due to the pull of his own inward desires, which can be enormously attractive. His own desire takes hold of him, and that produces sin. And sin in the long run means death—make no mistake about that, brothers of mine ! But every good endowment that we possess and every complete gift that we have received must come from above, from the Father of all lights, with Whom there is never the slightest variation or shadow of inconsistency. By His own wish He made us His own sons through the word of Truth, that we might be, so to speak, the first specimens of His new creation.

Hear God's Word and put it into practice :
that is real religion 1 : 19

In view of what He has made us then, dear brothers, let every man be quick to listen but slow to use his tongue, and slow to lose his temper. For man's temper is never the means of achieving God's true goodness.

Have done, then, with impurity and every other evil which touches the lives of others, and humbly accept the message that God has sown in your hearts, and which can save your souls. Don't, I beg you, hear the message only, but put it into practice. The man who simply hears and does nothing about it is like a man catching the reflection of his own face in a mirror. He sees himself, it is true, but he goes on with whatever he was doing without the slightest recollection of what sort of person he saw in the mirror. But the man who looks into the perfect mirror of God's Law, the Law of liberty, and makes a habit of so doing, is not the man who sees and forgets. He puts that Law into practice and he wins true happiness.

If anyone appears to be " religious " but cannot control his tongue, he deceives himself and we may be sure that his religion is useless. Religion that is pure and genuine in the sight of God the Father will show itself by such things as visiting orphans and widows in their distress and keeping oneself uncontaminated by the world.

Avoid snobbery : keep the Royal Law   II : I

Don't ever attempt, my brothers, to combine snobbery with faith in our Lord Jesus Christ ! Suppose one man comes into your meeting well dressed and with a gold ring on his finger, and another man, obviously poor, arrives in shabby clothes. If you pay special attention to the well-dressed man by saying, " Please sit here—it's an excellent seat," and say to the poor man, " You stand over there, please, or if you must sit, sit on the floor," doesn't that prove that you are making class-distinctions in your mind, and setting yourselves up to assess a man's quality ?—a very bad thing. For do notice, my brothers, that God chose poor men, whose only wealth was their faith, and made them heirs to the Kingdom promised to those who love Him. And if you behave as I have suggested, it is the poor man that you are insulting. Look around you. Isn't it the rich who are always trying to " boss " you, isn't it the rich who drag you into litigation ? Isn't it usually the rich who blaspheme the glorious Name by which you are known ?

If you obey the Royal Law, expressed by the Scripture, " Thou shalt love thy neighbour as thyself," all is well. But once you allow any invidious distinctions to creep in, you are sinning, you have broken God's Law. Remember that a man who keeps the whole Law but for a single exception is none the less a Law-breaker. The One Who said, " Thou shalt not commit adultery," also said, " Thou shalt do no murder." If you were to keep clear of adultery but were to murder a man you would have become a breaker of God's whole Law.

Anyway, you should speak and act as men who will be judged by the Law of freedom. The man who makes no allowances for others will find none made for him. It is still true that " mercy smiles in the face of judgment."

The relation between faith and action   II : 14

Now what use is it, my brothers, for a man to say he " has faith " if his actions do not correspond with it ? Could that sort of faith save anyone's soul ? If a fellow man or woman has no clothes to wear and nothing to eat, and one of you say, " Good luck to you, I hope you'll keep warm and find enough to eat," and yet give them nothing to meet their physical needs, what on earth is the good of that ? Yet that is exactly what a bare faith without a corresponding life is like—useless and dead. If we only " have faith " a man could easily challenge us by saying, " You say that you have faith and I have merely good actions. Well, all you can do is to show me a faith without corresponding actions, but I can show you by my actions that I have faith as well."

To the man who thinks that faith by itself is enough I feel inclined to say, " So you believe that there is one God ? That's fine. So do all the devils in hell, and shudder in terror ! " For, my dear short-sighted man, can't you see far enough to realise that faith without the right actions is dead and useless ? Think of Abraham, our ancestor. Wasn't it his action which really justified him in God's sight when his faith led him to offer his son Isaac on the altar ? Can't you see that his faith and his actions were, so to speak, partners—that his faith was implemented by his deed ? That is what the Scripture means when it says :

> And Abraham believed God,
> And it was reckoned unto him for righteousness ;
> And he was called the friend of God.

A man is justified before God by what he does as well as by what he believes. Rahab, who was a prostitute and a foreigner, has been quoted as an example of faith, yet surely it was her action that pleased God, when she welcomed Joshua's reconnoitring party and got them safely back by a different route.

Yes, faith without action is as dead as a body without a soul.

The responsibility of a teacher's position   III : I

Don't aim at adding to the number of teachers, my brothers, I beg you! Remember that we who are teachers will be judged by a much higher standard.

The danger of the tongue   III : 2

We all make mistakes in all kinds of ways, but the man who can claim that he never says the wrong thing can consider himself perfect, for if he can control his tongue he can control every other part of his personality! Men control the movements of a large animal like the horse with a tiny bit placed in its mouth. And in the case of ships, for all their size and the momentum they have with a strong wind behind them, a very small rudder controls their course according to the helmsman's wishes. The human tongue is physically small, but what tremendous effects it can boast of! A whole forest can be set ablaze by a tiny spark of fire, and the tongue is as dangerous as any fire with vast potentialities for evil. It can poison the whole body, it can make the whole of life a blazing hell.

Beasts, birds, reptiles and all kinds of sea-creatures can be, and in fact are, tamed by man, but no one can tame the human tongue. It is an evil always liable to break out, and the poison it spreads is deadly. We use the tongue to bless our Father, God, and we use the same tongue to curse our fellowmen, who are all created in God's likeness. Blessing and curses come

out of the same mouth—surely, my brothers, this is the sort
of thing that never ought to happen! Have you ever known
a spring give sweet and bitter water simultaneously? Have
you ever seen a fig-tree with a crop of olives, or seen figs growing on a vine? It is just as impossible for a spring to give fresh
and salt water at the same time.

Real, spiritual, wisdom means
humility, not rivalry   III : 13

Are there some wise and understanding men among you?
Then your lives will be an example of the humility that is
born of true wisdom. But if your heart is full of rivalry and
bitter jealousy, then do not boast of your wisdom—don't
deny the truth that you must recognise in your inmost heart.
You may acquire a certain superficial wisdom, but it does not
come from God—it comes from this world, from your own
lower nature, even from the Devil. For wherever you find
jealousy and rivalry you also find disharmony and all other
kinds of evil. The wisdom that comes from God is first
utterly pure, then peace-loving, gentle, approachable, full of
tolerant thoughts and kindly actions, with no breath of
favouritism or hint of hypocrisy. And the wise are peace-
makers who go on quietly sowing for a harvest of righteousness—in other people and in themselves.

Your jealousies spring from love of
what the world can give   IV : 1

But what about the feuds and struggles that exist among
you—where do you suppose they come from? Can't you see
that they arise from conflicting passions within yourselves?
You crave for something and don't get it, you are jealous and
envious of what others have got and you don't possess it
yourselves. Consequently, in your exasperated frustration
you struggle and fight with one another. You don't get what
you want because you don't ask God for it. And when you
do ask He doesn't give it to you, for you ask in quite the
wrong spirit—you only want to satisfy your own desires.

You are like unfaithful wives, flirting with the glamour of

this world, and never realising that to be the world's lover
means becoming the enemy of God! Anyone who deliberately chooses to love the world is thereby making himself
God's enemy. Do you think what the Scriptures have to say
about this is a mere formality? Or do you imagine that this
spirit of passionate jealousy is the Spirit He has caused to live
in us? No, He gives us grace potent enough to meet this and
every other evil spirit, if we are humble enough to receive it.
That is why He says:

> God resisteth the proud,
> But giveth grace to the humble.

You should be humble, not proud   IV : 7
Be humble then before God. But resist the Devil and you'll
find he'll run away from you. Come close to God and He will
come close to you. Realise that you have sinned and get your
hands clean again. Realise that you have been disloyal and
get your hearts made true once more. As you come close to
God you should be deeply sorry, you should be grieved, you
should even be in tears. Your laughter will have to become
mourning, your high spirits will have to become heartfelt
dejection. You will have to feel very small in the sight of
God before He will set you on your feet once more.

It is for God to judge, not for us   IV : 11
Never pull each other to pieces, my brothers. If you do you
are judging your brother and setting yourself up in the place
of God's Law; you have become in fact a critic of the Law.
Yet if you start to criticise the Law instead of obeying it you
are setting yourself up as judge, and there is only One Judge,
the One Who gave the Law, to Whom belongs absolute
power of life and death. How can you then be so silly as to
imagine that you are your neighbour's judge?

It is still true that man proposes,
but God disposes   IV : 13

Just a moment, now, you who say "We are going to such-and-such a city to-day or to-morrow. We shall stay there a year doing business and make a profit!" How do you know what will happen even to-morrow? What, after all, is your life? It is like a puff of smoke visible for a little while and then dissolving into thin air. Your remarks should be prefaced with, "If it is the Lord's Will, we shall still be alive and will do so-and-so." As it is, you get a certain pride in yourself in planning your future with such confidence. That sort of pride is all wrong.

No doubt you agree with the above in theory. Well, remember that if a man knows what is right and fails to do it, his failure is a real sin.

Riches are going to prove a liability,
not an asset, to the selfish   V : 1

And now, you plutocrats, is the time for you to weep and moan because of the miseries in store for you! Your richest goods are ruined, your hoard of clothes is moth-eaten, your gold and silver are tarnished. Yes, their very tarnish will be the evidence of your wicked hoarding and you will shrink from them as if they were red-hot. You have made a fine pile in these last days, haven't you? But look, here is the pay of the reaper you hired and whom you cheated, and it is shouting out against you! And the cries of the other labourers you swindled are heard by the Lord of Hosts Himself. Yes, you you have had a magnificent time on this earth, and have indulged yourselves to the full. You have picked out just what you wanted like soldiers looting after battle. You have condemned and ruined innocent men in your career, and they have been powerless to stop you.

Ultimate justice will surely come :
be patient meanwhile   V : 7

But be patient, my brothers, as you wait for the Lord to come. Look at the farmer quietly awaiting his precious harvest. See how he has to possess his soul in patience till the land has had the early and late rains. So must you be patient, resting your hearts on the ultimate certainty. The Lord's coming is very near.

Don't make complaints against each other in the meantime, my brothers—you may be the one at fault yourself. The Judge Himself is already at the door.

For our example of the patient endurance of suffering we can take the prophets who have spoken in the Lord's name. Remember that it is usually those who have patiently endured to whom we accord the word " blessed." You have heard of Job's patient endurance and how God dealt with him in the end, and therefore you have seen that the Lord is merciful and full of understanding pity for us men.

Don't emphasise with oaths : speak
the plain truth   V : 12

It is of the highest importance, my brothers, that your speech should be free from oaths (whether they are " by " Heaven or earth or anything else). Your yes should be a plain yes, and your no a plain no, and then you cannot go wrong in the matter.

Prayer is a great weapon   V : 13

If any of you is in trouble let him pray. If anyone is flourishing let him sing praises to God. If anyone is ill he should send for the Church elders. They should pray over him, anointing him with oil in the Lord's name. Believing prayer will save the sick man ; the Lord will restore him and any sins that he has committed will be forgiven. You should get into the habit of admitting your sins to each other, and praying for each other, so that if sickness comes to you you may be healed.

Tremendous power is made available through a good man's earnest prayer. Do you remember Elijah ? He was a man like us but he prayed earnestly that it should not rain. In fact, not a drop fell on the land for three and a half years. Then he prayed again, the heavens gave the rain and the earth sprouted with vegetation as usual.

A concluding hint   V : 19

My brothers, if any of you should wander away from the Truth and another should turn him back on to the right path, then the latter may know that in turning a man back from his wandering course he has rescued a soul from death, and his loving action will " cover a multitude of sins."

JAMES

THE FIRST LETTER OF PETER

AUTHOR. *Peter, one of the original Twelve, writing probably from Rome, symbolically described as " Babylon." It is thought that Silvanus, or Silas, did the actual writing of the letter.*

DATE. *Almost certainly 64.*

DESTINATION. *This letter, like that of James, is addressed to the Christian Jews scattered, by persecution or force of circumstance, to various parts of Asia Minor.*

THEME. *We are here largely concerned with the Christian's attitude towards undeserved suffering, possibly because persecution of Christians was becoming common. It also contains advice to Christian husbands and wives and direction for Christian servants and Christian citizens.*

The passages in III, 18-21, about Christ preaching to " imprisoned spirits," is obscure and many speculations have arisen from it.

PETER, Messenger of Jesus Christ, sends this letter to the exiles of the Dispersed Tribes (in Pontus, Galatia, Cappadocia, Asia and Bithynia), whom God the Father knew and chose long ago to be made holy by His Spirit, that they might obey Jesus Christ and be cleansed by His blood : may you know more and more of God's grace and peace.

Your faith is being tested, but
your future is magnificent   I : 3

Thank God, the God and Father of our Lord Jesus Christ
that in His great mercy we men have been born again into a
life full of hope, through Christ's rising again from the dead !
You can now hope for a perfect inheritance beyond the reach
of change and decay, " reserved " in Heaven for you. And in
the meantime you are guarded by the power of God operating
through your faith, till you enter fully into the salvation
which is all ready for the dénouement of the last day. This
means tremendous joy to you, I know, even though at
present you are temporarily harassed by all kinds of trials and
temptations. This is no accident—it happens to prove your
faith, which is infinitely more valuable than gold, and gold,
as you know, even though it is ultimately perishable, must
be purified by fire. This proving of your faith is planned to
bring you praise and honour and glory in the day when Jesus
Christ reveals Himself. And though you have never seen
Him, yet I know that you love Him. At present you trust
Him without being able to see Him, and even now He brings
you a joy that words cannot express and which has in it a hint
of the glories of Heaven ; and all the time you are receiving
the result of your faith in Him—the salvation of your own
souls. The prophets of old did their utmost to discover and
obtain this salvation. They did not find it, but they prophesied
of this grace that has now come to you. They tried hard to
discover to what time and to what sort of circumstances the
Spirit of Christ working in them was referring. For He foretold the sufferings of Christ and the glories that should follow
them. It was then made clear to them that they were dealing
with matters not meant for themselves, but for you. It is
these very matters which have been made plain to you by
those who preached the Gospel to you by the same Spirit sent
from Heaven—and these are facts to command the interest of
the very angels !

Consider soberly what God has done for you   I : 13

So brace up your minds, and, as men who know what they

L.Y.C.   H are doing, rest the full weight of your hopes on the grace that will be yours when Jesus Christ reveals Himself. Live as obedient children before God. Don't let your character be moulded by the desires of your ignorant days, but be holy in every department of your lives, for the One Who has called you is Himself Holy. The Scripture says:

> Ye shall be holy; for I am Holy.

If you pray to a Father Who judges men by their actions without the slightest favouritism, then you should spend the time of your stay here on earth with reverent fear. For you must realise all the time that you have been " ransomed " from the futile way of living passed on to you by your fathers' traditions, not with some money payment of transient value, but by the costly shedding of blood. The price was in fact the life-blood of Christ, the unblemished and unstained Lamb of Sacrifice. It is true that God chose Him to fulfil this part before the world was founded, but it was for your benefit that He was revealed in these last days—for you who found your faith in God through Christ. And God raised Him from the dead and gave Him unimaginable splendour, so that all your faith and hope might be centred in God.

Let your life match your high calling   I : 22
Now that you have, by obeying the truth, made your souls clean enough for a genuine love of your fellows, see that you do love each other, fervently and from the heart. For you are sons of God now; the live, permanent Word of the living God has given you His own indestructible heredity. It is true that:

> All flesh is as grass,
> And all the glory thereof as the flower of grass.
> The grass withereth, and the flower falleth:
> But the Word of the Lord abideth for ever.

The word referred to, as far as you are concerned, is the message of the Gospel that was preached to you.

Have done, then, with all evil and deceit, all pretence and jealousy and slander. You are babies, new-born in God's family, and you should be crying out for unadulterated spiritual milk to make you grow! And so you will, if you have already tasted the goodness of the Lord.

To change the metaphor, you come to Him, as living stones to the immensely valuable Living Stone (Which men rejected but God chose), to be built up into a spiritual House of God, in which you, like holy priests, can offer those spiritual sacrifices which are acceptable to God by Jesus Christ. There is a passage to this effect in Scripture, and it runs like this :

Behold I lay in Zion a chief corner stone, elect, precious :
And he that believeth on Him shall not be put to shame.

It is to you who believe in Him that He is " precious," but to those who disobey God, it is true that :

The stone which the builders rejected,
The same was made the head of the corner.

And He is, to them,

A stone of stumbling and a rock of offence.

Yes, they stumble at the Word of God for in their hearts they are unwilling to obey it—which makes stumbling a foregone conclusion. But you are God's " chosen generation," His " royal priesthood," His " holy nation," His " peculiar people "—all the old titles of God's People now belong to you. It is for you now to demonstrate the goodness of Him Who has called you out of darkness into His amazing Light. In the past you were not " a people " at all : now you are the People of God. In the past you had no experience of His mercy, but now it is intimately yours.

Your behaviour to the outside world   II : II

I beg you, as those whom I love, who live in this world as strangers and "temporary residents," to keep clear of the desires of your lower natures, for they are always at war with your souls. Your conduct among the surrounding peoples in your different countries should always be good and right, so that although they may in the usual way slander you as evil-doers yet when disasters come, they may glorify God when they see how well you conduct yourselves.

Obey every man-made authority for the Lord's sake—whether it is the Emperor, as the supreme ruler, or the Governors whom he has appointed to punish evil-doers and reward those who do good service. It is the Will of God that you may thus silence the ill-informed criticism of the foolish. As free men you should never use your freedom as an excuse for doing something that is wrong, for you are at all times the servants of God. You should have respect for everyone, you should love our brotherhood, fear God and honour the Emperor.

A word to household servants   II : 18

You who are servants should submit to your masters with proper respect—not only to the good and kind, but also to the difficult. A man does something valuable when he endures pain, as in the sight of God, though he knows he is suffering unjustly. After all, it is no credit to you if you are patient in bearing a punishment which you have richly deserved ! But if you do your duty and are punished for it and can still accept it patiently, you are doing something worthwhile in God's sight. Indeed this is part of your calling. For Christ suffered for you and left you a personal Example, and wants you to follow in His steps. He was guilty of no sin or the slightest prevarication. Yet when He was insulted He offered no insult in return. When He suffered He made no threats of revenge. He simply committed His cause to the One Who judges fairly. And He personally bore our sins in His own body on the Cross, so that we might be dead to sin and be alive for all that is good. It was the suffering that He bore which has healed you. You had wandered away like so many sheep, but now you have returned to the Shepherd and Guardian of your souls.

A word to married Christians   III : I

In the same spirit you married women should adapt your-selves to your husbands, so that even if they do not obey the Word of God they may be won to God without any word being spoken, simply by seeing the pure and reverent behaviour of you, their wives. Your beauty should not be dependent on an elaborate coiffure, or on the wearing of jewellery or fine clothes, but on the inner personality—the unfading loveliness of a calm and gentle spirit, a thing very precious in the eyes of God. This was the secret of the beauty of the holy women of ancient times who trusted in God and were submissive to their husbands. Sara, you will remember, obeyed Abraham and called him her lord. And you have become, as it were, her true descendants to-day as long as you too live good lives and do not give way to hysterical fears.

Similarly, you husbands should try to understand the wives you live with, honouring them as physically weaker yet equally heirs with you of the grace of eternal life. If you don't do this, you will find it impossible to pray properly.

Be good to each other—and to all men   III : 8

To sum up, you should all be of one mind living like brothers with true love and sympathy for each other, generous and courteous at all times. Never pay back a bad turn with a bad turn or an insult with another insult, but on the contrary pay back with good. For this is your calling—to do good and one day to inherit all the goodness of God. For :

> He that would love life,
> And see good days,
> Let him refrain his tongue from evil,
> And his lips that they speak no guile :
> And let him turn away from evil, and do good ;
> Let him seek peace and pursue it.

> For the eyes of the Lord are upon the righteous,
> And his ears unto their supplication :
> But the face of the Lord is against them that do evil.

Do good, even if you suffer for it   III : 13

After all, who in the ordinary way is likely to injure you for being enthusiastic for good ? And if it should happen that you suffer " for righteousness' sake," that is a privilege. You need neither fear their threats nor worry about them ; simply concentrate on being completely devoted to Christ in your hearts. Be ready at any time to give a quiet and reverent answer to any man who wants a reason for the hope that you have within you. Make sure that your conscience is perfectly clear, so that if men should speak slanderously of you as rogues they may come to feel ashamed of themselves for libelling your good Christian behaviour.

If it is the Will of God that you should suffer it is really better to suffer unjustly than because you have deserved it. Remember that Christ the just suffered for us the unjust, to bring us to God. That meant the death of His body, but He came to life again in the Spirit. It was in the Spirit that He went and preached to the imprisoned souls of those who had been disobedient in the days of Noah—the days of God's great patience during the periods of the building of the ark, in which eventually only eight souls were saved in the Flood. And I cannot help pointing out what a perfect illustration this is of the way you have been admitted to the safety of the Christian " ark " by baptism, which means, of course, far more than the mere washing of a dirty body : it means the ability to face God with a clear conscience. For there is in every true baptism the virtue of Christ's rising from the dead. And He has now entered Heaven and is at God's right hand, with all angels, authorities and powers subservient to Him.

Following Christ will mean pain   IV : 1

Since Christ had to suffer physically for you, you must fortify yourselves with the same inner attitude that He must have had. You must realise that to be dead to sin inevitably means pain, and you should not therefore spend the rest of your time here on earth indulging your physical nature, but in doing the will of God. Our past life may have been good enough for pagan purposes, though it meant sensuality, lust, drunkenness, orgies, carousals and worshipping forbidden gods. Indeed your former companions may think it very queer that you will no longer join with them in their riotous excesses, and accordingly say all sorts of unpleasant things about you. Don't worry : they are the ones who will have to explain their behaviour before the One Who is prepared to judge all men, whether living or dead. (For that is why the dead also had the Gospel preached to them—that it might judge the lives they lived as men and give them also the opportunity to share the eternal life of God in the spirit.)

Your attitude in these last days   IV : 7

We are near the end of all things now, and you should therefore be calm, self-controlled men of prayer. Above everything else be sure that you have real deep love for each other, remembering how love can " cover a multitude of sins." Be hospitable to each other without secretly wishing you hadn't got to be ! Serve one another with the particular gifts God has given each of you, as faithful dispensers of the magnificently varied grace of God. If any of you is a preacher then he should preach his message as from God. And in whatever way a man serves the Church he should do it recognising the fact that God gives him his ability, so that God may be glorified in everything through Jesus Christ. To Him belong praise and power for ever, Amen !

Your attitude to persecution   IV : 12

And now, dear friends of mine, I beg you not to be unduly alarmed at the fiery ordeals which come to test your faith, as though this were some abnormal experience. You should be glad, because it means that you are called to share Christ's sufferings. One day, when He shows Himself in full splendour to men, you will be filled with the most tremendous joy. If you are reproached for being Christ's followers, that is a great privilege, for you can be sure that God's Spirit of glory, unseen by you, is resting upon you. But take care that none of your number suffers as a murderer, or a thief, a rogue or a spy! If he suffers as a Christian he has nothing to be ashamed of and may glorify God in Christ's Name.

The time has evidently arrived for God's judgment to begin, and it is beginning at His own House. And if it starts with us, what is it going to mean to those who refuse to obey the Gospel of God? If even the good man is only just saved, what will be the fate of the wicked and the sinner? And if it is true that we are living in a time of judgment, then those who suffer according to God's Will can only commit their souls to their faithful Creator, and go on doing all the good they can.

A word to your leaders v : 1

Now may I who am myself an elder say a word to you my fellow-elders? I speak as one who actually saw Christ suffer, and as one who will share with you the glories that are to be unfolded to us. I urge you then to see that your "flock of God" is properly fed and cared for. Accept the responsibility of looking after them willingly and not because you feel you can't get out of it, doing your work not for what you can make, but because you are really concerned for their well-being. You should aim not at being "little tin gods" but as examples of Christian living in the eyes of the flock committed to your charge. And then, when the Chief Shepherd reveals Himself, you will receive that crown of glory which cannot fade.

Learn to be humble and to trust v : 5

You younger members must also submit to the elders. Indeed all of you should defer to one another and wear the "overall" of humility in serving each other. God is always against the proud, but He is always ready to give grace to the humble. So, humble yourselves under God's strong Hand, and in His own good time He will lift you up. You can rest the weight of all your anxieties upon Him, for you are always in His care.

Resist the Devil : you are in God's hands   V : 8

Be self-controlled and vigilant always, for your enemy the
Devil is always about, prowling like a lion roaring for its prey.
Resist him, standing firm in your faith and remember that the
strain is the same for all your fellow-Christians in other parts
of the world. And after you have borne these sufferings a
very little while, God Himself (from Whom we receive all
grace and Who has called you to share His Eternal Splendour
through Christ) will make you whole and secure and strong.
All power is His for ever and ever, Amen !

Final greetings   V : 12

I am sending this short letter by Silvanus, whom I know to
be a faithful brother, to stimulate your faith and assure you
that the above words represent the true grace of God. See
that you stand fast in that grace !

Your sister-Church here in " Babylon " sends you greetings,
and so does my son Mark. Give each other a handshake all
round as a sign of love.

Peace be to all true Christians.

                                                            PETER

THE SECOND LETTER OF PETER

AUTHOR. *The authenticity of this letter was sharply disputed by the
early Church, and it is still viewed with suspicion by many. This is
partly because one section appears to be copied from the letter of
Jude, partly because the general character is different from the first
letter of Peter, and partly because competent scholars consider there
are references in it to events which happened after Peter's death in
approximately 64. It is, of course, possible that we have here parts
of a genuine letter of Peter with considerable later additions.*

DATE. *About 130 ? (very uncertain.)*

DESTINATION. *A particular, but unknown, Church.*

THEME. *The letter stresses the observed facts upon which the*

Christian faith rests. It contains a stern warning and violent attack against false teachers, and a reminder that Christ will certainly return in Person, even though His coming appears to men to be long delayed.

SIMON PETER, servant and Messenger of Jesus Christ, sends this letter to those who have been given a faith as valuable as ours in the righteousness of our God, and Saviour Jesus Christ. May you know more and more of grace and peace as your knowledge of God and Jesus our Lord grows deeper.

God has done His part : see that you do yours   1 : 3

He has by His own action given us everything that is necessary for living the truly good life, in allowing us to know the One Who has called us to virtue and glory. It is through Him that God's greatest and most precious promises have become available to us men, making it possible for you to escape the inevitable disintegration that lust produces in the world and to share God's essential nature. For this very reason you must do your utmost from your side, and see that your faith carries with it real goodness of life. Your goodness must be accompanied by knowledge, your knowledge by self-control, your self-control by the ability to endure. Your endurance too must always be accompanied by a real trust in God ; that in turn must have in it the quality of brotherliness, and your brotherliness must lead on to Christian love. If you have these qualities existing and growing in you then it means that knowing our Lord Jesus Christ has not made your lives either complacent or unproductive. The man whose life fails to exhibit these qualities is short-sighted —he can no longer see the reason why he was cleansed from his former sins.

Set your minds, then, on endorsing by your conduct the fact that God has called and chosen you. If you go along the lines I have indicated above, there is no reason why you should stumble, and if you have lived the sort of life I have recommended God will open wide to you the gates of the eternal Kingdom of our Lord and Saviour Jesus Christ.

Truth will bear repetition   1 : 12

I shall not fail to remind you of things like this although you know them and are already established in the truth. I consider it my duty, as long as I live in the temporary dwelling of this body, to stimulate you by these reminders. I know that I shall have to leave this body at very short notice, as our Lord Jesus Christ made clear to me. Consequently I shall make the most of every opportunity, so that after I am gone you will remember these things.

We were not following a cleverly written-up story when we told you about the power and eventual coming of our Lord Jesus Christ—we actually saw His majesty with our own eyes. He received honour and glory from God the Father Himself when that Voice said to Him, out of the sublime glory of Heaven, "This is my beloved Son, in Whom I am well pleased." We actually heard that Voice speaking from Heaven while we were with Him on the sacred mountain. The word of prophecy was fulfilled in our hearing ! You should give that word your closest attention, for it shines like a lamp amidst all the dirt and darkness of the world, until the Day dawns, and the Morning Star rises in your hearts.

False prophets will flourish, but
only for a time   1 : 20

But you must understand this at the outset, that no prophecy of scripture arose from an individual's interpretation of the truth. No prophecy came because a man wanted it to : men of God spoke because they were inspired by the Holy Spirit. But even in those days there were false prophets, just as there will be false teachers among you to-day. They will be men who will subtly introduce dangerous heresies. They will thereby deny the Lord Who redeemed them, and it will not be long before they bring on themselves their own downfall. Many will follow their pernicious teaching and thereby bring discredit on the way of truth. In their lust to make converts these men will try to exploit you too with their bogus arguments. But judgment has been for some time hard on their heels and their downfall is inevitable. For if God did not spare angels who sinned against Him, but banished them to the dark imprisonment of Hell till Judgment Day : if He did not spare the ancient world but only saved Noah (the solitary voice that cried out for righteousness) and his seven companions, when He brought the Flood upon the world in its wickedness ; and if God reduced the entire cities of Sodom and Gomorrah to ashes (when He sentenced them to destruction as a fearful example to those who wanted to live in defiance of His laws), and yet saved Lot the righteous man, in acute mental distress at the filthy lives of the godless—Lot, remember, was a good man suffering spiritual agonies day after day at what he saw and heard of their lawlessness—then you may be absolutely certain that the Lord knows how to rescue a good man surrounded by temptation, and how to reserve His punishment for the wicked until His day comes.

Let me show you what these men are really like   II : 10
His judgment is chiefly reserved for those who have indulged all the foulness of their lower natures, and have nothing but contempt for authority. These men are arrogant and presumptuous—they think nothing of scoffing at the glories of the unseen world. Yet even angels, who are their superiors in strength and power, do not bring insulting criticism of such things before God.

But these men, with no more sense than the unreasoning brute beasts which are born to be caught and killed, scoff at things outside their own experience, and will most certainly be destroyed in their own corruption. Their wickedness has earned them an evil end and they will be paid in full.

These are the men who delight in daylight self-indulgence ; they are foul spots and blots, playing their tricks at your very dinner-tables. Their eyes cannot look at a woman without lust, they captivate the unstable ones, and their technique of getting what they want is, through long practice, highly developed. They are born under a curse, for they have abandoned the right road and wandered off to follow the old trail of Balaam, son of Beor, the man who had no objection to wickedness as long as he was paid for it. But he, you remember, was sharply reprimanded for his wickedness—by a donkey, of all things, speaking with a human voice to check the prophet's wicked infatuation!

These men are like wells without a drop of water in them, like the changing shapes of whirling storm-clouds, and their fate will be the black night of utter darkness. With their high-sounding nonsense they use the sensual pull of the lower passions to attract those who were just on the point of cutting loose from their companions in misconduct. They promise them liberty. Liberty!—when they themselves are bound hand and foot to utter depravity. For a man is the slave of whatever masters him. If men have escaped from the world's contaminations through knowing our Lord and Saviour, Jesus Christ, and then become entangled and defeated all over again, their last position is far worse than their first. It would be better for them not to have known the way of goodness at all, rather than after knowing it to turn their backs on the sacred commandments given to them. Alas, for them, the old proverbs have come true about the " dog returning to his vomit," and " the sow that had been washed going back to wallow in the muck."

God delays the last day, in His Mercy　　　　　III : 1

This is the second letter I have written to you, dear friends of mine, and in both of them I have tried to stimulate you, as men with minds uncontaminated by error, by simply reminding you of what you really know already. For I want you to remember the words spoken of old by the holy prophets as well as the commands of our Lord and Saviour Jesus Christ, given to you through His Messengers.

You should never forget that in the last days mockers will undoubtedly come—men whose only guide in life is what they want for themselves—and they will say, " What has happened to His promised Coming ? Since the first Christians fell asleep, everything remains exactly as it was since the beginning of creation!" They are deliberately shutting their eyes to a fact that they know very well, that there were, by God's command, heavens in the old days and an earth formed out of the water and surrounded by water. It was by water that the world of those days was deluged and destroyed, but the present heavens and earth are, also by God's command, being carefully kept and maintained for the fire of the Day of Judgment and the destruction of wicked men.

But you should never lose sight of this fact, dear friends, that time is not the same with the Lord as it is with us—to Him a day may be a thousand years, and a thousand years only a day. It is not that He is dilatory about keeping His own Promise as some men seem to think; the fact is that He is very patient towards you. He has no wish that any man should be destroyed: He wishes that all men should come to repent. Yet it remains true that the Day of the Lord will come as suddenly and unexpectedly as a thief. In that Day the heavens will disappear in a terrific tearing blast, the very elements will disintegrate in heat and the earth and all that is in it will be burnt up to nothing.

Never lose sight of the eternal world

III : 11

In view of the fact that all these things are to be dissolved, what sort of people ought you to be? Surely men of good and holy character, who live expecting and earnestly longing for the coming of the Day of God. True, this Day will mean that the heavens will disappear in fire and the elements disintegrate in fearful heat, but our hopes are set not on these but on the new heavens and the new Earth which He has promised us, and in which nothing but good shall live.

Because, my dear friends, you have a hope like this before you, I urge you to make certain that such a Day would find you at peace with God and man, clean and blameless in His sight. Meanwhile, consider that God's patience is meant to be man's salvation, as our dear brother Paul pointed out in his letter to you, written out of the wisdom God gave him. In that letter, as indeed in all his letters, he referred to these matters. There are, of course, some things in his letters which are difficult to understand, and which, unhappily, ill-informed and unbalanced people distort (as they do the other scriptures), and bring disaster on their own heads.

But you, my friends whom I love, are forewarned, and should therefore be very careful not to be carried away by the errors of wicked men and so lose your proper foothold. On the contrary, you should grow in grace and in your knowledge of our Lord and Saviour Jesus Christ—to Him be glory now and until the dawning of the Day of Eternity!

THE FIRST LETTER OF JOHN

AUTHOR. *John, one of the original Twelve, or John the Elder, a close companion of his. It is believed that he wrote it from Ephesus, when a very old man.*

DATE. *Uncertain, possibly about 90.*

DESTINATION. *Augustine refers to this letter as " The Epistle of John to the Parthians," but there is no other evidence of a Church in what would now be called Persia or Iran. Many scholars think that this letter is addressed to the local churches round about Ephesus.*

THEME. *This letter emphasises the fact that Christ really did become man, and did not merely " appear " to be human as the heresy of " docetism " maintained. It speaks in the strongest possible language of men being able to live " in " God, and of the fact of God being " in " those who believe in Him. God is Light and Love and Life.*

WE are writing to you about something which has always existed yet which we ourselves actually saw and heard: something which we had opportunity to observe closely and even to hold in our hands, and yet, as we know now, was something of the very Word of Life Himself! For it was *Life* which appeared before us: we saw it, we are eye-witnesses of it, and are now writing to you about it. It was the very Life of all Ages, the Life that has always existed with God the Father, which actually became visible in Person to us mortal men. We repeat, we really saw and heard what we are now writing to you about. We want you to be with us in this—in this fellowship with God the Father, and Jesus Christ his Son. We must write and tell you about it, because the more that fellowship extends the greater the joy it brings to us who are already in it.

Experience of living " in the Light "   1 : 5

Here, then, is the message we heard Him give: GOD IS LIGHT, and not the faintest shadow of darkness can exist in Him. Consequently, if we were to say that we enjoyed fellowship with Him and still went on living in darkness, we should be both telling and living a lie. But if we really are living in the same light in which He eternally exists, then we have true fellowship with each other, and the blood which He shed for us keeps us clean from any and every sin. If we are silly enough to refuse to admit that we are sinners, then we live in a world of illusion and truth becomes a stranger to us. But if we freely admit that we have sinned, we find God utterly reliable and straightforward—He forgives our sins and makes us thoroughly clean from all that is evil. For if we take up the attitude, " we have not sinned," we flatly deny God's diagnosis of our conditions and cut ourselves off from what He has to say to us.

Love and obedience are essentials
for living in the Light   II : I

I write these things to you (may I call you " my children "— for that's how I think of you), to help you to avoid sin. But if a man should sin, remember that our Advocate before God is Jesus Christ the Righteous, the One Who made personal atonement for our sins (and for those of the rest of the world as well). It is only when we obey God's laws that we can be quite sure that we really know Him. The man who claims to know God but does not obey His laws is not only a liar, but

lives in self-delusion. In practice, the more a man learns to
obey God's laws the more truly and fully does he express his
love for Him. Obedience is the test of whether we really live
" in God " or not. The life of a man who professes to be
living in God must bear the stamp of Christ.

I am not really writing to tell you of any new command,
brothers of mine. It is just the old, original command. You
may think that the original message is old, and yet as I give it
to you again I know that it is always new and always true—in
your life as it was in His. For the darkness is beginning to lift
and the true Light is now shining in the world. Anyone who
claims to be " in the light " and hates his brothers is, in fact,
still in complete darkness. The man who loves his brother
lives and moves in the light, and has no reason to stumble.
But the man who hates his brother is shut off from the light
and gropes his way in the dark without seeing where he is
going. To move in the dark is to move blindfold.

As I write I visualise you, my children   II : 12

I write this letter to you all, as my dear children, because
your sins are forgiven for Christ's Name's sake. I write to
you who are now fathers, because you have known Him Who
has always existed. And to your vigorous young men I am
writing because you have been strong in defeating the Evil
One. Yes, I have written these lines to you all, dear children,
because you know the Father ; to you fathers because of your
experience of the One Who has always existed, and to you
young men because you have all the vigour of youth, because
you have a hold on God's truth and because you have defeated
the Evil One.

See the " world " for what it is   II : 15

Never give your hearts to this world or to any of the things
in it. A man cannot love the Father and love the world at the
same time. For the whole world-system, based as it is on men's
primitive desires, their greedy ambitions and the glamour of
all that they think splendid, is not derived from the Father at
all, but from the world itself. The world and all its passionate

desires will one day disappear. But the man who is following God's Will is part of the Permanent and cannot die.

Little anti-christs are abroad already   II : 18

Even now, dear children, we are getting near the end of things. You have heard, I expect, the prophecy about the coming of anti-Christ. Believe me, there are anti-christs about already, which confirms my belief that we are near the end. These men went out from our company, it is true, but they never really belonged to it. If they had really belonged to us they would have stayed. In fact, their going proves beyond doubt that men like that were not " our men " at all.

Be on your guard against error   II : 20

God has given you a certain amount of spiritual insight, and indeed I have not written this warning as if I were writing to men who don't know what error is. I write because your eyes are clear enough to discern a lie when you come across it. And what, I ask you, is the crowning Lie ? Surely the denial that Jesus is God's Anointed One, His Christ. I say, therefore, that any man who refuses to acknowledge the Father and the Son is an anti-christ. The man who will not recognise the Son cannot possibly know the Father ; yet the man who believes in the Son will find that he knows the Father as well.

For yourselves I beg you to stick to the original teaching. If you do, you will be living in fellowship with both the Father and the Son. And that means sharing His own Life for ever, as He has promised.

It is true that I felt I had to write the above about men who would dearly love to lead you astray. Yet I know that the touch of His Spirit never leaves you, and you don't really need a human teacher. You know that the Spirit teaches you in everything. Remember that His teaching urges you to live " in Christ." So that if He were suddenly to reveal Himself we should still know exactly where we stand, and should not have to shrink away from His Presence.

What it means to be sons of God   II : 29

You all know that God is really Good. You may be just as sure that the man who leads a really good life is a true child of God.

Consider the incredible love that the Father has shown us in allowing us to be called " children of God "—and that is not just what we are called, but what we *are*. Our heredity on the God-ward side is no mere figure of speech—which explains why the world will no more recognise us than it recognised Christ.

Oh, dear children of mine (forgive the affection of an old man !), have you realised it ? Here and now we *are* God's children. We don't know what we shall become in the future. We only know that, if reality were to break through, we should reflect His likeness, for we should see Him as He really is !

Everyone who has at heart a hope like that keeps himself pure, for he knows how pure Christ is.

Conduct will show who is a man's spiritual father   III : 4

Everyone who commits sin breaks God's law, for that is what sin is, by definition—a breaking of God's law. You know, moreover, that Christ became Man for the purpose of removing sin, and that He Himself was quite free from sin. The man who lives " in Christ " does not habitually sin. The regular sinner has never seen or known Him. You, my children, are younger than I am, and I don't want you to be taken in by any clever talk just here. The man who lives a consistently good life is a good man, as surely as God is good. But the man whose life is habitually sinful is spiritually a son of the Devil, for the Devil is behind all sin, as he always has been. Now the Son of God came to earth with the express purpose of liquidating the Devil's activities. The man who is really God's son does not practise sin, for God's nature is in him, for good, and such a heredity is incapable of sin.

Here we have a clear indication as to who are the children of God and who are the children of the Devil. The man who does not lead a good life is no son of God, and neither is the man who fails to love his brother. For the basic command, as you know, is that we should love one another. We are none of us to have the spirit of Cain, who was a son of the Devil and murdered his brother. Have you realised his motive? It was just because he realised the goodness of his brother's life and the rottenness of his own. Don't be surprised, therefore, if the world hates you.

Love and life are inter-connected   III : 14

We know that we have crossed the frontier from death to life because we do love our brothers. The man without love for his brother is living in death already. The man who actively hates his brother is a potential murderer, and you will readily see that the eternal Life of God cannot live in the heart of a murderer.

We know and, to some extent realise, the love of God for us because Christ expressed it in laying down His life for us. We must in turn express our love by laying down our lives for those who are our brothers. But as for the well-to-do man who sees his brother in want but shuts his eyes—and his heart—how could anyone believe that the love of God lives in him? My children, let us love not merely in theory or in words—let us love in sincerity and in practice!

Living in love means confidence in God   III : 19

If we live like this, we shall know that we are children of the truth and can reassure ourselves in the sight of God, even if our own hearts make us feel guilty. For God is infinitely greater than our hearts, and He knows everything. And if, dear friends of mine, when we realise this our hearts should stop their accusation, we may have the utmost confidence in God's presence. We receive whatever we ask for, because we are obeying His orders and following His plans. His orders are that we should put our trust in the Name of His Son, Jesus Christ, and love one another—as we used to hear Him say in person.

The man who does obey God's commands lives in God and

God lives in him, and the guarantee of His presence within us is the Spirit He has given us.

I repeat my warning against false teaching IV : 1

Don't trust every spirit, dear friends of mine, but test them to discover whether they come from God or not. For the world is full of false prophets. You can test them in this simple way : every spirit that acknowledges the fact that Jesus, God's Christ, actually became Man, comes from God, but the spirit which denies this fact does not come from God. The latter comes from the anti-Christ, which you were warned would come and which is already in the world.

You, my children, who belong to God have already defeated this spirit, because the One Who lives in you is far stronger than the anti-Christ in the world. The agents of the anti-Christ are children of the world, they speak the world's language and the world, of course, pays attention to what they say. We are God's children and only the man who knows God hears our message ; what we say means nothing to the man who is not himself a child of God. This gives us a ready means of distinguishing the true from the false.

Let us love : God has shown us love at its highest IV : 7

To you whom I love I say, let us go on loving one another, for love comes from God. Every man who truly loves is God's son and has some knowledge of Him. But the man who does not love cannot know Him at all, for God is love.

To us, the greatest demonstration of God's love for us has been His sending His only Son into the world to give us Life through Him. We see real love, not in the fact that we loved God, but that He loved us and sent His Son to make personal atonement for our sins. If God loved us as much as that, surely we, in our turn, should love each other !

It is true that no human being has ever had a direct vision of God. Yet if we love each other God does actually live within us, and His love grows in us towards perfection. And, as I wrote above, the guarantee of our living in Him and His living in us is the share of His own Spirit which He gives us.

Knowing Christ means more love and
confidence, less and less fear   IV : 14

We ourselves are eye-witnesses able and willing to testify to
the fact that God did send the Son to save the world. Everyone who acknowledges that Jesus is the Son of God finds that
God lives in Him, and he lives in God. So have we come to
know and trust the love God has for us. God *is* love, and the
man whose life is lived in love does, in fact, live in God, and
God does, in fact, live in him. So our love for Him grows
more and more, filling us with complete confidence for the
Day when He shall judge all men—for we realise that our life
in this world is actually His life lived in us. Love contains no
fear—indeed fully-developed love expels every particle of fear,
for fear always contains some of the torture of feeling guilty.
This means that the man who lives in fear has not yet had his
love perfected.

Yes, we love Him because He first loved us. If a man says,
"I love God" and hates his brother, he is a liar. For if he
does not love the brother before his eyes how can he love the
One beyond his sight? And in any case it is His explicit command that the one who loves God must love his brother too.

Only real faith in Christ as God's Son can make
a man confident, obedient and loving   V : 1

Everyone who really believes that Jesus is God's Christ
proves himself one of God's family. The man who loves the
Father cannot help loving the Father's own Son.

The test of the genuineness of our love for God's family lies
in this question—do we love God Himself and do we obey
His commands? And honestly, these commands of His are
not burdensome, for God's "heredity" within us will always
conquer the world outside us. In fact, this faith of ours is the
only way in which the world has been conquered. For who
could ever be said to conquer the world, in the true sense,
except the man who really believes that the Jesus who entered
the world is God's Son? Jesus Christ came with the double
sign of water and blood—the water of His Baptism as Man
and the blood of the atonement that He made by His death.

It is a mistake to think of Him as only the perfect Man—He made the perfect Atonement as well. The Spirit within us endorses this as true (as might be expected when we remember that He is the Spirit of truth). The witness therefore is a triple one—the Spirit in our own hearts, the signs of the water of baptism and the blood of atonement—and they all say the same thing about Jesus, that He is God's Christ. If we are prepared to accept human testimony, God's own testimony concerning His own Son is surely infinitely more valuable. The man who really believes in the Son of God will find God's testimony in his own heart. The man who will not believe God is making Him out to be a liar, because he is deliberately refusing to accept the testimony concerning His own Son that God is prepared to give him. This is, that God has given men eternal life and this real life is to be found only in His Son. It follows naturally that any man who has genuine contact with Christ has this life ; and if he has not, then he does not possess this life at all.

I have written like this to you who already believe in the Name of God's Son so that you may be quite sure that, here and now, you possess eternal life. We have such confidence in Him that we are certain that He hears every request that is made in accord with His own Plan. And since we know that He invariably gives His attention to our prayers, whatever they are about, we can be quite sure that our prayers will be answered.

Help each other to live without sin   v : 16

If any of you should see his brother committing a sin (I don't mean deliberately turning his back on God and embracing evil), he should pray to God for him and secure fresh life for the sinner. It is possible to commit sin that is a deliberate embracing of evil and that leads to spiritual death—that is not the sort of sin I have in mind when I recommend prayer for the sinner. Every failure to obey God's laws is sin, of course, but there is sin that does not preclude repentance and forgiveness.

Our certain knowledge   V : 18

We know that the true child of God does not sin, he is in the charge of God's own Son and the evil one must keep his distance.

We know that we ourselves are children of God, and we also know that the world around us is under the power of the evil one. We know too that the Son of God has actually come to this world, and has shown us the way to know the One Who is True. We know that our real life is in the True One, and in His Son Jesus Christ. This is the Real God and this is Real, Eternal Life.

But be on your guard, my dear children, against every false god!

JOHN

THE SECOND LETTER OF JOHN

AUTHOR. *Although the author calls himself simply " the Elder " there is no real reason to suppose that he is not the same person as the author of the first letter. An old "retired apostle " might in his humility call himself by such a title.*

DATE. *Uncertain, possibly 90.*

DESTINATION. *Either a Christian lady and her family, or a church and its members. Nobody now knows which.*

THEME. *This brief letter expresses the writer's joy at the true faith exhibited by some members of the family he has met. He urges them to continue in Christian love and to set their faces sternly against teachers of a false Christianity.*

THIS letter comes from the Elder to a certain Christian lady and her children, held in the highest affection not only by me but by all who know the Truth. For that Truth's sake (which even now we know and which will be our companion for ever) I wish you, in all love and sincerity, grace, mercy and peace from God the Father and the Lord Jesus Christ, the Father's Son.

Let us love, but have no dealings with lies   4

I was overjoyed to find some of your children living the life of truth, as the Father Himself instructed us. I beg you now, dear lady, not as though I were issuing any new order but simply reminding you of the original one, to see that we continue to love one another. Real love means obeying the Father's orders, and you have known from the beginning that you must live in obedience to Him. For the world is becoming full of impostors—men who will not admit that Jesus the Christ really became man. Now this is the very spirit of deceit and is anti-Christ. Take care of yourselves ; don't throw away all the labour that has been spent on you, but persevere till God gives you your reward.

Have nothing to do with false teachers   9

The man who is so " advanced " that he is not content with what Christ taught, has in fact no God. The man who bases his life on Christ's teaching, however, has both the Father and the Son as his God. If any teacher comes to you who is disloyal to what Christ taught, don't have him inside your house. Don't even wish him " God-speed," unless you want to share in the evil that he is doing.

Personal   12

I have a lot that I could write to you, but somehow I find it hard to put down on paper. I hope to come and see you personally, and we will have a long talk together—and how we shall enjoy that ! You sister's children send their love.

JOHN

THE THIRD LETTER OF JOHN

AUTHOR. *The same author as the Second Letter of John.*

DATE. *Uncertain, possibly about 90.*

DESTINATION. *The letter is addressed personally to Gaius, possibly the leader of a small church in Asia Minor. Gaius was such a common name that it is impossible to say whether the reference is to any of those of that name mentioned elsewhere in the New Testament.*

THEME. *The letter deals with the Christian duty and privilege of entertaining those who are busy carrying the Gospel from place to place. It roundly condemns the conceited behaviour of Diotrephes, and commends the excellent character of Demetrius.*

The Elder sends this letter to his very dear friend Gaius with sincere love.

I thank God for you and pray for you 2

My heartfelt prayer for you, my very dear friend, is that you may be as healthy and prosperous in every way as you are in soul. I was delighted when the brothers arrived and spoke so highly of the sincerity of your life—obviously you are living in the Truth. Nothing brings me greater joy nowadays than hearing that " my children " are living " in the Truth."

Your actions have been just right 5

You are doing a fine faithful piece of work, dear friend, in looking after the brothers who come your way, especially as you have never seen them before. It is a fine thing to help them on their way—it shows you realise the importance of what they are doing. They set out on this work, as you know, for the sake of " the Name " and they accept no help from

non-Christians. We ought to give such men a real welcome
and prove that we too are co-operating with the Truth.

I know about Diotrephes   9
I did write a letter to the Church, but Diotrephes, who
wants to be head of everything, does not recognise us ! If I do
come to you, I shall not forget his actions nor the slanderous
things he has said against us. And it doesn't stop there, alas,
for although he wants to be leader he refuses the duty of
welcoming the brothers himself, and stops those who would
like to do so—he even excommunicates them !

A little piece of advice : and I shall
soon be seeing you personally   11
Never let evil be your example, dear friend of mine, but
always good. The man who does good is God's man, but the
man who does evil does not know God at all.

Everyone has a good word to say for Demetrius, and the
very Truth speaks well of him. He has our warm recommendation also, and you know you can trust what we say about
anyone.

There is a great deal I want to say to you but I can't put it
down in black and white. I hope to see you before long, and
we will have a heart-to-heart talk. Peace be with you. All our
friends here send love : please give ours personally to all our
friends at your end.

JOHN

THE LETTER OF JUDE

AUTHOR. *It may still reasonably be held that this letter was written
by Jude (Judas), the brother or step-brother of Jesus. Like his
brother James, he did not believe in the divinity of Jesus until after
the Resurrection.*

DATE. *Between 70 and 80, or possibly as late as 2nd century.*

DESTINATION. *Some unknown church, where false teaching was prevalent, or possibly for general circulation.*

THEME. *This letter is almost entirely a terrific condemnation of false teachers, with scathing comparisons with evil characters in the Old Testament. It concludes with an exhortation to loyalty to the truth, and with the well-known " doxology."*

JUDE, the servant of Jesus Christ and brother of James, to those who have obeyed the Call, who are loved by God the Father and kept in the faith by Jesus Christ—may you ever experience more and more of mercy, peace and love !

The reason for this letter   3

I fully intended, dear friends, to write to you about our common salvation, but I feel compelled to make my letter to you an earnest appeal to put up a real fight for the faith which has been once and for all committed to those who belong to Christ. For there are men who have surreptitiously entered the Church but who have for a long time been heading straight for the condemnation I shall plainly give them. They have no real reverence for God, and they abuse His grace as an opportunity for immorality. They will not recognise the only Master, Jesus Christ our Lord.

Past history warns us that the unfaithful
have mingled with the faithful   5

I want to remind you of something that you really know already : that although the Lord saved all the people from the land of Egypt, yet afterwards He brought to their downfall those who would not trust Him. And the very angels who failed in their high duties and abandoned their proper sphere have been deprived by God of both light and liberty until the judgment of the Great Day. Sodom and Gomorrah and the adjacent cities who, in the same way as these men to-day, gave themselves up to sexual immorality and perversion, stand in their punishment as a permanent warning of the fire of judgment. Yet these men are defiling their bodies by their filthy fantasies in just the same way; they show utter contempt for Authority and make a jest of the heavenly glories. But I would remind you that even the Archangel Michael when he was contending with the Devil in the dispute over the body of Moses did not dare to condemn him with mockery. He simply said, the Lord rebuke you!

These fellows, however, are ready to mock at anything that is beyond their immediate knowledge, while in the things that they know by instinct like unreasoning beasts they have become utterly depraved. I say, Woe to them! For they have taken the road of Cain; for what they could get they have rushed into the same error as Balaam; they have destroyed themselves by rebelling against God as did Korah long ago.

Be on your guard against these wicked men   12

These men are a menace to the good-fellowship of your feasts, for they eat in your company without a qualm yet they care for no one but themselves. They are like clouds driven up by the wind, but they bring no rain. They are like trees with the leaves of autumn but without a single fruit—they are doubly dead for they have no roots either. They are like raging waves of the sea producing only the spume of their own shameful deeds. They are like stars which follow no orbit, and their proper place is the everlasting blackness of the regions beyond the light. It was of men like these that Enoch (seventh descendant from Adam) prophesied when he said:

Behold, the Lord came with ten thousands of His holy ones, to execute judgment upon all, and to convict all the ungodly of all their works of ungodliness which they have ungodly wrought, and of all the hard things which ungodly sinners have spoken against Him.

These are the men who complain and curse their fate while trying all the time to mould life according to their own desires: they " talk big " but will pay men great respect if it is to their own advantage.

Forewarned is forearmed 17

Now do remember, dear friends, the words that the Messengers of Jesus Christ gave us beforehand when they said " there will come in the last days mockers who live according to their own godless desires." These are the men who split communities, for they are led by human emotions and never by the Spirit of God.

Look after your own faith : save whom you can 20

But you, dear friends of mine, build yourselves up on the foundation of your most holy faith and by praying through the Holy Spirit keep yourselves within the love of God. Wait patiently for the mercy of our Lord Jesus Christ which will bring you to the life eternal. For some of these men you can feel pity and you can treat them differently. Others you must try to save by fear, snatching them as it were out of the fire while hating the very garments their deeds have befouled.

Ascription 24

Now to Him Who is able to keep you from falling and to present you before His glory without fault and with unspeakable joy, to the only God, our Saviour, be glory and majesty, power and authority, through Jesus Christ our Lord, before time was, now, and in all ages to come, Amen.

JUDE

LETTERS AND PAPERS FROM PRISON
DIETRICH BONHOEFFER

These documents, smuggled out of prison under the nose of the Gestapo, have a clear and shining unity—so that they make an opening into fresh worlds of thought.

A HANDBOOK OF CHRISTIAN THEOLOGY
EDITED BY HALVERSON AND COHEN

Over a hundred essays by leading theologians on the concise terms used in current Christian theology.

CHRISTIANITY AND HISTORY
HERBERT BUTTERFIELD

"As crystal clear as it is wise and compelling. There are sentences on every page which cry out to be quoted." SPECTATOR

THE YOUNG CHURCH IN ACTION
J. B. PHILLIPS

Luke's work rendered into contemporary English for new readers, and for those who no longer read their Bible because of its familiarity.

SCIENCE AND CHRISTIAN BELIEF
C. A. COULSON

Professor Coulson shows that science is essentially a religious activity, playing its part in the unfolding of the nature and purpose of God.

SACRED WRITINGS
GÜNTER LANCZKOWSKI

A guide to the literature of the great religions of the world.
ILLUSTRATED

THE PERENNIAL PHILOSOPHY
ALDOUS HUXLEY

"It opens doors into many aspects of life and thought which most people would never have discovered for themselves."
NATIONAL REVIEW

THE EPISTLE OF PAUL TO THE ROMANS
C. H. DODD

Professor Dodd makes this great Epistle live for the layman as well as the theologian in a way that no other commentary does or is likely to do.